DISCARD

MANUAL OF SOUND RECORDING

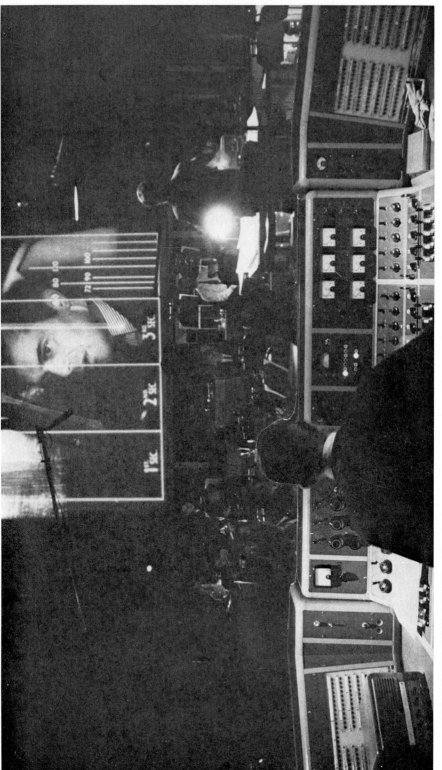

RECORDING FILM MUSIC. The Author seated at a music making console can see the orchestra and the screen, on which a music timing film is synchronously projected on top of the film being scored. The Conductor watches a pointer moving towards the instant of starting a music section, and the final second is marked in metronome timing so that he can begin his beat at the correct moment whatever the tempo. *Photo: James Clark.*

MANUAL OF
SOUND
RECORDING

John Aldred
M.B.K.S.T.S.

FOUNTAIN PRESS LTD

First Edition   *1963*
Second Enlarged Edition 1971

ISBN 0 852 42001 3

*Published in Great Britain by Fountain
Press Limited, 46–47 Chancery Lane,
London, WC2A 1JU and printed in
Great Britain by The Whitefriars Press
Limited, London and Tonbridge.*

Contents

INTRODUCTION 9

I BASIC SOUND PRINCIPLES 12
Sound Velocity (12) Wavelength (13) Amplitude (14)
Phase (14) Beat Frequency (14) Combination Tones (15)
Obstacle Effect (15) Masking (16) Echo (16) The Ear
(17) Intensity Scale (17) Threshold of Hearing (18)
Threshold of Feeling (18) Sense of Direction (19)
Frequency (19) Fundamental Frequency (20) Harmonics
(20) Octaves (22) Doppler Effect (22) Speech Waves
(22) Loudness (24) Voice Effort (24) Signal-to-Noise
Ratio (25) Dynamic Range (26) Distortion (26) Re-
sonance (27) Hi-Fi (28)

II BASIC ELECTRICAL PRINCIPLES 30
Ohm's Law (30) Electrical Power (31) Division of Units
(31) Capacitance (32) Inductance (32) Alternating
Current (33) Impedance (34) Resonant Frequency (34)
The Decibel (35) Audio Oscillator (36) A.C. Voltmeter
(37)

III MAGNETIC RECORDING AND REPRODUCTION 39
Theory of Magnetic Sound (39) The Need for Bias (40)
High Frequency Bias (41) Bias Oscillator (42) Bias
Rejection Filter (43) Magnetic Frequency Response (43)
Frequency Correction Standards (45) Magnetic Tape (47)
Tape Selection (48) Print-Through (50) Modulation
Noise (50) Magnetic Heads (51) Record Head (51)
Replay Head (52) Erase Head (52) Multi-Track Heads
(53) Crossfield Head (53) Hum Bucking Coil (54) Tape
Transport Mechanism (54) Recording Speeds (56)
Standard Track Dimensions (56) Alignment of Heads (58)
Azimuth Setting (58) Fringe Effect (59) Quick Loading
Systems (59) Demagnetization (62) Magnetic Rever-
beration Units (63) Videotape (64) Tape Joining (64)

IV DISC RECORDING AND REPRODUCTION 66
Recording Machine (67) Recording Head (68) Cutting
Stylus (68) Groove Dimensions (69) Radius Com-
pensation (71) Recording Frequency Response (71)

Standard Recording Characteristic (72)   Cutting a Stereo
Disc (73)   Processing (74)   Disc Pressings (75)   Turntable Units (75)   Stroboscope Disc (76)   Pick-up Arms
(77)   Reproducing Stylus (78)   Stylus Pressure (79)
Pick-up Cartridges (80)   Semi-Conductor Cartridge (81)
Photocell Cartridge (81)   Stereo Pick-ups (82)   Frequency Correction (83)   Low Pass Filter (83)   Rumble
Filter (84)   Frequency Test Discs (84)   Record Wear
(84)

V   MICROPHONES   86
Pressure Operation (86)   Pressure Gradient Operation
(87)   Polar Distribution (88)   Cardioid Microphones (90)
Carbon Microphones (91)   Crystal Microphones (91)
Dynamic Microphones (93)   Ribbon Microphones (94)
Condenser Microphones (95)   Directional Microphones
(98)   Contact Microphones (102)   Lip Microphones (102)
Lavalier Microphones (103)   Radio Link (104)   Micro-
phone Loading (105)   Microphone Sensitivity (106)
Microphone Cables (109)

VI   AMPLIFIERS AND FILTERS   112
Voltage Amplifier (112)   Power Amplifiers (114)   Transistor
Amplifiers (116)   Basic Transistor Configurations (117)
Field Effect Transistor (119)   Photo Transistor (120)
Compression and Limiting (121)   Noise Reduction System
(123)   Printed Circuits (124)   Integrated Circuits (124)
Filters (125)   High Pass Filter (126)   Low Pass Filter (126)
Hi-Lo Equalizer (126)   Band Stop Filter (127)   Telephone
Simulator (128)   Dialogue Equalizer (128)   Dynalizer
(128)   Film Loss Equalizer (129)   Presence Equalizer (129)
Rumble Filter (129)

VII   LOUDSPEAKERS   130
Early Types (130)   Moving Coil Loudspeakers (131)
Horn Loudspeakers (134)   Re-entrant Horn (135)   Dual
Concentric Loudspeaker (136)   Electrostatic Loudspeaker
(137)   Impedance Matching (137)   Frequency Dividing
Networks (138)   Loudspeaker Enclosures (140)   A Small
Domestic Loudspeaker (143)   Acoustical Resistance Unit
(144)   Column Loudspeakers (144)   Cinema Loudspeaker
Systems (144)   Acoustic Lens (145)

VIII RECORDING STUDIOS   146
Reverberation (146)   Conditions for Recording (147)
Sound Isolation (147)   Air-borne Sound (148)   Studio
Acoustics (149)   Flutter Echoes (151)   Standing Waves
(151)   Helmholtz Resonators (151)   Panel Absorbers (152)
Membrane Absorbers (152)   Reverberation Chambers
(152)   Alternative Reverberation Units (154)   Studio Lay-
out (156)   Drama Studio (158)   Monitoring Room (159)
Mixing Consoles (159)   Volume Indicators (161)   Monitor
Loudspeaker Volume (163)

 IX MUSIC RECORDING   165
String Instruments (165)   Woodwind Instruments (166)
Wind Instruments (167)   Brass Instruments (167)   Percussion Instruments (168)   A Music Studio (168)   Acoustic
Treatment (169)   Vocal Room (170)   Monitoring Room
(171)   Orchestral Combination (172)   Orchestral Lay-out
(172) (176)   Multi-Microphone Technique (174)   Recording Choirs (179)   Organ Music (180)   Electronic Organs
(181)   Mechanical Organs (181)   Electronic Music (181)
Music Concrete (183)

  X STEREOPHONIC SOUND   184
The Basic Principle (184)   Stereo Microphone Techniques
(187)   Coincident Microphone Pair (189)   Panoramic
Potentiometer (190)   Sum and Difference Method (191)
Width Control (194)   Spaced Microphone Technique (195)
Wandering Stereo Image (196)   Recording Equipment
(197)   Magnetic Reduction Transfers (199)   Stereophonic
Listening Conditions (199)   Stereophonic Broadcasts (202)
Quadrasonics (202)

 XI MOTION PICTURE SOUND   204
Double Film System (204)   Single Film System (205)
Compiling a Film Sound Track (206)   Post-Synchronization (207)   Recording Commentaries (208)   Sound Effects
(209)   Music   Recording   (209)   Re-recording   (210)
Optical Sound Recording (213)   Noise Reduction (215)
Optical Frequency Response (215)   Signal-to-Noise Ratio
(217)   Negative Exposure (217)   Sound Film Processing
(218)   Sensitometry (218)   Cross Modulation (219)

Intermodulation (220)   Direct Positives (221)   Interlock
Motor Systems (222)   Principle of Synchro-Start (222)
Magnetic Film Recording (223)   Magnetic Film Path
(223)   Magnetic Frequency Response (224)   Magnetic
Track Standards (224)   Magnetic Stripe (225)   Recording
Equipment (226)   Pulse Synchronization (227)   Wide
Screen Film Processes (229)   Frequency Response (231)
Multi-Track Recordings (232)   Electronic Printing (233)

XII   MICROPHONE TECHNIQUES   234
Microphone Connectors (234)   Microphone Directivity
(235)   Announcements and Commentaries (236)   Lectures
and Speeches (237)   Plays and Drama (238)   Dialogue
Recording (239)   Dialogue Quality (240)   Volume Level
(241)   Dialogue Perspective (242)   Recording Out of
Doors (242)   Explosions and Gunfire (244)   Quiet
Sounds (244)   The Piano (245)   Copyright (246)

APPENDIX   248

INDEX   261

Introduction

SOUND as heard by the ear is a disturbance of air particles caused by a series of vibrations. Before the turn of this century several eminent gentlemen were concurrently pursuing the idea of designing and building a machine which would record these vibrations and reproduce them as audible sound. The name of Thomas Edison springs to mind with his Phonograph, which he produced in America during 1877. This device consisted of a sheet of tin foil attached to the cylindrical surface of a drum which was rotated by a handle, and a cutting stylus connected to a diaphragm and horn. As the handle was turned the stylus moved across the rotating drum, cutting a continuous spiral groove which was modulated by shouting into the horn!

After a recording had been made, the drum and stylus were returned to their first positions and the handle turned again at the same speed as before. The recorded impression was then audibly reproduced, rather distorted but just intelligible. The original sound vibrations had been impressed into the tin foil by varying the depth of the groove, a method known as *hill and dale* recording. In later models of the Phonograph the tin foil was abandoned in favour of a wax cylinder, also separate stylus and diaphragm assemblies for recording and playing back.

At about the same time a German named Berliner conceived the idea of using a flat disc instead of a wax cylinder, with a spiral groove cut from inside to outside. The reason for starting on the inside was probably one of convenience, since the waste material extruded from the groove would lay on the inside of the stylus and not get in the way. The groove was modulated from side to side, a method known today as *lateral cut* recording. Berliner's early machines used 5 in. (14·5 cm) discs running at 70 r.p.m. and lasting about $1\frac{1}{2}$ minutes. He called his invention the Gramophone!

But it was a Dane called Valdemar Poulsen who produced a rather more scientific device called the Telegraphone, which was capable of recording sound by means of magnetism. Basically it consisted of a steel piano wire about $1\frac{1}{2}$ metres in length, along which was passed an electromagnet in close contact. The coil of the magnet was connected in series with a battery and a carbon microphone from a telephone. By speaking into the microphone the piano wire became magnetized along its length in sympathy with the speech waves. By connecting the magnet coil to a telephone receiver, a minute electrical current was induced into the coil as the magnet pole faces were passed along the magnetized wire, causing speech to be heard in the receiver.

Poulsen also discovered that the sensitivity of the wire could be improved by first adding a direct current to the speech signal, although this produced a rather high background noise as well. In 1898 it was not possible to amplify the signals beyond headphone strength, as the thermionic valve had not yet been invented. So although the Telegraphone worked it remained little more than a novelty for a number of years: but the principle of magnetic recording had been firmly established.

The development of the valve amplifier revived interest in Poulsen's original experiments, and the $1\frac{1}{2}$ metre length of piano wire had grown to a spool of much thinner wire, several hundred feet in length. It was found that this thin wire was inclined to twist and did not always stay in the same plane on subsequent playings. So a flat metal tape was introduced and used in a large recorder developed by Blattner, called the Blattnerphone. The B.B.C. installed one for pre-recording plays in the early 1930s, but the steel tape snapped easily and was impossible to join. A paper based recording tape was then introduced, coated with iron oxide, and this was soon preferred as a recording medium. It maintained its popularity until the development of plastic based tapes, with which everybody is familiar today.

Parallel with progress made in disc and tape recording was the problem of giving a voice to the popular silent films of the early 1920s. Experiments in actually photographing sound waves were made in 1876, when a certain Professor Blake threw a beam of light on to a small mirror attached to a microphone diaphragm. Vibrations of the diaphragm caused a flickering light to be photographed on a moving photographic plate, but the resulting image was of little use. In 1906 an altogether different approach was made by a Frenchman, Eugene Lauste, who had once worked in Edison's studio. Lauste's method was to record sound photographically alongside the picture, and on the same piece of 35 mm film. Inside his camera he fitted an exposure lamp and an electro-magnet with a slit diaphragm, which he fed with speech signals from the telephone type microphone of the period. The speech signals were sufficient to vibrate the diaphragm assembly (which he called a light-valve in his 1907 patent) causing a variation in the intensity of light falling on the film.

To reproduce this sound track Lauste had to construct a projector with an exciter lamp and selenium cell, which converted the photographic trace back into electrical signals. It is worthy of note that the sound track occupied at least 50 per cent of the width of the film, a situation which would not be tolerated today. Dr. Lee de Forest takes the credit for making sound films a commercial possibility with his photo-electric cell. By using his cell, together with valve amplifiers and loudspeakers, he was able to demonstrate talking films in 1923.

But it was 1928 before silent films were given a jolt by the appearance of Al Jolson singing and talking in a Warner Brothers film called 'The Jazz Singer'. This was closely followed by other musicals such as 'The Singing Fool' and 'Broadway Melody'. Sound for these films was recorded on a 16 in. (40 cm) disc, running at 33⅓ r.p.m., with a turntable mechanically coupled to the picture projector. This system was employed because of the various teething troubles with the mass production of photographic type sound tracks, and projection equipment of the day was designed to handle sound-on-disc or sound-on-film.

World War Two produced a sudden spurt in the field of electronics, which naturally included sound recording. Germany was in the lead with the Magnetophon tape recorder, using a plastic based tape running at 22 i.p.s. (56 cm per second). The quality was so good that disc recording companies took an interest in tape during the late 1940's, with a view to using it as a recording medium. They then found that the 78 r.p.m. discs of the day were poor by comparison with the master tape recording, and the outcome was a move towards a slower speed, long playing disc pressed with improved materials. The first long playing disc appeared in 1946 and gave excellent sound quality; in fact it showed the need for a far better type of sound reproducer. A major boom in high fidelity recording and reproduction was under way.

Sound recording today is no longer practised only by the professional engineer, and in the majority of homes the tape recorder rivals the television set in popularity. It is the purpose of this Manual to provide a full understanding of sound recording, with an accurate description of the methods and techniques used in the current state of the art.

CHAPTER I

Basic Sound Principles

SOUND RECORDING can be considered as a manufacturing process, since energy is being transformed from one medium to another for use at a later date. This process involves electricity, magnetism, mechanics, and other branches of physics, so that an elementary knowledge of these subjects is desirable if the problems associated with recording are to be fully understood.

Sound as heard by the ear is a disturbance of air particles caused by a series of vibrations. These vibrations set up alternate areas of compression and rarefaction of air particles called sound waves, which travel in all directions from the source of origin of the sound. An analogy here is the dropping of a stone into a pond. Ripples of water or waves are sent out from the point at which the stone hit the water to the edge of the pond. If there was no edge to the pond, these waves could theoretically go on for ever. But in practice they decrease in intensity (or volume) en route, due to the dispersal of power when travelling through a medium, and finally disappear altogether.

Sound will also travel in both liquids and solids, although these mediums are not so elastic as air. In fact they offer less resistance to sound waves. But in all mediums the actual particles do not travel out with the wave. They merely vibrate where they are and pass on energy due to the elastic coupling that exists between them. The only medium through which sound waves will not travel is a vacuum, since there are no particles of matter to vibrate.

Sound Velocity

The speed or *velocity* of sound waves depends on the density and temperature of the medium through which they are travelling. Under normal conditions the velocity of sound in air is 1,120 feet per second, or 763 m.p.h. Compare this with light and radio signals, which are waves travelling through space at a velocity of 186,000 miles per second. The relatively slow speed of sound becomes apparent when watching a football match. We see a player kick the ball but we do not hear anything until a fraction of a second later. One watches a jet fighter streak across the sky, but the sound made by the aircraft seems to emanate from a point some distance behind.

These facts work to our advantage, since the slower sound velocity plays an important part in our everyday hearing by helping us to have a sense of direction (see page 19). It also enables designers to give us microphones with directional characteristics (see page 98). Furthermore, if sound travelled at the same velocity as light we would not be able to appreciate stereophony, since this depends on time differences between the same sound reaching the left and right ears (see page 184).

Sound velocity is virtually independent of *frequency*, and remains constant throughout the entire audible frequency range. Humidity also has a negligible effect, although the velocity is slightly faster in saturated air than in dry air. But temperature does affect sound velocity, to the extent of approximately 2 ft. per second for every degree centigrade rise or fall. This is borne out in practice by the tuning of wind instruments in an orchestra, which tend to become sharp with a temperature rise and go flat with a temperature fall.

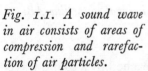

Fig. 1.1. A sound wave in air consists of areas of compression and rarefaction of air particles.

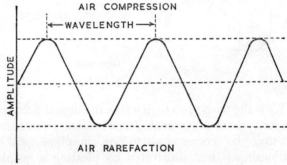

Wavelength
A sound wave in air bears a close resemblance to the ripples of water in the pond, and the distance between one wave crest and the next is called a *wavelength*. In fact a wavelength can be measured from any point in a wave formation to a similar point in the adjacent wave. This distance is also called a *cycle*, and contains an area of air compression and an equal area of air rarefaction as shown in Fig. 1.1. We seldom describe a particular sound by its wavelength, since we are more interested in frequency. Sound wave frequency is no longer expressed in terms of cycles per second, but in terms of Hertz (Hz) per second. Heinrich Hertz was a 19th century German who concerned himself with the study of sound and radio waves. Hence the terms Hz and kHz (1000 Hz). To determine frequency, divide velocity by wavelength. For example a wavelength of 2 ft. (0·6 m) has a frequency of 1,120 divided by 2, which is 560 cycles (expressed as 560 Hz).

In sound recording we usually know the frequency of the sound we are dealing with, and it is merely a question of establishing wavelength. By simple substitution we divide velocity by frequency, so that a 120 cycle (Hz) note has a wavelength of 1,120 divided by 120, or 10 ft. (3 m).

Amplitude

The maximum displacement of any particle of matter from its normal position is called its *amplitude*. It follows therefore that the greater the amplitude of a sound wave the louder will be the resultant sound. One of the arts of sound recording is to maintain the amplitude of the original waveform throughout the recording and reproducing chain, although this is not always possible.

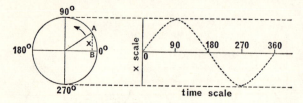

Fig. 1.2. Wave motion plotted along a time scale has a phase relationship to a circle. Wave amplitude is equal to the line AB.

Phase

This is the term used to describe the actual point reached by a sound wave in its cycle of movement. *Phase* is always measured in degrees of a circle, so that 360° corresponds to one complete cycle of movement. Phase relationship is best illustrated by plotting a graph showing wave motion along a time scale (Fig. 1.2). It will be seen that the start of any one wave is exactly 360° away from its neighbour, and this means that all crests can be said to be in phase with each other. Similarly all valleys are separated by 360°, and they too can be said to be in phase. But the crests are said to be out of phase with the valleys, since their phase relationship differs by 180°. The important lesson to be learnt here is that all *in phase* sounds are additive and will easily combine, whereas all *out of phase* sounds are subtractive and tend to cancel each other. This situation assumes significance when combining sounds of different character, and also when dealing with a stereophonic installation.

Beat Frequency

When two sound waves of slightly different frequency are combined together, they produce a third and new waveform which is known as the *beat frequency*. This is the direct result of the addition and subtraction of the various peaks and valleys, or areas of compression and rarefaction, of the two waveforms (Fig. 1.3). If the beat frequency is higher than about

20 Hz, the ear hears this as a musical note or tone. But as the beats become more rapid, due to an increase in the difference between the two basic frequencies, they also become less distinguishable. When the beat frequency is completely eliminated, the two original sound waves are known to be of identical frequency, or one is an exact multiple of the other. This occurs when two musical notes are said to be in tune.

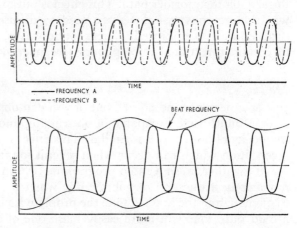

Fig. 1.3. Two sound waves of slightly different frequency combine to produce a beat frequency.

One problem often encountered is when two sound waves identical in frequency have their waveforms occurring at slightly different points on the time scale. This results in a partial elimination of sound due to the cancelling effect of one wave upon another, causing *phase distortion* with a complex waveform.

Combination Tones

When two sound waves A and B, whose frequency difference is within the limits of the audible frequency range, are superimposed, *combination tones* are produced equal in frequency to A + B, and *difference tones* equal in frequency to A—B. These tones are clearly heard by the ear as musical notes and not as beat frequencies. When many frequencies are heard simultaneously, one imagines that there are many additional frequencies also present. This makes a complex waveform difficult to analyse.

Obstacle Effect

When sound waves in air strike an object in their path, they are reflected like a beam of light. But the amount of reflection depends on the frequency of the sound and the size of the object. This phenomenon is known as the *obstacle effect,* and the amount of reflection will be very small if the size of the object is less than the wavelength of the sound.

Since the wavelengths of audible sounds extend from 50 ft. to under one inch, articles such as furniture, studio fittings, and people have a marked effect at different frequencies. High frequencies tend to be reflected more than low frequencies, the latter tending to become only slightly bent and to carry on their former path. This effect is put to good use in studio design where large convex surfaces are used to diffuse sound waves. Concave surfaces are also employed to focus sound waves, a principle which is used in certain directional microphones (see page 99).

Masking

Just as a person standing in front of you can obstruct your line of vision, so one sound wave is capable of obstructing another—particularly if the frequency of both waves is similar. This effect is known as *masking,* and is a condition which can occur when several sounds are intentionally combined together, as in a radio programme or film sound track. Masking is not merely a question of volume, for when the masking tone differs in frequency from the masked tone the problem is not so severe. Furthermore a loud pure tone will more easily mask one of a higher frequency. You have to decide which is the more important sound, and therefore which sound should be clearly heard by the listener.

Echo

An *echo* is caused by the reflection of a sound wave after striking the surface of some medium which is considerably denser than air. In order for the echo or reflected sound wave to become audible, the reflecting surface must be large compared with the wavelength of the sound. Common examples are echoes heard between buildings, amongst trees, or across a valley.

When sound waves are reflected by a number of suitably placed surfaces, a number of echoes will be heard for some time and overlapping into each other. This multiple reflection is known as *reverberation,* and is the principle employed in the design and construction of reverberation chambers. These chambers are used for adding reflected sound waves artificially during recording, to change the character of the original sound (see page 152).

Since the final assessment of all sound recording is made by the ear, it becomes necessary to understand the rather special capabilities of the ear and its reaction to sound waves.

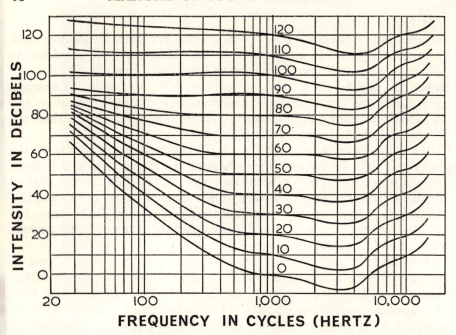

Fig. 1.4. Contour lines showing the frequency response of the ear at various sound intensities (Fletcher's Curves).

represents the lowest volume of a 1000 Hz tone which is on the threshold of hearing, and 120 db represents the loudest acceptable volume on the threshold of feeling.

Threshold of Hearing

When any sound becomes just audible it is said to be on the *threshold of hearing*. At low volume levels the ear is not very sensitive to frequencies below 500 Hz, and a 40 Hz tone must be a lot louder than a 500 Hz tone before it reaches the threshold of hearing. As the sound intensity increases, so does the ear's appreciation of bass frequencies, and in fact the frequency response of the ear is almost flat as we approach the threshold of feeling.

Threshold of Feeling

When a sound becomes deafening it is said to be on the *threshold of feeling*, because any increase in sound intensity results in a feeling of pain rather than a sensation of sound. Since there is no sharp dividing line between hearing sound and feeling pain, some people (and animals) express

BASIC SOUND PRINCIPLES

The Ear

When a sound enters the outer portion of the ear down the *audit*
minute changes of air pressure are set up which cause the ear
vibrate. These vibrations are transmitted by small bones to a liqu
inner ear, and finally to a membrane containing the nerves of
This rather delicate and efficient mechanism is extremely sensi
capable of accepting an astonishing volume range, far greater
average recording system can handle.

The *frequency range* to which the ear is sensitive depends largel
individual. The lowest frequency which can be appreciated as a
tone is roughly 16 Hz, whilst at the other end of the scale the
frequency audible to a pair of young ears is between 17,000 and 18
As we grow older our appreciation of the upper frequencies bec
and less, although for most of our life we should be able to identify
of frequencies covering ten octaves.

But before a sound wave becomes audible it must attain a
minimum intensity, and this minimum varies with the frequenc
sound wave. Low frequencies require a considerable intensity be
are audible, and so do extremely high frequencies. The ear
sensitive in the range between 1000 Hz and 6000 Hz, due to *reso*
page 27) in the narrow auditory canal. A graph containing equ
tivity curves for average hearing is shown in Fig. 1.4. These cont
are known as Fletcher's curves, and represent the locus of all poir
a large number of observers indicated to be of equal loudness. Th
of curves becomes necessary since the frequency response of the e
with sound intensity or volume.

Intensity Scale

Our appreciation of loudness can be calculated logarithmically
of 10. If we increase the intensity of sound by ten, the sound wil
to the ear to have doubled in volume. If we increase the intensity
ten times, the sound will again appear to have doubled in volu
unit which relates these changes is called the *Bel*. In practice th
too large so we divide by 10 to obtain the *Decibel* (expressed as db
good listening conditions, the minimum change in intensity tha
detected by a pair of trained ears is 1 db at a frequency of 1000

Since Fig. 1.4 shows us that apparent intensity varies with fr
we cannot use the decibel to express intensity at all frequencies
called the *Phon* is therefore employed to indicate aural loudness.
of any frequency is said to have a loudness of N/phons when it
equally loud to a 1000 Hz tone which is N/db above *zero level*. Z

annoyance of certain high frequency sounds even though they are nowhere near the threshold of feeling. This effect varies with individuals, and no two persons will necessarily be irritated by exactly the same frequency.

Sense of Direction

Whilst a single ear can give a certain amount of information concerning the direction of a sound source, two ears are necessary to establish the direction and exact location of a sound source. It is interesting to note how this is achieved, since a *sense of direction* is required to appreciate stereophonic sound, which is dealt with in a later chapter.

Two principles are involved in the ear's direction finding methods. Sounds having a frequency below approximately 1000 Hz are located by an out of phase effect, due to the signal reaching one ear being at a different point on its waveform to the signal reaching the other ear. But at frequencies above 1000 Hz the distance between the ears becomes greater than the wavelength of the sound, and each ear hears a signal that is in phase, in other words occurring at the same point on the signal waveform. Since the head is solid it has a shielding effect, causing each ear to receive the in phase signal at a slightly different volume or intensity. By turning the head until each ear appears to be receiving the same intensity, an accurate assessment of direction can be made. Therefore we are more aware of the direction of high frequencies than of low frequencies, the latter often being difficult to locate.

Frequency

In order to appreciate everyday sounds as we are accustomed to hearing them, we must obtain a faithful recording over a *frequency range* of approximately 40 Hz to 14,000 Hz. For practical reasons it is not necessary to record frequencies as low as 16 Hz, the lowest audible frequency, and not always as high as 18,000 Hz, the upper limit of audibility. In the ten octaves audible to the ear, quite a large number of frequencies can be distinguished by careful listening. We can recognize all the notes on the musical scale, and also tones in between these notes. This facility enables us to appreciate when a musical note is sharp or flat. Special training or an inherent musical talent is not necessary to enable these small frequency changes to be observed; it merely assists in making judgment easier.

Generally speaking, to create a pleasing sound the frequency response of the recording and reproducing systems must always be equally balanced over the entire audible range. Any extension or opening up of the high frequencies must be accompanied by an equivalent extension of the bass frequencies. Since the middle of the audible range is in the region of 800

Hz, it is usual practice in any sound system to reproduce as many octaves above this frequency as there are below. Therefore if your equipment will record frequencies as high as 16,000 Hz, it must also be capable of recording down to 40 Hz, a range of four and a half octaves on either side of 800 Hz. The ideal condition is when the highest frequency multiplied by the lowest frequency equals 640,000, and some typical frequency ranges in use today are shown in Fig. 1.5.

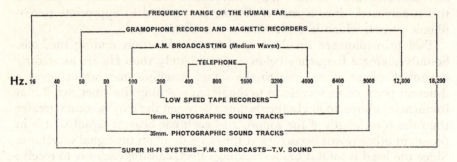

Fig. 1.5. Some typical frequency responses.

Fundamental Frequency

If we strike middle C on a piano keyboard, the sound vibrations we hear as a musical note will have a frequency of 256 Hz (assuming that the piano is in tune), and this is known as the *fundamental frequency* of the note. Multiples of the fundamental frequency are also generated, although to a lesser extent, and these are called *overtones* or *harmonics*. But it is the fundamental frequency which determines the pitch of a note, thus informing us whether the note is high or low on the musical scale. Fig. 1.6 shows a scale of orchestral and vocal compasses, which clearly illustrates the range of fundamental frequencies generated by a variety of musical instruments. The dotted lines indicate the harmonic content of each instrument, and these extend up to a frequency of 16,000 Hz.

Harmonics

The actual quality of any sound is determined by the presence of harmonics, which are always exact multiples of the fundamental frequency. The second harmonic is double the fundamental, the third harmonic is three times the fundamental, and so on up to the fifth or sixth, each successive harmonic diminishing in power or intensity. Harmonics are not confined to musical sounds or notes, although these do contain

The Ear

When a sound enters the outer portion of the ear down the *auditory canal*, minute changes of air pressure are set up which cause the ear drum to vibrate. These vibrations are transmitted by small bones to a liquid in the inner ear, and finally to a membrane containing the nerves of hearing. This rather delicate and efficient mechanism is extremely sensitive and capable of accepting an astonishing volume range, far greater than the average recording system can handle.

The *frequency range* to which the ear is sensitive depends largely on the individual. The lowest frequency which can be appreciated as a definite tone is roughly 16 Hz, whilst at the other end of the scale the highest frequency audible to a pair of young ears is between 17,000 and 18,000 Hz. As we grow older our appreciation of the upper frequencies becomes less and less, although for most of our life we should be able to identify a range of frequencies covering ten octaves.

But before a sound wave becomes audible it must attain a certain minimum intensity, and this minimum varies with the frequency of the sound wave. Low frequencies require a considerable intensity before they are audible, and so do extremely high frequencies. The ear is most sensitive in the range between 1000 Hz and 6000 Hz, due to *resonance* (see page 27) in the narrow auditory canal. A graph containing equal sensitivity curves for average hearing is shown in Fig. 1.4. These contour lines are known as Fletcher's curves, and represent the locus of all points which a large number of observers indicated to be of equal loudness. The family of curves becomes necessary since the frequency response of the ear varies with sound intensity or volume.

Intensity Scale

Our appreciation of loudness can be calculated logarithmically to a base of 10. If we increase the intensity of sound by ten, the sound will appear to the ear to have doubled in volume. If we increase the intensity a further ten times, the sound will again appear to have doubled in volume. The unit which relates these changes is called the *Bel*. In practice this unit is too large so we divide by 10 to obtain the *Decibel* (expressed as db). Given good listening conditions, the minimum change in intensity that can be detected by a pair of trained ears is 1 db at a frequency of 1000 Hz.

Since Fig. 1.4 shows us that apparent intensity varies with frequency, we cannot use the decibel to express intensity at all frequencies. A unit called the *Phon* is therefore employed to indicate aural loudness. A sound of any frequency is said to have a loudness of N/phons when it appears equally loud to a 1000 Hz tone which is N/db above *zero level*. Zero level

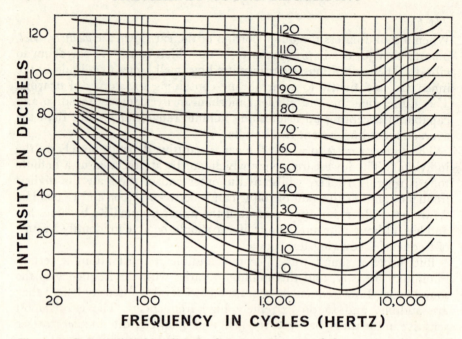

Fig. 1.4. Contour lines showing the frequency response of the ear at variovs sound intensities (Fletcher's Curves).

represents the lowest volume of a 1000 Hz tone which is on the threshold of hearing, and 120 db represents the loudest acceptable volume on the threshold of feeling.

Threshold of Hearing

When any sound becomes just audible it is said to be on the *threshold of hearing*. At low volume levels the ear is not very sensitive to frequencies below 500 Hz, and a 40 Hz tone must be a lot louder than a 500 Hz tone before it reaches the threshold of hearing. As the sound intensity increases, so does the ear's appreciation of bass frequencies, and in fact the frequency response of the ear is almost flat as we approach the threshold of feeling.

Threshold of Feeling

When a sound becomes deafening it is said to be on the *threshold of feeling*, because any increase in sound intensity results in a feeling of pain rather than a sensation of sound. Since there is no sharp dividing line between hearing sound and feeling pain, some people (and animals) express annoyance of certain high frequency sounds even though they are nowhere near the threshold of feeling. This effect varies with individuals, and no two persons will necessarily be irritated by exactly the same frequency.

Sense of Direction

Whilst a single ear can give a certain amount of information concerning the direction of a sound source, two ears are necessary to establish the direction and exact location of a sound source. It is interesting to note how this is achieved, since a *sense of direction* is required to appreciate stereophonic sound, which is dealt with in a later chapter.

Two principles are involved in the ear's direction finding methods. Sounds having a frequency below approximately 1000 Hz are located by an out of phase effect, due to the signal reaching one ear being at a different point on its waveform to the signal reaching the other ear. But at frequencies above 1000 Hz the distance between the ears becomes greater than the wavelength of the sound, and each ear hears a signal that is in phase, in other words occurring at the same point on the signal waveform. Since the head is solid it has a shielding effect, causing each ear to receive the in phase signal at a slightly different volume or intensity. By turning the head until each ear appears to be receiving the same intensity, an accurate assessment of direction can be made. Therefore we are more aware of the direction of high frequencies than of low frequencies, the latter often being difficult to locate.

Frequency

In order to appreciate everyday sounds as we are accustomed to hearing them, we must obtain a faithful recording over a *frequency range* of approximately 40 Hz to 14,000 Hz. For practical reasons it is not necessary to record frequencies as low as 16 Hz, the lowest audible frequency, and not always as high as 18,000 Hz, the upper limit of audibility. In the ten octaves audible to the ear, quite a large number of frequencies can be distinguished by careful listening. We can recognize all the notes on the musical scale, and also tones in between these notes. This facility enables us to appreciate when a musical note is sharp or flat. Special training or an inherent musical talent is not necessary to enable these small frequency changes to be observed; it merely assists in making judgment easier.

Generally speaking, to create a pleasing sound the frequency response of the recording and reproducing systems must always be equally balanced over the entire audible range. Any extension or opening up of the high frequencies must be accompanied by an equivalent extension of the bass frequencies. Since the middle of the audible range is in the region of 800

Hz, it is usual practice in any sound system to reproduce as many octaves above this frequency as there are below. Therefore if your equipment will record frequencies as high as 16,000 Hz, it must also be capable of recording down to 40 Hz, a range of four and a half octaves on either side of 800 Hz. The ideal condition is when the highest frequency multiplied by the lowest frequency equals 640,000, and some typical frequency ranges in use today are shown in Fig. 1.5.

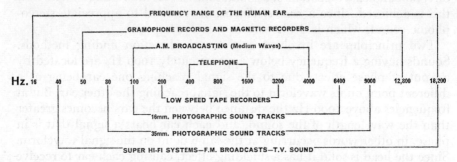

Fig. 1.5. Some typical frequency responses.

Fundamental Frequency

If we strike middle C on a piano keyboard, the sound vibrations we hear as a musical note will have a frequency of 256 Hz (assuming that the piano is in tune), and this is known as the *fundamental frequency* of the note. Multiples of the fundamental frequency are also generated, although to a lesser extent, and these are called *overtones* or *harmonics*. But it is the fundamental frequency which determines the pitch of a note, thus informing us whether the note is high or low on the musical scale. Fig. 1.6 shows a scale of orchestral and vocal compasses, which clearly illustrates the range of fundamental frequencies generated by a variety of musical instruments. The dotted lines indicate the harmonic content of each instrument, and these extend up to a frequency of 16,000 Hz.

Harmonics

The actual quality of any sound is determined by the presence of harmonics, which are always exact multiples of the fundamental frequency. The second harmonic is double the fundamental, the third harmonic is three times the fundamental, and so on up to the fifth or sixth, each successive harmonic diminishing in power or intensity. Harmonics are not confined to musical sounds or notes, although these do contain harmonics as part of their overtone structure. It is the very presence of harmonics which determines the sound quality or *timbre* of every note on every instrument, and enables us to differentiate between one instrument and another—even though they may both be producing the same note and emitting the same fundamental frequency. But harmonics must not be confused with musical *overtones*, some of which are not exact multiples of the fundamental.

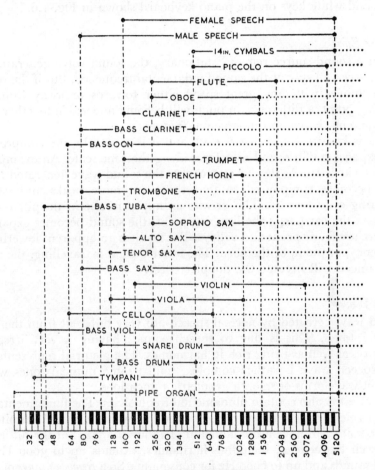

FREQUENCY IN CYCLES PER SECOND

Fig. 1.6. A scale of orchestral and vocal compasses related to a piano keyboard. Dotted lines show harmonic content of each instrument, which can extend up to 16 kHz.

Octaves

Standard musical notation is always expressed in *octaves*, and any two notes which are an octave apart have a frequency ratio of 2 to 1. From this statement it will be obvious that the first harmonic of any note is equal to the fundamental frequency of the same note one octave higher on the musical scale. These two notes played together are said to be in tune. Each octave is divided into 12 notes, called *semitones*, which are visible as black and white keys on the piano keyboard shown in Fig. 1.6.

Doppler Effect

Whilst a sound source remains stationary, the sound wave generated by that source will stay at the same fundamental frequency. But if the sound source moves with any great speed either towards or away from the listening point, a difference in pitch will become noticeable together with an apparent change in fundamental frequency.

This is known as the *doppler effect*, and it is caused by the compression and expansion of a sound waveform along the time scale. An example of this is a car horn. As the car approaches the sound wave generated by its horn becomes compressed so that there are more peaks and valleys occurring every second. This creates an apparent rise in the pitch of the horn. As the car passes the listening point, the sound becomes expanded so there are fewer peaks and valleys. The result is an apparent lowering in frequency, or pitch, of the horn. The faster the car is travelling, the more pronounced will become the doppler effect.

Speech Waves

Sound waves created by normal speech are very different from the pure musical tones. This is due to speech sounds having a very irregular intensity, as well as being rich in harmonics. The pictorial representation of a speech wave is rather complex, unlike some musical tones which contain waveforms of smooth geometric dimensions.

Speech waves also contain fundamental frequencies. The fundamental for a deep voiced male is in the region of 120 Hz, whilst a fairly high pitched female voice will have a fundamental of about 400 Hz. But the full range of speech frequencies, including harmonics, extends up to 3000 Hz for vowel sounds and up to 6000 Hz for consonants. So a *frequency range* of from 60 Hz to 6000 Hz is the minimum that can be tolerated if we are to record and reproduce speech with any realism. This explains why it is sometimes hard to recognize familiar voices when speaking on the telephone, which has a very limited frequency response.

Some of the cheaper domestic tape recorders make an excellent job of speech recording, although they do not always possess an adequate frequency response for high quality music. We have already seen that music requires a recording system with a frequency range of 40 Hz to 16,000 Hz for lifelike reproduction, and of course a good loudspeaker outside the tape recorder cabinet. Such a recorder would also make an excellent job of speech recording.

Decibels	Type of Noise
140	Threshold of Feeling or Pain
120	Jet Aircraft close
115	Pneumatic Drill
100	Aircraft Engine
95	Noisy Tube Train
85	Ship's Siren close
75	Symphony Orchestra
70	Factory Workshop
65	Train with open window, Shouting
60	Loud Speech, Heavy Traffic
55	Quiet Train, Normal Traffic
50	Normal Conversation
45	Car Passing
40	Quiet Restaurant or Street
35	Distant Traffic
30	Quiet Room, Clock Ticking
25	Cinema Audience
20	Hospital, or Quiet Garden
10	Recording Studio, Quiet Whisper
0	Threshold of Hearing

Fig. 1.7. Approximate noise levels in decibels of everyday sounds.

The fundamental frequency of any voice is determined by the length, thickness, and tension of the *vocal chords*, situated in the wind pipe. These chords vibrate as air is forced between them by the lungs, and a pulsating air column enters the cavities formed by the mouth and nose. It is the shape of these cavities which determines the general character or *timbre* of the voice, and the variation of cavity resonances by movement of the tongue and lips controls the harmonic content of the voice and enables us to form vowels and consonants.

In order to record speech waves faithfully, it is essential that the microphone is in line with the speaker's mouth (either slightly above or below) so as to obtain the natural voice quality without colouration due to room or studio acoustics. In practice high frequencies tend to be emitted in an upward direction, so this is the favoured position. The volume range of speech is considerable, as shown in Fig. 1.7.

Loudness

Returning to the piano once more, if we strike middle C several times, each time a little harder, we shall produce sound vibrations becoming stronger and stronger, although still of the same fundamental frequency of 256 Hz. More and more power is being given to the waveform which means that the wave height is increased. This wave height is called the amplitude of the wave, and the greater the amplitude the louder the sound will appear to the listener.

Quiet speech is measured at about 20 db above the threshold of hearing, whilst normal conversation is around 50 db. A large symphony orchestra playing fortissimo would be somewhere in the middle of the ear's volume range if you were sitting 30 ft. away in a concert hall, whilst a pneumatic drill heard fairly close by would be on the threshold of feeling at 140 db. No recording system can possibly hope to accommodate such a large volume range, using equipment available today, and so a compromise is sought by raising the volume of low intensity sounds and lowering the volume of high intensity sounds. This statement might be alarming to perfectionists seeking an exact reproduction of waveform and amplitude, but the ear readily adapts itself to prevailing conditions and accepts a reduced volume range in recorded sound.

There are limits to the quietest sound that can be recorded before either the residual amplifier noise or the studio background noise begins to predominate, or possibly becoming louder than the sound signal itself. Likewise very loud sound intensities are liable to push the amplifier or recording device into severe overload, unless there is some control over the volume range of sound passing through the recording system. The compromise sought is the one where the quietest sounds are clearly heard above the inherent background noise of the system, and the loudest sounds are reduced or compressed sufficiently to prevent overload occurring in any part of the recording and reproducing systems.

The large symphony orchestra in the concert hall can produce volume changes of 60 db between quiet and loud passages. Since the usual volume range of a recording system is slightly less than this figure, some degree of compression has to take place. On the other hand speech is usually confined to a volume range of only 25 db to 30 db, except for shouts and screams, so speech can be recorded satisfactorily without any artificial compression. Nevertheless compression is used occasionally to improve intelligibility (see page 121).

Voice Effort

An interesting point about the human voice is that its frequency content alters considerably according to the amount of *voice effort* used. This has the effect of altering the pitch of the voice with varying degrees of loudness or intensity. Compared with normal conversation, soft speech lowers the middle frequencies and gives the impression of a drop in pitch. Shouted, declamatory speech raises the middle frequencies and severely reduces the bass content, giving the impression of a rise in pitch. In addition the frequency response curves of the ear at different volume levels must be taken into account (Fig. 1.4), from which it will be apparent that less bass is heard at low volume levels than at high levels.

Another situation arises when speech is being reproduced at a higher acoustic volume level than the acoustic volume level of the original sound, as in a cinema. Under these conditions the bass frequencies will become accentuated unless some correction has been made in the recording to restore the *timbre* of the voice. But the same recording played over a domestic television set would sound thin and lacking in bass, since the acoustic volume would be similar to the acoustic volume of the dialogue as spoken in the studio.

Music is nearly always reproduced at approximately the same acoustic volume level as the original performance. If the reproduced volume is lower, a reduction of bass frequencies takes place which is sometimes corrected by a loudness control (not a volume control) on an amplifier. In fact music which has been recorded with an amplifier system that has been compensated for dialogue will often sound thin and strident, and is difficult to correct. Certain microphones contain frequency compensation arrangements for speech and music (see page 91), and removing this compensation can sometimes help to restore the bass content of a shouted voice.

Signal-to-Noise Ratio

The volume range available in any sound recording or reproducing system is governed by the *signal-to-noise ratio* of that system. This ratio is expressed in dbs, and gives an indication of the volume range which exists between the loudest sound that it is possible to record and the inherent background noise of the recording system. The signal-to-noise ratio of an average domestic tape recorder is about 40 db to 45 db, and a professional tape recorder is regarded as good at 60 db. A modern amplifier by itself will have a figure of 70 db in its specification. It is worthy of note that motion picture sound using an optical or photographic type of sound track, which was once considered the best medium for sound quality during the 1930's, now comes off as the worst medium with a signal-to-noise ratio of approximately 35 db. It also has a restricted frequency response. This does not of course apply to magnetic sound tracks as used on large screen 70 mm pictures, and certain pictures in the Cinemascope format.

Dynamic Range

The useful volume range in a recording or reproducing system is called the *dynamic range*. This is always less than the signal-to-noise ratio of a system since we do not wish to record sound which is anywhere near the background noise level. The dynamic range of a recording is sometimes varied to suit a particular set of listening conditions, such as overseas broadcasting where the listener has to contend with extra noise and interference on short wave radio. Normal broadcasts on V.H.F. have a dynamic range of only 40 db, whilst magnetic tape recordings and long playing records will accept a greater dynamic range.

Distortion

If we choose to ignore the limits imposed by the dynamic range of a recording system and attempt to modulate more than 100%, *distortion* will become evident even to the casual listener. Distortion in any form is seldom pleasant, especially when it occurs in original sound recordings. Although overload is the most common form of distortion it is by no means the only one. If any additions are made to the main features of the original sound wave, or if any features are absent from the recording in part or in whole, then such alterations constitute distortion in one form or another.

Frequency Distortion—caused by unequal amplification of frequencies within the audible range, or the omission of certain frequencies at either end of the range. This form of distortion is always present to a minor degree, but it only becomes detectable when there is a severe unbalance between bass and treble, either in amplitude or frequency range. But it is not always desirable to record and reproduce frequencies over the entire audible range: in fact an extended frequence response in a recording is only acceptable to the ear when all other forms of distortion are at a minimum.

Harmonic Distortion—caused by non-linearity of the input/output characteristic of a sound recording or reproducing device, which either introduces harmonics which were not present in the original waveform or eliminates certain harmonics altogether. If any of the harmonics are suppressed, or unevenly amplified, the recording will be unlike the original sound. The ear is quite critical of quality changes in reproduced sound, although it soon becomes accustomed to an inferior sound quality.

Intermodulation—a form of distortion which is introduced when two sounds of different frequency are superimposed, resulting in the modulation of one frequency by another and the production of unwanted beat frequencies and combination tones. Intermodulation can occur when a loudspeaker attempts to reproduce sounds of high and low frequency at the same time, resulting in distortion of the higher frequency since this is the one which usually contains less power. The effects of intermodulation are used to determine the optimum processing conditions when recording photographic sound tracks of variable density (see page 220).

Spatial Distortion—an effect peculiar to stereophony, occurring when the image created by stereophonic sound reproduction appears to be misplaced in relation to the position of the original sound waves. The cause is usually some irregularity in microphone placement, in the positioning of sounds occurring in front of the microphones, or in the balancing of the microphone volume controls during recording. The stereophonic image can also be distorted by being reproduced on a wider or narrower scale than the original sound source. Spatial distortion is further explained on page 196.

Transient Distortion—caused by the inability of any part of a sound recording or reproducing system to provide an exact copy of the steep wave fronts occurring in the original sound waveform. The usual items of equipment which give transient distortion are those which transfer energy from one medium to another, such as microphones and loudspeakers. After reproducing a very loud transient, loudspeaker cones can sometimes suffer a 'hangover' before resuming their normal position. This is known as *ringing* and can cause a slight amplitude distortion to the following part of the sound wave.

Volume Distortion—due to operating a loudspeaker at a different volume level to that of the original sound. This distortion often exists, sometimes intentionally, and is accepted by the average ear. In home surroundings, for example, it is seldom desirable to listen to an orchestral concert at the same volume level as the orchestra would create in the concert hall itself. Whispered speech is often reproduced at an increased volume level for reasons of intelligibility, although this sounds perfectly natural to the ear.

Resonance

Since all sound waves consist of vibrating air particles, they are capable of causing anything standing in their path to vibrate in sympathy. Articles having both mass and stiffness will be forced to vibrate more freely at one particular frequency than at any other, and this condition is known as *resonance*. The power of sound waves at resonance is well demonstrated by the shattering of glass when a large window vibrates freely at the same frequency as the sound waves which strike it. Similarly a wine glass can be made to reveal its resonant frequency by passing a slightly moistened finger around the circumference of the glass.

Another practical test is to feed a continuous tone through a loudspeaker, varying the frequency of the tone from one end of the audible range to the other. Note the various objects nearby which rattle and vibrate as their resonant frequency is reproduced.

Resonance is, strictly speaking, a form of frequency distortion; although its presence can cause some of the other forms of distortion previously mentioned. Rooms themselves contain pronounced resonances, due to sound waves being reflected between parallel walls or surfaces which are half a wavelength apart, or multiples of half a wavelength. Consequently the frequency of resonances depends on the size and shape of the room and the gradual build up of sound into a continuous wave motion is called *a standing wave*. These standing waves are most troublesome at low frequencies, and can cause a colouration of sound quality in a small untreated studio. When designing a recording studio, steps are usually taken to absorb any standing waves of this nature (see page 151).

Mechanical resonances are also present in microphones, gramophone pick-up arms, loudspeakers, and other electro-mechanical devices. The exact resonant frequency depends entirely on the mass and stiffness of any moving parts; the greater the mass the lower the frequency, the stiffer the mass the higher the frequency. Electrical circuits can also be made to resonate by introducing elements of *resistance*, *capacitance*, and *inductance*, thus making them frequency selective. Capacitors and inductors can be arranged in certain configurations to produce circuits tuned to resonate at specific frequencies; and these circuits form the basis of many forms of frequency correction equalisers used in sound recording systems.

Hi-Fi

This modern expression is used indiscriminately when referring to almost any sound recording or reproducing system, or part thereof. *Hi-Fi* means high fidelity, reproducing an exact copy of the original sound waves, as far as is humanly and electrically possible, without any colouration due to any form of distortion.

High fidelity is a purely relative term, since recordings which were considered excellent in 1940 are not rated very highly today. In another 20 years time we shall probably be wondering what was so marvellous about sound in the 70's. It remains a fact that no two persons can ever seem to agree as to what constitutes good, faithful sound reproduction. One person may take great pains to ensure that all the high frequencies are accurately reproduced, whilst another person will express resentment if the reproduction contains too much top, or high frequencies. One reason for this is that everybody's hearing is slightly different, so that sound quality is best assessed by a group of persons to simulate a pair of average ears.

Even with magnetic recording there are limits to the frequency response and volume range which can be used to create lifelike sound reproduction. Furthermore a single channel or *monophonic* system can only reproduce sound waves from a single point source, even though these waves were originally generated from a number of point sources over a wide front. A general improvement can be heard in stereophonic recordings which employ two separate channels, each feeding separate loudspeaker systems. Not only do we hear sound reproduced from two point sources, but also from various positions between each point source. This results in greater fidelity, added realism, and a feeling of closer contact with the original sound source. Large screen films possess as many as six magnetic sound tracks feeding six loudspeaker systems, but even this does not provide an accurate replica of sound as heard live in a concert hall since five of the loudspeakers are behind the screen. An illusion of 'live' sound can best be demonstrated by a four channel system feeding four loudspeakers, one stereo pair in front of the listener and one stereo pair behind (see Quadrasonics on page 202).

CHAPTER II

Basic Electrical Principles

SOUND RECORDING consists of collecting acoustical energy and converting it into electro-magnetic energy (magnetic recording), mechanical energy (disc recording), or photographic waveforms (film recording). This energy is stored until required, and then transformed back into acoustical energy when we wish to hear the information we have recorded. This process involves numerous electrical principles which, together with the measurement thereof, form the basis of a recording and reproducing system.

Electricity consists of free electrons moving through a metal wire conductor in the form of an electric current, and the force required to maintain this current is called the electromotive force which is measured in *volts*. The rate at which the electrons pass a given point in a circuit determines the amount of current, and this is measured in *amperes* or *amps*. The direction of current flow is always away from a positive terminal (coloured red) towards a negative terminal (coloured black); whilst the electron flow is the exact opposite to this as the electron is a negatively charged particle. The number of amps which will flow through a circuit fed with a specific number of volts depends on the *resistance* of the circuit. Resistance is always measured in ohms, which brings us to the elementary principle of *Ohm's law*.

Ohm's Law

This states that the current in amps which will flow through any given circuit can be found by dividing the electromotive force in volts by the resistance in ohms. For convenience 1 amp will flow through a 1 volt circuit when the resistance is 1 ohm. From this statement it will be evident that resistors can be specifically introduced into a circuit to control the current flow, and also (by applying Ohm's law) to obtain a different voltage from the supply voltage.

For example if 12 volts are applied to a circuit consisting of a 3 ohm resistor, the current flowing will be 4 amps (12 divided by 3). But 12 volts across a 6 ohm resistor will reduce the current flow to 2 amps. If two 3 ohm resistors are connected in series, their values are added to determine the current flow—which will again be 2 amps. But using Ohm's law we can obtain a new voltage at the junction of the two resistors, namely 6 volts, and such a circuit is termed a *potential divider*. If instead of two fixed resistors we substitute a single resistor with an additional sliding contact, we can arrange a simple voltage control circuit which can be employed as a volume control.

Now if the two 3 ohm resistors were connected in parallel and then wired to a 12 volt supply, the current flow would be divided into two paths passing 4 amps each (12 divided by 3), a total of 8 amps. This means that the effective resistance across the supply is now only $1\frac{1}{2}$ ohms. In cases where two resistors of unequal value are connected in parallel, the effective resistance can be found by the formula—

$$\frac{1}{R} = \frac{1}{R_1} + \frac{1}{R_2}$$

Electrical Power

The amount of effort used by an electrical current in a circuit is called power, and the unit of power is a *watt*. The number of watts being consumed at any given moment is found by multiplying the voltage across the circuit by the current flowing through it. This gives the formula W = VI, where W is watts, V is volts, and I is the current in amps. Using Ohm's law we can also find the power by two other variations thus—

$$W = I^2R \text{ or } W = \frac{V^2}{R}$$

Although we talk of power being consumed or expended in a circuit, the energy involved does not entirely disappear. It is a natural law that when energy is used it must reappear in some other form, and electricity usually reappears in the form of heat, light, or motion. A prime example of motion is the cone of a loudspeaker, which vibrates when converting electrical currents into audible sound waves.

Division of Units

The units of measurement mentioned so far are quite satisfactory for dealing with electrical matters. But for sound recording measurements these units are too large and we sub-divide them into one thousand and one million parts, designated by these symbols.

1 thousandth of a volt	= 1 millivolt	(1 mV)
1 millionth of a volt	= 1 microvolt	(1 μV)
1 thousandth of an amp	= 1 milliamp	(1 mA)
1 millionth of an amp	= 1 microamp	(1 μA)
1 thousandth of a watt	= 1 milliwatt	(1 mW)
1 millionth of a farad	= 1 microfarad	(1 μF)
1 millionth of a microfarad	= 1 picofarad	(1 pF)
1 thousandth of a henry	= 1 millihenry	(1 mH)
1 millionth of a henry	= 1 microhenry	(1 μH)
1 tenth of a bel	= 1 decibel	(1 db)

Units which are too small may be multiplied thus—

1 thousand volts	= 1 kilovolt	(1 kV)
1 thousand watts	= 1 kilowatt	(1 kW)
1 thousand ohms	= 1 kilohm	(1 k/ohm)
1 million ohms	= 1 megohm	(1 meg)
1 thousand cycles (Hz)	= 1 kilohertz	(1 kHz)
1 million cycles (Hz)	= 1 megahertz	(1 mHz)

Capacitance

A *capacitor* consists basically of two thin metal plates separated by an insulator such as air, mica, or paper. Therefore no direct current can actually flow from one plate to another, although a charge of electrons can be built up and stored between them. If a circuit is connected across the plates, electrons are released in the form of energy. This ability of storing electrons is called capacitance, and the unit of measurement is a *Farad*. The number of Farads in any given capacitor is directly proportional to the area of the plates, and inversely proportional to the distance between the plates. In practice a Farad is found to be too large, and a *microfarad* (expressed as 1 μF) which is 1 millionth of a Farad is normally employed, also a *picofarad* (1 pF) which is 1 millionth of a microfarad.

Capacitors are employed in amplifiers as a blocking device between two electron streams, and for stabilising power supplies. They are also used in tone control circuits since capacitors are frequency selective and can adjust audio signal voltages. A capacitor is also the basis of the capsule in a condenser microphone, where the microphone diaphragm forms one plate and the fixed back plate of the capsule is the other (see page 95).

Inductance

When an electrical current is passed along a wire conductor, a magnetic field is produced in the vicinity of the wire. If the wire is wound into a coil the magnetic field is increased, and becomes similar to the field surrounding a bar magnet. Building up this magnetic field requires energy, which the coil takes in the form of an increase in current. When the magnetic field is complete, the current is at a minimum. On removing the supply of current the magnetic field collapses, and the coil momentarily dispenses energy. The coil of wire therefore reacts to changes in current passing through it, a property called inductance for which the unit of measurement is a Henry. This is sometimes too large for practical purposes, and use is made of a *millihenry* (1 mH) which is 1 thousandth of a Henry. Such a coil is termed an *inductor*.

The building up and collapse of the magnetic field produces a voltage across the coil terminals, which is determined by the coil inductance. The inductance will be increased if the coil is wound around an iron core, and this is the construction of an electromagnet used for relays and transformers. In a transformer two coils of wire, called primary and secondary windings, are wound on to the same core. Changes in the magnetic field surrounding the primary winding will induce a voltage into the secondary winding. The voltage in the secondary can be made higher or lower than the voltage in the primary, depending on the number of turns in the two coils and the ratio between them. This is the principle of step-up or step-down mains transformers.

In sound recording use is also made of special *hybrid transformers* which have one primary winding and two or more secondary windings. They are constructed in such a way that the secondary windings do not react upon each other, and these hybrid transformers are employed for isolating speech or signal circuits. Since inductors, like capacitors, are frequency selective, they are also used in tone control circuits.

But an inductor has many other applications. For example if the coil is wound around a magnet and the magnet is moved in relation to the coil, a voltage will be produced across the coil which is the principle of a simple electric generator. Similarly if the coil is moved in relation to the magnet, we have the principle of a moving coil microphone. Conversely when an electric current is passed through the coil and the magnet is fixed, the coil will move and we have the basis of a moving coil loudspeaker.

Alternating Current

So far the only electrical currents described are those which flow through a circuit in one direction only. These are called direct currents (d.c.) and the power source is usually a battery or a special d.c. generator. But in sound recording the signals dealt with are mainly currents which are continually reversing their direction of flow, and these are called *alternating currents* (a.c.). The rate at which these alternating currents change their direction is called frequency, which is analogous to the theory of sound wave motion described in the previous chapter. The obvious example is the frequency of the a.c. mains supply, which is detectable as a 50 or 60 Hz hum in the loudspeaker of a poorly designed or faulty a.c. amplifier.

Since sound waves in electrical terms are a.c. and not d.c., the behaviour of resistors, capacitors, and inductors in a.c. circuits is important.

When a.c. is passed through a resistor the power dissipated is not the peak value as determined by Ohm's law, but an average value called the root mean square (r.m.s.) which is approximately 0·7 times the peak value.

But the current passing through a resistor is the same at all frequencies, since resistors are not frequency selective.

Connecting an a.c. supply to a capacitor causes an electron charge to appear first on one plate and then on the other, with a rapidity equal to the frequency of the a.c. supply. Therefore a.c. can be said to flow in and out of a capacitor in the process of charging it, and the amount of current flow will increase with an increase in capacitance, or with an increase in frequency, or both. This makes a capacitor frequency selective to a.c. Capacitors are also rated either for a peak operating voltage or an r.m.s. operating voltage, and it is important to distinguish between these two if component failure is to be avoided.

Since an inductor opposes change in the flow of a direct current, it offers even more opposition to the change in flow of an alternating current. This opposition increases with an increase in inductance, or with an increase in frequency, or with both. This makes an inductor frequency selective to a.c.

To sum up, raising the capacitance or frequency increases the current flow through a capacitor; but raising the inductance or frequency decreases the current flow through an inductor. This property is called *reactance*, and is peculiar to these two components. Resistors maintain the same value and pass the same current at all frequencies.

Impedance

When a particular component (or a circuit containing several components) has both reactance and resistance, their combined effect is known as *impedance*. This is made abundantly clear by a loudspeaker voice coil which is described as having an impedance, say, of 15 ohms. The measured d.c. resistance may only be in the region of 5 or 6 ohms, whilst the remainder is comprised of reactance to a.c. due to the inductance present in the coil.

All sources of voltage including amplifiers, batteries, gramophone pick-ups, and microphones have an output impedance. This is due to a combination of their internal resistance and reactance. These voltage sources will only deliver their maximum amount of power into a circuit when the impedance of source and circuit is correctly matched. In cases where an impedance match is not possible there will be an inevitable loss of power. But conditions are usually such that this power loss is negligible when compared with the power gained by the following circuit.

Resonant Frequency

Since the reactance of a capacitor decreases as frequency increases, and the reactance of an inductor increases as frequency increases, it is obvious that there will be one spot frequency at which the reactance of two specific components will be the same. This is known as their *resonant frequency*, and the capacitor and inductor may be connected to form a tuned circuit.

It has been found that reactances cancel each other out when such components are wired in series, so that the current passing through rises to a maximum at the resonant frequency. When the components are wired in parallel, the reactances become additive and the current passing through falls to a minimum at the resonant frequency. The degree of sharpness at resonance depends on the amount of resistance present, which can be increased to form a broadly tuned circuit or reduced to form a sharply tuned circuit. Tuned circuits are employed in equalizers for frequency correction, as well as in radio and television receivers.

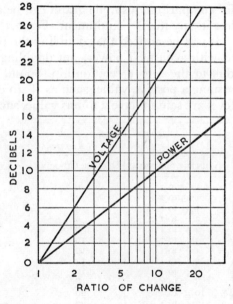

Fig. 2.1. A graph showing the relationship in decibels of voltage and power changes.

The Decibel

It has already been explained that a *decibel* is actually one tenth of a rather large unit of loudness called the *Bel*. A decibel can be defined as the logarithmic ratio between two different sound volume levels or powers; and since the sensation of hearing also follows a logarithmic scale, the usual formula for calculating the relationship in decibels between two sound volumes is—

$$10 \log \frac{\text{Volume A}}{\text{Volume B}}$$

In order to express a power ratio we must have a reference volume level. Acoustically zero db is measured at the point when a 1000 Hz note reaches the threshold of hearing, but a different term of reference exists for measuring sound waves in their electrical form. Here the decibel merely expresses a power or voltage ratio, and it has no absolute value such as an ohm, an amp, or a volt.

When passing through any amplifier system, sound signals comprise an a.c. voltage of a certain power, usually rated in watts or milliwatts. Zero level, or 0 dbm, has been firmly established as being 1 mW dissipated across a 600 ohm resistor. But the decibel is also employed to express voltage ratios, and in this case the reference level of zero dbv is taken as 0·775 V measured across a 600 ohm resistor. Since the relationship between volts and power (in watts) is always 2 to 1, using the same value of resistor for comparison, a simple graph can be drawn to show the decibel gain or loss in any item of equipment (Fig. 2.1).

It will be noticed that doubling the power causes a 3 db rise in volume as with acoustical power, but doubling the voltage produces a 6 db rise due to the 2 to 1 relationship. Sound volumes above zero level always assume a positive value, such as + 40 db; but sound volumes below zero level are said to have a minus value, such as − 6 db.

DECIBEL TABLE No. 1

VOLTAGE CHANGE	DECIBEL CHANGE
1 to 1	0
1·25 to 1	2
1·6 to 1	4
2 to 1	6
2·5 to 1	8
3·2 to 1	10
4 to 1	12
5 to 1	14
6·4 to 1	16
8 to 1	18
10 to 1	20
12·5 to 1	22
16 to 1	24
20 to 1	26
25 to 1	28

DECIBEL TABLE No. 2

POWER CHANGE	DECIBEL CHANGE
1 to 1	0
2 to 1	3
3 to 1	5
4 to 1	6
5 to 1	7
6 to 1	8
8 to 1	9
10 to 1	10
20 to 1	13
25 to 1	14

Fig. 2.2A. A table showing the decibel change for a given voltage change.

Fig. 2.2B. A table showing the decibel change for a given power change.

Audio Oscillator

Since such importance is placed on the subjects of sound volume in decibels, and signal frequency in Hertz per second, it is essential to have some form of tone generator to use when setting up or making adjustments to a sound recording system or installation. A simple tuning fork will emit a single standard frequency, but for our purpose we need a generator which will produce any desired frequency over the entire audible range, and sometimes beyond. At the same time it is necessary to have accurate control over the intensity or volume of these frequencies, in order to allow accurate measurements to be made in dbs.

Such a generator is called an *audio oscillator*, and it should be capable of producing a pure sine wave to simulate any fundamental frequency, and without any harmonics. Oscillators of this type generate tones with frequencies from 1 or 2 cycles (Hz) up to 100 kHz or more, either with a series of continuous sweeps in 4 or 5 ranges or switched to give a succession of spot frequencies. A volume level or db meter is included so that the output voltage from the oscillator may be kept constant, and the output impedance is usually 600 ohms. To control the amount of power being fed into the equipment under test, and prevent overloading the input circuit, there is a switched attenuator. Such an attenuator should have at least two controls, variable in 1 db and 10 db steps respectively. Other output impedances can be matched with a transformer.

Some audio oscillators are available in dual waveform versions, and contain special shaping circuits for producing square waves in addition to sine waves. Square waves are rich in harmonics, and can therefore be used for examining harmonic distortion in audio amplifying equipment by observing the waveform on an oscilloscope. Square waves are also used in the production of electronic music. Both mains and battery operated oscillators are in general use, the former containing valves as their active components and the latter type transistors.

A.C. *Voltmeter*

To measure the output signal of equipment under test, one would assume that an *a.c. voltmeter* is all that is required. This is true when considering amplifier outputs where the signal assumes a level of several volts: but measurements will often be required on passive items of equipment such as equaliser circuits which have no amplification. In fact equalizers introduce a signal loss, which is called their insertion loss, and is measured in dbs. If equalizers have been designed to operate in low level circuits, only a small signal can be passed through them without overload. Therefore amplification will have to take place before measurement, and the device for doing this is either a *valve voltmeter* or a *transistor voltmeter*.

Typical commercial models have a sensitivity range of from $5\mu V$ to $500V$, and they give accurate readings over a frequency range of from

1 Hz to 3 mHz. Meter scales are calibrated in decibels from − 20 db to + 2 db or + 3db, as well as in volts, millivolts, and microvolts, which makes a very comprehensive instrument. Sometimes it is also convenient to hear the signal frequency being measured, and a monitor outlet is then fitted for this purpose. The input impedance of a valve or transistor voltmeter is intentionally kept high so that it does not load the circuit being measured, which would give a false reading.

CHAPTER III

Magnetic Recording and Reproduction

MAGNETIC RECORDING as we know it today is the result of development work on recording heads and magnetic tape carried out in Germany during the second world war, and of considerable research in Europe and America since that time. One of the most notable achievements was the addition of a high frequency bias to the audio signal during recording, which gave a vast improvement to the sound quality. But magnetic recording is far from being a linear process, since it consists of converting electrical energy into an electromagnetic field, which is then imparted by induction on to the coating of a plastic base tape. Such conversions do not follow a linear law, and severe harmonic distortion occurs unless suitable precautions are taken. There is also a loss of high frequencies due to self demagnetization of the tape as it passes over the record head, and a severe attenuation of bass frequencies during playback. These problems, and others, have been successfully overcome so that excellent sound quality can be obtained from modern recorders. In fact the reproduced sound is often indistinguishable from the original sound source.

Theory of Magnetic Sound

In order to understand the theory of magnetic sound recording and reproduction it will be necessary to refer to the basic principles of electricity and magnetism. The effect of passing an electrical current through a coil of wire wound round a core of soft iron is generally known. The iron will be induced with a certain amount of magnetism, the exact amount depending on the strength of the current through the coil. The result is the formation of a magnetic field containing north and south poles, although this field collapses when the current is switched off since soft iron will not retain its magnetism. If the core of iron is shaped to form a circle with only a very small gap between the ends, current passing through the coil will create a field with a strong magnetic flux across the gap. This is the basic design of a magnetic recording head.

The signals we wish to record already exist in the form of electrical currents, varying in frequency and amplitude according to the original sound waveform. If these signal currents are passing through the coil of wire, and a plastic tape with a magnetic coating is drawn evenly past the gap, the magnetic flux existing at any given moment will be imparted to the tape. The tape coating completes the magnetic path across the gap, and the special qualities of the coating—an iron oxide lacquer—enable it

39

to retain the magnetism it receives. The result is the formation of numerous permanent magnets along the length of the tape.

Tape playback is the exact opposite of the recording process. It is the magnetism inherent in the tape coating which produces a varying magnetic flux as it is drawn past the gap in the head. The head coil has a minute a.c. voltage induced into it by the flux, and this voltage is fed into an amplifier and finally reproduced as audible sound.

Why should magnetic tape retain its magnetism indefinitely, and yet the metal core of a record head lose its magnetic field so quickly? The answer lies in the *coercivity* of the material used. Coercivity denotes magnetic hardness, and is measured in *Oersteds*. Magnetic heads have a low coercivity, which means that they are magnetically soft and incapable of retaining any magnetic flux. Conversely tape oxide coatings have a high coercivity and are magnetically hard, so recorded information due to an induced magnetic flux may be stored for as long as required. All magnetic heads and tape coatings are manufactured from high *permeability* materials, meaning that they have a low resistance to the flow of magnetic flux lines.

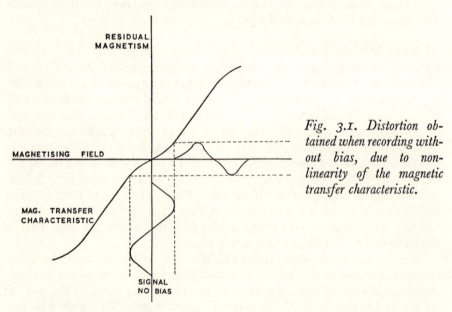

Fig. 3.1. Distortion obtained when recording without bias, due to nonlinearity of the magnetic transfer characteristic.

The need for Bias

It has already been established that magnetic recording is a non-linear process, which is illustrated by the shape of the *magnetic transfer characteristic* (or remanence curve) in Fig. 3.1. This shows the magnetic field of a sine wave applied to the central point of the transfer characteristic, and the resulting waveform induced on to the tape. Distortion of the third harmonic is indicated, which must be avoided at all costs. Sounds of low volume would not be recorded at all under these conditions, and sounds of normal and high volume would not be at all intelligible. The answer is to remove the operating point away from the curved part of the transfer characteristic and place it on a more linear section.

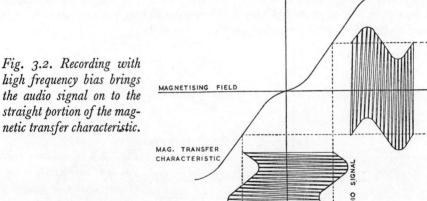

Fig. 3.2. Recording with high frequency bias brings the audio signal on to the straight portion of the magnetic transfer characteristic.

High Frequency Bias

The superimposition of a *high frequency bias* voltage causes the audio signal modulations to be applied along the straight portions of the transfer characteristic (Fig. 3.2). This eliminates distortion and effectively increases the sensitivity of the tape. Another effect of high frequency bias is that tape background noise is reduced since the signal-to-noise ratio has been increased.

The frequency of the bias voltage must be sufficiently above the highest audible frequency to avoid the generation of any beat frequencies or combination tones. The usual frequency employed is 60 kHz. The amount of bias voltage required depends on the type of tape in use, and can vary considerably with different brands even when used on the same recording machine. The optimum value of bias for any particular tape is a compromise which gives the most satisfactory frequency response with the minimum of distortion, together with a good signal-to-noise ratio. A low bias setting tends to accentuate the response at high frequencies and to introduce distortion, whilst a high bias setting causes a falling off in high frequency response and a reduction in the signal-to-noise ratio. The usual method of alignment is to record a 1 kHz tone and adjust the bias until the output from the playback (or monitor) head is at a maximum. The bias is then further increased until the playback output falls by 1 db.

In early magnetic recorders it was common practice to apply a direct current bias which moved the operating point to one side of the transfer characteristic (Fig. 3.3). Although this allowed satisfactory recordings to be made, it caused a high background noise due to the tape particles being magnetized in one direction only, also a restriction in the volume of sound it was possible to record without distortion. Direct current bias is only used today in certain domestic portable recorders.

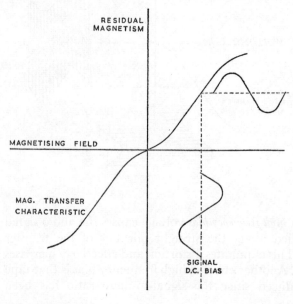

RESIDUAL MAGNETISM

MAGNETISING FIELD

MAG. TRANSFER CHARACTERISTIC

SIGNAL D.C. BIAS

Fig. 3.3. Recording with d.c. bias only uses one half of the available magnetic transfer characteristic, giving a poor signal-to-noise ratio.

Bias Oscillator

High frequency bias is obtained from a special tuned circuit in the recording amplifier which is called the *bias oscillator*. The frequency is usually several times the value of the highest frequency being recorded, which means between 60 kHz and 80 kHz. The oscillator must generate a pure sine waveform, since odd harmonics of the bias frequency can seriously interfere with the content of the audio signal being recorded.

Both halves of the sine wave must also be symmetrical, otherwise a small d.c. component will be present which is liable to introduce unwanted noise. Great care is taken in the design of bias oscillators, and a push-pull circuit is often employed to ensure a clean waveform. In cases where the application of bias gives rise to an uneven tape background noise, radio frequency filters are fitted to the oscillator output to remove all traces of harmonics and to further improve the waveform.

The bias oscillator is also used to supply current for an erase head where one is fitted. The erase current is always greatly in excess of the record bias current, and is often obtained from a separate winding on the oscillator coil. This enables the maximum amount of power to be obtained when the erase head and record head are of different impedances.

Bias Rejection Filter

It is important to prevent any bias from finding its way back into the recording amplifier, since this would constitute a partial short circuit of the oscillator output and lower its efficiency. This condition is prevented by a simple tuned circuit called a *bias rejection filter*, which acts as a high impedance barrier to the oscillator frequency. It is inserted in series with the lead from the amplifier to the record head, and offers a low impedance to signals of audio frequency with no insertion loss.

The filter consists of a suitable inductor which is approximately tuned to the bias frequency by a small capacitor. The inductor has a variable ferrite core for vernier tuning, and the filter is easily aligned for maximum bias rejection.

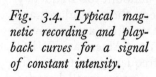

Fig. 3.4. Typical magnetic recording and playback curves for a signal of constant intensity.

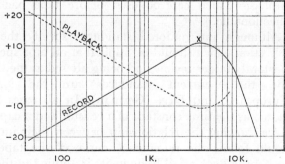

Magnetic Frequency Response

In addition to obtaining a linear magnetic transfer characteristic there is the problem of obtaining a flat overall frequency response in a record/replay system. Magnetic recording follows the law of induction which means that the impedance of the record head increases as the recorded frequency increases, causing a decrease in head efficiency at high frequencies. During replay the output from a magnetic head is also proportional to frequency. Fig. 3.4 shows the frequency response curve of a tape system obtained with un-equalized amplifiers, and the dotted line shows the frequency correction required during replay to obtain a level characteristic. The shape of the recording curve will remain the same for all tape speeds, except that the turnover point (x) will vary its position on the frequency scale according to the tape speed in use. Values for x are as follow: $1\frac{7}{8}$ i.p.s. = 2 kHz, $3\frac{3}{4}$ i.p.s. = 4 kHz, $7\frac{1}{2}$ i.p.s. = 8 kHz, 15 i.p.s. = 14 kHz.

In order to provide sufficient flux density at high frequencies to fully load the tape, high frequency pre-emphasis is applied during recording. The exact amount of pre-emphasis is adjusted for each tape speed, so as to obtain the best frequency response without distortion due to over-modulation. The upper limit of the frequency response occurs when the wavelength of the signal frequency approaches the space available on the tape. Above the optimum wavelength more than one complete cycle will appear and result in virtual demagnetization of the tape at high frequencies.

When playing back a tape recording, the signal voltage induced into the head winding is fully dependant on frequency, and increases by 6 db for each octave rise. Therefore bass lift becomes necessary to maintain a level output from the head at all frequencies. High frequency emphasis is also used to combat losses which occur as the recorded wavelength becomes comparable with the dimensions of the gap in the replay head, especially at slow tape speeds. But there is a limit to the amount of emphasis which can be used before tape background noise becomes objectionable.

Although international standards specify the amount of frequency correction which should be applied at all tape speeds, these standards are constantly under review and being altered as the state of the art improves. The three current standards are the NAB (American), IEC (European), and DIN (German). In all cases frequency correction is quoted as the time constant of a resistor and a capacitor in parallel, and a curve showing the relationship between their impedance and frequency should follow the remanence curve of the tape. This assumes that a constant voltage at all frequencies is applied to the input of the recording chain. In addition there is now a small amount of bass lift applied during recording, so as to reduce the amount of bass lift required during replay, and this is quoted as the time constant of a resistor and a capacitor in parallel. In all cases the corresponding replay characteristic is that which gives a flat response when reproducing each recording condition. Time constants are given in micro-seconds.

Frequency Correction Standards

Tape Speed	Standard	Time Constant (µs.)
15 i.p.s.	NAB	35 (high), 3180 (low)
	IEC	35 (high), 3180 (low)
	DIN	35 (high), 3180 (low)
7½ i.p.s.	NAB	50 (high), 3180 (low)
	IEC	70 (high), 3180 (low)
	DIN	100 (high), 3180 (low)
3¾ i.p.s.	NAB	100 (high), 3180 (low)
	IEC	140 (high), 3180 (low)
	DIN	120 (high), 3180 (low)
1⅞ i.p.s.	DIN	120 (high), 1590 (low)

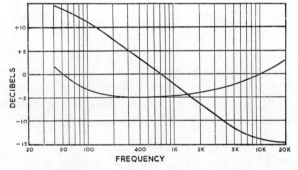

Fig. 3.5. Typical record and replay amplifier curves for a tape speed of 15 i.p.s.

Typical record and replay amplifier curves for a tape speed of 15 i.p.s. are shown in Fig. 3.5, and remain the same for all three frequency correction standards. However the amount of equalization required may **vary** slightly with different equipment, according to the specification of

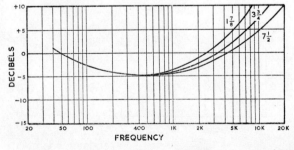

Fig. 3.6. Typical recording curves for a three-speed domestic machine.

the record and replay heads, the type of tape used, the amount of record bias, and any other small losses which require compensation.

In multi-speed domestic recorders the problem is more complex since several different curves must be provided. Fig. 3.6 shows the three frequency response curves of a recording amplifier in a three speed machine, and Fig. 3.7 shows the corresponding frequency response curves of a replay amplifier. It is customary for the required curve to be selected automatically by the speed change switch on the recorder.

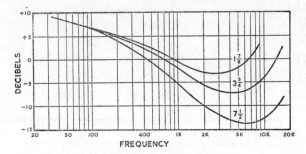

Fig. 3.7. Typical replay curves for a three-speed domestic machine.

Since the three frequency standards have different time constants at slower tape speeds, additional equalization is provided on some recorders so that tapes recorded to different standards may be replayed correctly. Similar results can usually be achieved by using tone control circuits in a replay amplifier.

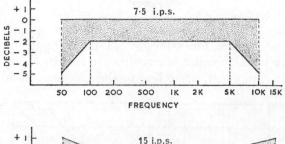

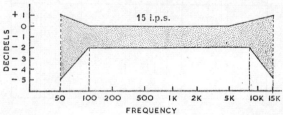

Fig. 3.8. Tolerances in overall frequency response for a magnetic recording and reproducing system.

For each tape speed of each frequency correction standard there is a pre-recorded test tape available commercially. These *calibration tapes* contain a series of spot frequencies for adjustment of the replay equalizer, so that a level frequency response can be obtained. Then the record amplifier is adjusted to give the same result as the calibration tape, and the recorder is known to be correctly aligned. Some latitude is permissible in any recording system, and the overall limits laid down by the British Standards Institution for tape speeds of $7\frac{1}{2}$ i.p.s. and 15 i.p.s. are shown in Fig. 3.8.

Magnetic Tape

Magnetic recording tape consists of a backing material, which is usually a plastic base, coated with a lacquer containing finely ground iron oxide particles (Fe_2O_3) and a binding agent. This description is perhaps an over-simplification since the oxide lacquer may contain as many as 17 ingredients. The oxide particles comprise numerous permanent magnets which have a random formation in a piece of un-recorded tape. When recording takes place the applied magnetic field causes the oxide particles to become re-orientated to form a magnetic pattern of north and south poles. The stronger the field the greater the amplitude of the recorded waveform, since more particles will become affected. Tape saturation occurs when all the oxide particles have been magnetized.

Tape base is manufactured in five different thicknesses, and is referred to as Standard play (0·002 in.), Long play (0·0015 in.), Douple play (0·001 in.), Triple play (0·00075 in.), and Quadruple play (0·0005 in.). Materials used include Polyvinyl Chloride, Polyester, and occasionally Cellulose Acetate. Tape base must possess a high tensile strength to withstand normal handling, and yet be supple enough to maintain good contact with a recording head. These properties should not be affected by extremes of humidity and temperature, and the base should possess a fairly good resistance to stretch. In fact some of the thinner Polyester based tapes are pre-stretched (also called pre-tensilized) during manufacture to resist further stretching during use. All tape bases should be non-inflammable and unaffected by ageing, since recordings may often be stored for a considerable length of time.

Tape coatings have several mechanical and magnetic properties. The surface of the tape must be extremely smooth and flat to maintain a good contact with the record head, and most modern tapes undergo a finishing treatment consisting of a special polishing technique. This ensures that the tape is capable of recording a good high frequency response, and causes the minimum of head wear. The iron oxide particles must also be dispersed at an even density throughout the coating, otherwise variations in sensitivity could occur resulting in the sudden reduction or loss of the recorded signal. This condition is known as a *drop-out*, which can also be caused by impurities in the tape coating or even a speck of foreign matter embedded in the tape. The binding properties of the lacquer must also be efficient, otherwise oxide particles will become detached from the coating and deposited as a brown dust in the tape path of the recorder.

Not all tapes are suitable for all recorders as tape coatings vary considerably in their magnetic characteristics. All tapes must have a high *coercivity* which is the ability to retain the magnetic flux applied during recording, and they must also possess a high *remanence* in order to give the tape a high sensitivity to induction. But it is the high frequency recording bias which places the audio signal on the linear portion of the magnetic transfer characteristic, and it is this characteristic which must be matched to suit different brands of oxide coatings. This means that different makes of tape will require different bias settings to obtain maximum output with the minimum of distortion, and the correct frequency response.

Professional recorders have the facility for bias adjustment, also a means of quickly checking performance at any given bias setting. But not all domestic recorders have the same facilities, and they should preferably only be used with the particular brand of tape recommended by the manufacturer.

Tape Selection

The importance of selecting the correct tape is emphasized when remembering the following facts. If the recording bias is too high for a particular tape, the high frequency response and signal-to-noise ratio will be worse although distortion and absence of drop-outs will be improved. If the record bias is low, the high frequency response will be enhanced but distortion, drop-outs, and signal-to-noise ratio will be worse. This brings to light the fallacy of attempting to improve high frequency response by intentionally using a low bias setting, and shows the need for accurately adjusting a recorder for use with the selected brand of tape.

Quite apart from variations in the magnetic characteristics of different oxide coatings, the physical properties of the various base thicknesses must be considered, together with their suitability for various recording applications.

Standard play—easy to handle and has a high mechanical strength. Used on all professional equipment where tape to head contact is not a problem, and is ideal for general use at $7\frac{1}{2}$ i.p.s. and 15 i.p.s. It is also the best tape to use when editing is contemplated. Not suitable at all for four-track recorders, or for slow speed recording on twin-track machines.

Long play—an equally strong tape but more supple, also used professionally when longer playing time is required. Suitable for four-track machines, both mains operated and battery portable types.

Double play—an extremely supple tape which is eminently suitable for all four-track recorders at all tape speeds. Tape joins can be made, but general editing is difficult.

Triple play—originally manufactured for extended playing times on portable recorders with small spool sizes. Print-through from one layer to the next is sometimes troublesome. Used extensively in cassette recorders.

Quadruple play—used for maximum playing time with portable and cassette recorders. Extremely delicate to handle, easily damaged at the edges. Print-through factor is reasonable unless overmodulated.

SPOOL SIZES IN INS. AND CMS—CONTENTS IN FEET AND METRES							
Spool Size	3 in. 8 cm	3¼ in. 9 cm	4 in. 10 cm	4¼ in. 11 cm	5 in. 13 cm	5¾ in. 15 cm	7 in. 18 cm
Standard Play Tape	150 ft. 45 m	175 ft. 53 m	300 ft. 90 m	410 ft. 125 m	600 ft. 180 m	850 ft. 255 m	1200 ft. 360 m
Long Play Tape	225 ft. 70 m	350 ft. 105 m	450 ft. 135 m	560 ft. 158 m	900 ft. 270 m	1200 ft. 360 m	1800 ft. 540 m
Double Play Tape	300 ft. 90 m	400 ft. 122 m	600 ft. 180 m	800 ft. 240 m	1200 ft. 360 m	1800 ft. 540 m	2400 ft. 720 m
Triple Play Tape	450 ft. 135 m	600 ft. 180 m	900 ft. 270 m	1200 ft. 360 m	1800 ft. 540 m	2400 ft. 720 m	3600 ft. 1080 m
Quadruple Play Tape	600 ft. 180 m	800 ft. 240 m	1200 ft. 360 m	—	—	—	—

TAPE RUNNING TIMES							
	150 ft. 45 m	300 ft. 90 m	450 ft. 135 m	600 ft. 180 m	1200 ft. 240 m	800 ft. 360 m	1800 ft. 540 m
1⅞ i.p.s. 4·75 cm	16 min.	32 min.	48 min.	1 hr. 4 m.	1 hr. 26 m.	2 hr. 8 m.	3 hr. 12 m.
3¾ i.p.s. 9·5 cm	8 min.	16 min.	24 min.	32 min.	43 min.	1 hr. 4 m.	1 hr. 36 m.
7½ i.p.s. 19 cm	4 min.	8 min.	12 min.	16 min.	21 min.	32 min.	48 min.
15 i.p.s. 36 cm	2 min.	4 min.	6 min.	8 min.	11 min.	16 min.	24 min.

Print-Through

Once a tape has received a recording, the induced magnetism will be retained indefinitely without losing any of the original signal strength. But loud signals cause a greater degree of magnetism, some of which causes *print-through* from one layer of tape to the next as the tape is fairly tightly wound. This effect can increase with temperature, and also with length of storage, and becomes audible as a faint pre-echo of a loud signal. Print-through is only generally noticeable in moments of comparative silence between sounds of high intensity.

The remedy for print-through is to rewind tapes at frequent intervals and store them in a fairly cool place away from radiators. Overmodulated tapes will naturally suffer most, in spite of the low *print-through factor* achieved by tape manufacturers. This is usually better than 55 db between adjacent layers of tape with 100 per cent modulation, measured after 24 hours at a temperature of approximately 20°C. The fact that long play tapes have a much thinner base does not necessarily mean a poorer print-through factor, although this often is the case.

Tapes which have been stored for a considerable period of time and already possess print-through can sometimes be improved by passing the tape over a very weak bar magnet. Special magnetized tape guides have been sold for this purpose. An alternative method is to run the tape through a recorder with the erase head disconnected and a very low value of bias passing through the record head. A certain amount of experimenting is required to obtain a bias setting which gives the desired amount of print-through correction, so do not use valuable and irreplacable tapes until you know in advance what the result will be.

Modulation Noise

Another side effect of magnetic sound is called *modulation noise*, which is present to some extent on all magnetic tape and magnetic film recordings. This appears as little bursts of background noise which are generated in synchronism with the audio signal during the recording process, due to the non-homogeneous nature of the tape coating. Modulation noise is most noticeable as a slight fuzziness of high frequency sounds, although this type of noise is also present on signals of medium and low frequency.

Some tape coatings produce more modulation noise than others, and the characteristics of coatings are continually being improved. Should this effect become troublesome, a change of tape brand could produce better results. One method of reducing modulation noise, especially at medium and low frequencies, is to use a compressor/expander circuit such as the noise reduction system described on page 123.

Magnetic Heads

In magnetic recording equipment designed for professional use, separate record and replay amplifiers are fitted together with separate record and replay heads. This permits continuous monitoring of the audio signal a few milliseconds after it has been recorded. It is known as on/off tape monitoring, or alternatively A/B monitoring when A = direct sound and B = the recorded sound. In most domestic tape recorders a combined record/replay head is fitted for the sake of economy. An erase head is also fitted to domestic recorders, but not always on professional equipment.

The design of a magnetic head is rather more complicated than the brief explanation already given on page 39. The core of iron is not used in practice, but a stack of laminations made from high permeability materials such as mu-metal, radiometal, etc. This ensures that the magnetizing force will flow freely and the head core will not retain any magnetism once the magnetizing force has ceased. The two ends of the laminated core are known as *pole pieces*, and the gap between them is filled with a thin shim of gold, beryllium copper, or phosphor bronze. These materials have a low permeability and therefore offer a high magnetic resistance.

There is also a second gap at the rear of the laminations, usually of air, which increases the resistance of the magnetic circuit. Its purpose is to tilt the shape of the magnetic transfer characteristic and extend the linear portions of the curve. It also helps to keep the magnetizing force constant, and is useful during playback to minimize hum picked up in the windings from stray magnetic fields. The complete head system is assembled with a separate coil on each lamination stack, and then potted with a synthetic resin inside a mu-metal container which acts as a magnetic shield.

The coil of wire wound around the laminations presents a case for impedance matching. For recording purposes the impedance of the coils should be low to ensure a constant current which is independent of frequency. But for replay purposes the coils should have a high impedance with a large number of turns in order to obtain the maximum output voltage from the tape. When separate record and replay heads are used, each can be designed for its optimum operating conditions. Combined record/replay heads are usually of medium impedance, although low impedance heads used for replay have an impedance matching transformer between the head and the following amplifier input circuit.

Record Head

Recording takes place across the gap between the pole pieces, due to the magnetic flux taking the less resistive path offered by the oxide coating on the tape. The gap dimensions in a record head are not critical, since it is only the trailing edge of the pole pieces which governs the amplitude of the recorded signal at any frequency. But the gap must be accurately formed along its width, and of even dimensions throughout.

Replay Head

The construction of a replay head is similar to a record head except that the gap width must be smaller than the wavelength of the highest frequency it is desired to reproduce. In theory it is possible to attain an upper limit of 15 kHz at a tape speed of $7\frac{1}{2}$ i.p.s. if the gap width is 0·0005 in. But in practice the effective gap width is slightly reduced, and a gap of 0·00025 in. is required to adequately reproduce a frequency of 15 kHz. Slower tape speeds require replay heads with correspondingly smaller gaps, and a figure of 0·0001375 in. is not uncommon.

Since tolerances in head construction are so small as to be almost non-existent, modern methods of manufacture include plating the two pole pieces with a thin film of gold or copper, and even vacuum spraying. This allows accurate control over the thickness of the material deposited, and consequently control of the gap width dimensions.

Erase Head

Magnetic heads designed for erasing purposes are basically of the same construction as record and replay heads. The only difference is that the gap is made much wider to permit the tape to remain longer in the magnetic field existing between the pole pieces. Since the purpose of an erase head is to remove any residual magnetism from the tape, a magnetic field must be created which is strong enough to saturate the tape. To achieve this the current passing through the erase head winding is often considerable, and can result in the head reaching a high temperature.

Since modern tapes have a high remanence it has been found that satisfactory erasure was not always achieved with a single gap head. This has led to the introduction of erase heads with double gaps, giving an effective demagnetization of the tape amounting to over 75 db. Both gaps are of different dimensions and spaced about one-eighth of an inch apart on a common set of laminations.

The efficiency of an erase head also depends on the frequency of the current passing through it. Since efficiency is reduced as the frequency of the current is increased, and for economy reasons the high frequency bias oscillator usually supplies the erase current, pole-pieces made of *ferrite* are often employed to minimize losses. Screening of an erase head is not vitally important, in fact some erase heads are not screened at all and do not cause interference.

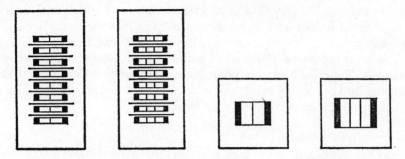

Fig. 3.9. Multi-track and single-track heads. L to R: 8-track record, 8-track erase, single-track record, single-track erase.

Multi-track Heads

It is frequently necessary to assemble a number of magnetic heads inside a single screened case for specialized applications. This is called a *stack* of heads, and a stack may contain two, three, four, six, eight, twelve, or sixteen heads, all mounted with their recording gaps in line. It is essential that the screening between each individual head winding is adequate to prevent *crosstalk*, that is interference between the signals in one head and its immediate neighbour. The pole pieces of each head must be accurately aligned with their gaps in phase, and they are usually potted in resin to prevent any movement. The final assembly is ground and lapped to give an even surface across the whole width of the tape.

Crossfield Head

When tape passes in front of a conventional record head, the bias field reaches a maximum in the centre of the gap, and decays as the tape leaves the influence of the field behind. This trailing bias field tends to demagnetize the tape and cause partial erasure of the high frequency content of the recording just made. An attempt by some manufacturers to improve this situation is the *crossfield head*, which is an additional head for applying the record bias through the base of the tape whilst the audio signal is applied at the front in the normal way.

The crossfield head is angled in such a way that the tape leaves the bias field more quickly, so that the effects of partial erasure are reduced. Although the bias head never actually touches the base of the tape, it is swung out of the way to facilitate tape threading.

Hum Bucking Coil

Where the arrangement of leads from a tape replay head to an amplifier are laid out in such a way that some a.c. mains hum is added to the audio signal, a small inductance is sometimes inserted into the audio lead and called a *hum bucking coil*. This coil also has hum induced into its windings, but it is arranged to be 180° out of phase so that the two hum currents cancel out. Tape deck motors often have a strong electrical field which penetrates into the replay head, and a hum bucking coil is used in addition to a mu-metal screen surrounding the head.

Tape Transport Mechanism

The mechanical design of the tape transport mechanism plays a large part in achieving high quality recordings, although the mechanism itself is basically simple. All the various components are mounted on a *tape deck*, and comprise spool hubs, tape guides, magnetic heads, capstan and pressure roller, drive motor, and drive belts or pulleys. Their main purpose is to transport the tape past the record and replay heads at a constant speed, without any of the speed fluctuations producing what is called *wow* and *flutter*. Wow is actually a long term speed variation caused by the uneven rotation of any moving part, which in itself can be due to normal wear or lack of cleaning. Flutter is a short term speed variation caused by worn or bent shafts, excessive friction between tape and heads, or uneven back tension by the feed spool.

Wow and flutter are always expressed as a percentage of the correct running speed, and are measured on a special wow and flutter meter. This compares the frequency of a recorded tone (usually 3 kHz) with the original signal and indicates any frequency variations. The short term variations are the ones which are most noticeable to the ear, especially if the repetition rate is in the region of 4 or 5 per second.

The professional size of spool has a diameter of 10½ inches, a 3 inch centre, and is fitted with a quick release hub. Such a spool will hold 2,400 ft. of standard play tape. The magnetic heads themselves are either positioned separately on the tape deck, or occasionally mounted all together in a *head block*. The block method enables an easy replacement to be made since each block is accurately located by dowel pins. No pressure pads or pressure tapes are necessary on professional recorders to keep the magnetic tape in intimate contact with the heads, since the heads are always arranged in an arc and there is sufficient back tension to operate a 'tight loop' system (Fig. 3.10). Pressure pads only become necessary at slow tape speeds when there is little or no back tension, as in the majority of domestic recorders.

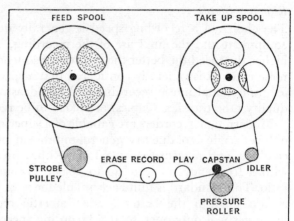

Fig. 3.10. Layout of a professional tape deck.

Adjacent to the head block is the driving spindle or *capstan*, which has a flywheel mounted on the same shaft to act as a mechanical filter against wow and flutter. The drive for the capstan is obtained via a rubber tyred wheel, positioned between a boss on the motor shaft and the rim of the flywheel. The boss is often stepped to provide different drive ratios for multi-speed recorders. An alternative method of drive is a belt from the motor to the flywheel, but this is not very satisfactory at slow speeds due to irregularities in the construction of the belt. The tape is held against the capstan by a rubber covered *pressure roller* or *pinch roller*, which is designed to provide good trcation without tape slip. The pressure roller should only be held in contact with the capstan when the tape transport mechanism is set in motion, and in fact most recorders are designed in this way. Leaving the pressure roller engaged causes an indent in the surface which could easily result in irregular running.

The tape is passed on to the take-up spool, usually via a spring loaded idler which prevents any variation in take-up tension being reflected back past the capstan and appearing at the record and replay heads. Provision is also made for the tape to be fast spooled forwards and backwards, and sometimes transported at slow speeds to assist in tape editing. Tape editing requires the tape to remain in contact with the replay head, but when spooling at high speeds the tape is usually lifted clear of the heads to avoid any unnecessary wear. A single motor of sufficient size can provide all the various drives required; or the work can be shared between three motors, one for the capstan and one each for the feed and take-up spool hubs.

Recording Speeds

The choice of a recording speed is generally determined by the type of equipment and the final use of the recording, bearing in mind that the higher the speed the better the recorded frequency response and signal-to-noise ratio. It is generally considered that a speed of 15 i.p.s. is necessary for professional music recording and broadcasting, especially if any high quality tape transfers (copies) are likely to be required.

Modern tape recorders are capable of a superior performance to those of only a decade ago, due to a general improvement in head design and tape coatings, and a recording speed of $7\frac{1}{2}$ i.p.s. produces high quality work with a frequency range of 40 to 16,000 Hz and a good signal-to-noise ratio. This standard is quite acceptable for a lot of professional work, and is also used in the better grade domestic recorders. Many domestic machines will only operate at a recording speed of $3\frac{3}{4}$ i.p.s., and a good frequency response is maintained by the use of equalizer circuits in the record and replay amplifiers. Even slower tape speeds are becoming more widely used, for example the popular compact cassette system which operates at $1\frac{7}{8}$ i.p.s. Here the frequency response has been maintained from 80 to 10,000 Hz, although the signal-to-noise ratio is below hi-fi standards. A speed of $\frac{15}{16}$ i.p.s. is also provided on certain multi-speed recorders, but this is only of some use for speech when an extremely long playing time is required.

It is obvious that in all recorders the tape must be transported as near to the stated speed as possible, to avoid pitch variations when material is passed from one machine to another. The generally accepted speed variations are $\pm$ 1 per cent for professional recorders, $\pm$ 2 per cent for all domestic recorders, and $\pm$ 3 per cent for battery operated portables. Also, since different frequency compensation is required for each tape speed, it is convenient to select compensation automatically on multi-speed recorders as the recording speed is changed.

Standard Track Dimensions

In order to make full use of the available signal-to-noise ratio in magnetic recording, the professional uses the full width of quarter-inch tape for any single recording. The only exception is where a second track has to be accommodated to carry a synchronizing pulse for certain types of film recording. Recording across only half the width of the tape effects a useful economy in tape consumption, with only a slight decrease in the signal-to-noise ratio, and this *twin-track* system is normally employed in the better domestic tape recorders. Further tape economy can be obtained with a *four-track* system, still using quarter-inch tape, which is considered perfectly adequate for amateur recordings of good quality. Fig. 3.11 shows the standard track dimensions of the twin-track and four-track systems, from which it will be seen that small safety margins or lanes are provided to assist in head alignment. They also prevent the pickup of information between adjacent tracks, thus reducing crosstalk.

Half-inch, one-inch and two-inch tapes are also to be seen in sound recording and broadcasting studios. Half-inch tape carries three tracks, each track being 0·1 in. wide, and one-inch tape carries from four to eight tracks. Two-inch tapes normally carry eight, sixteen, or twenty-four tracks. These wider tapes are most frequently used for music recording when several tracks are required simultaneously. Music master tapes must have a good signal-to-noise ratio, and consequently a reasonable track width must be employed.

The twin-track system offers an excellent standard for recording in stereo on quarter-inch tape. Numerous tape recorders are fitted with stacked heads aligned to this standard, and both head windings can be combined when necessary for single track working. The four-track system originated in America as a domestic standard for stereo recording. Tracks 1 and 3 are used on the first run of the tape, and tracks 2 and 4 on the second run after the tape has been reversed. One of the possibilities here is the unintentional scanning of an adjacent track, which will be heard running backwards. Recorder manufacturers have utilized the four-track system as a means of further tape economy, obtaining four separate single track recordings.

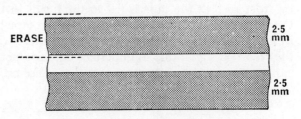

Fig. 3.11. Standard track dimensions on quarter-inch (6·35 mm) tape.

TWIN – TRACKS

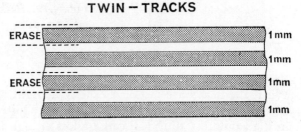

FOUR – TRACKS

An important point to remember is that twin-track and four-track recordings should be kept on separate reels of tape and not intermingled. A twin-track recording can be replayed on a four-track recorder, and a four-track recording can be replayed on a twin-track recorder if the two inside tracks are not used. But a four-track machine will only erase part of a twin-track recording, and this could cause confusion at a later date.

Alignment of Heads

All heads located in the tape path of a recorder must be accurately aligned to follow a definite and pre-determined tape track. This becomes extremely important when more than one track is being recorded on the same width of tape. It is usual for the erase head to overlap the track dimensions shown in Fig. 3.11 to ensure complete erasure even with a small amount of tape wander. When separate record and replay heads are fitted, these must be exactly in line with their gaps at right-angles to the edge of the tape.

Alignment tapes are available for twin-track and four-track recorders which allow correct head positioning. These tapes contain a recording made in the safety lanes, with a slight overspill into the track area on either side. This enables the height of the record/replay heads to be adjusted in relation to the tape, using a valve or transistor voltmeter to measure the output level from each track. The output will be equal from each track when head alignment is correct.

It is usual for tape guide pins or a tape channel to be fitted to the recorder so that the tape is fed to the heads in the correct plane and at the proper angle. It is also essential that the tape bears evenly on the head from top to bottom of the gap; otherwise there will be a loss of volume in the recorded signal due to imperfect tape contact across the length of the gap, and a deterioration in the signal-to-noise ratio.

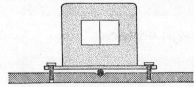

Fig. 3.12. Rocking-bar method of azimuth adjustment.

Azimuth Setting

When the heads are installed exactly at right angles to the direction of tape travel, they are said to be in *azimuth*. Quite a small amount of error in the azimuth setting will cause a loss of high frequency response, since the effect will be the same as using a replay head with an enlarged gap.

The degree of high frequency losses for a given azimuth error will depend on the width of the track. With full-track and twin-track recorders a small azimuth error simulates a very wide gap and produces a severe high frequency loss. But with a four-track recorder this effect is reduced and azimuth alignment becomes less critical.

To set up the heads a standard test tape containing a 9 kHz or 10 kHz tone is run through the recorder, and the head concerned is adjusted in angle until maximum output is attained. Alternatively a special azimuth alignment tape containing a wide range noise spectrum can be used, and an effective alignment can be achieved by ear without additional measuring instruments. A method of mounting the head on a rocking bar and tilting it by its fixing screws is illustrated in Fig. 3.12. Once the correct azimuth setting has been found, the fixing screws are sealed with a dab of paint or shellac. This treatment should normally last for the life of the head.

Fringe Effect

When tapes are replayed over a head having a narrower track width than the head which made the recording, stray magnetization coming from areas alongside the replay head cause a rise in response at low frequencies. This is called the *fringe effect*, which becomes greater as the track width is narrowed and the frequency is lowered. Therefore half-track and full-track recordings should not be replayed on machines with four-track heads, unless the fringe effect is taken into account and a correction factor applied. This can be evaluated by ear, or carried out more scientifically with magnetic test tapes.

Quick Loading Systems

Developments in tape transport methods have produced quick loading systems like the tape cassette and tape cartridge, which abolish tape threading as on conventional spool recorders. A *cassette* is a container in which tape runs from a feed core or spool to a take-up core or spool, and is manually turned over at the end of a run to reverse the direction of tape travel. A *cartridge* is a container which holds a single tape core and plate, and the tape ends are joined together to form a loop for continuous running. To avoid the possibility of jamming, or even tape breakage, the tape itself is lubricated with a coating of graphite.

Some cartridges use tape with a magnetic coating on both sides of the base support, a method which doubles the available playing time. The tape is then joined with a single twist to form a *mobius loop*, playing first one side of the tape and then the other. The main virtue of continuous play cartridges is for the reproduction of pre-recorded tapes, and the cassette system is more suitable for recording.

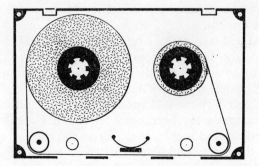

Fig 3.13. Philips Compact Cassette.

Compact Cassette

This is the name given to the very successful international cassette system originated by Philips, which is a double run cassette using tape $\frac{5}{32}$ in. (3·8 mm) wide at a tape speed of $1\frac{7}{8}$ i.p.s. Four tracks are recorded across the width of the tape, comprising two stereo pairs, and the track dimensions are shown in Fig. 3.14. Type C60 cassette holds 300 ft. (92 m) of triple play tape which gives 30 minutes playing time per track, type C90 cassette holds 450 ft. (133 m) of quadruple play tape which gives 45 minutes per track, and the type C120 cassette is loaded with quintuple play tape which gives 60 minutes per track.

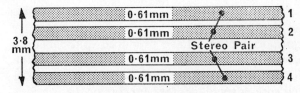

Fig. 3.14. Track location, compact cassette system.

All cassettes have built-in pressure pads, but the capstan and pressure roller remain as part of the recorder mechanism. The tape is wound oxide outward so that it makes contact with the heads as the cassette is inserted in the recorder, and it is the lower two tracks which are scanned as the tape travels from left to right. Since the two tracks of each stereo pair are adjacent they can be replayed with a single head (1·5 mm wide) scanning both tracks in compatible mono, in addition to normal stereo with stacked heads.

With any cassette system it is essential to give some form of protection against accidental erasure of pre-recorded tapes. The compact cassette has two small lugs moulded on to the back edge of the case which hold back a spring loaded tongue and allows the record button to be used. These lugs are omitted on cassettes containing pre-recorded material, and the tongue springs forward to prevent the record button from being operated.

D.C. International

This is another European cassette originated by Grundig and Telefunken, which is very similar to the compact cassette system. These cassettes are larger and will accommodate more tape, but the recording speed is non-standard at 2 i.p.s. Due to the lack of pre-recorded material, and the fact that Philips cassettes are not compatible, the D.C. International system is of limited use and not very popular.

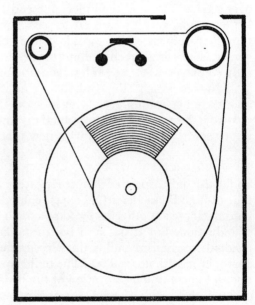

Fig. 3.15. Fidelipac Cartridge.

Fidelipac Cartridge

The most successful continuous run cartridge is the American *Fidelipac*, which is a plastic container loaded with quarter-inch tape and operating at a tape speed of 3¾ i.p.s. (Fig. 3.15). The cartridge slides into position on nylon guides, and closes a micro-switch which starts the tape transport mechanism. Pressure pads and pinch roller are contained within the cartridge, and the capstan is in the recorder. Either four or eight tracks

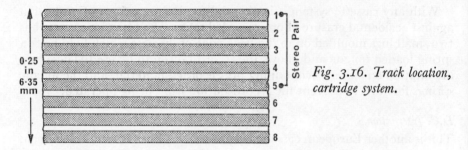

Fig. 3.16. Track location, cartridge system.

are recorded in stereo pairs (tracks 1 and 5, 2 and 6, 3 and 7, 4 and 8), and the replay head is automatically shifted from one pair to another by a solenoid and stepped cam mechanism operated by a metal stop foil.

Inside the cartridge the single reel of tape is loosely wound (oxide out) over a fixed hub, and the inner tape end is extracted from the centre and led past guides which cause it to pass across an opening in the case. The tape then returns to the outside of the coil, and the two ends joined together. There is a practical limit to the length of tape that can be successfully employed with the endless loop principle, and a coil 3 inches (76 mm) in diameter which allows about 20 minutes running time per track is about the maximum, even with lubricated tape. This type of multi-track system is best suited to reproduction, and recording should take place under controlled conditions with new tape on spool-to-spool recorders.

Demagnetization

So far the only aspect of demagnetization mentioned has been that of the tape at high frequencies (page 44), caused by numerous north and south poles facing each other in the tape coating and leading to a cancellation of induction. But it has also been established that a certain amount of residual magnetism builds up very gradually in the record and replay heads, even with normal use. The build-up increases with over modulation due to the continual saturation of the head core stampings. In the course of time this residual magnetism can become detrimental to the performance of the recorder, and result in increased background noise or 'mush' on the tape during recording. Similarly, any existing tapes already recorded can become magnetized by being played back only once over a magnetized head, since the induced background mush can never be removed.

The professional recording engineer is alive to this problem and makes a regular habit of demagnetizing his equipment. This is accomplished with an electromagnet having specially designed pole pieces, which fit right up against the head stampings and provide a concentrated a.c. field. This effectively demagnetizes the heads in a matter of seconds, the technique being to switch on when in position and then gradually draw the pole pieces away before switching off. The instrument is usually referred to as a *demagnetizer* or a *defluxer*, and can be put to other uses such as spot editing.

For example tape modulations can be fully erased if the dull (oxide) side of the tape is moved across the pole pieces of a demagnetizer. This must be done at an even rate or an alternative rumbling noise will be induced on to the tape. Joins which cause a 'plop' on replay can also be similarly treated, especially joins in film carrying a magnetic stripe.

A unique feature of magnetic recording is the ease with which recorded material can be completely erased and the tapes used over and over again. For the sake of convenience this erasure or demagnetizing is carried out at the time of recording by means of an erase head in the tape path. But the professional always uses clean tape which has been passed through the strong magnetic field of a *bulk eraser*. This is merely an electromagnet fed with an alternating current, which will neutralize any tape coating in a matter of seconds whilst the tape remains on its spool.

Magnetic Reverberation Units

Once a sound has been recorded on tape, it can be reproduced a few milliseconds later by placing a replay or monitor head in the tape path. The time delay introduced will depend on the speed at which the recorder is running and the spacing between the record and replay heads. By introducing a series of replay heads it is possible to have a number of delayed signals, each one with a different time constant. If the output from each successive head is gradually reduced, the effect of normal sound decay is simulated—which is equal to reverberation.

Ideally this method would involve a large number of heads in order to produce a smooth decay, instead of a decay consisting of several isolated echoes diminishing in volume level. But by careful adjustment of recording speed and head spacing, and feeding the output from the replay heads back into the record head, satisfactory results can be obtained from about four or five replay heads—including alteration of the reverberation characteristics to suit the nature of the work in hand. If the amplification in the feedback loop becomes greater than unity, the unit will become unstable and oscillations will occur.

Magnetic reverberation units should be used in conjunction with equalizers to adjust the frequency response of the reverberated signal before it is added to the original sound source. But there is usually a noticeable difference between the effect produced by a magnetic unit and a proper *reverberation chamber*.

Videotape

A logical development of magnetic recording is the use of *videotapes* for storing television programmes. When converted into electrical energy, video signals are basically the same as sound signals except that they are of a much higher frequency. A television picture of good definition contains frequencies up to 3 mHz, which with normal recording techniques would require a tape speed in the order of 30 ft. per second! To overcome this problem and permit the use of a more reasonable speed, a diagonal system of scanning is employed across a tape that is much wider than the tape normally used for sound recording. Two inch tape is usually used.

In the American Ampex recorder four heads are mounted on a drum at intervals of 90°. The drum rotates at speed and scans the two inch tape continuously, one head taking over where the previous head leaves the edge of the tape. The tape itself is slightly curved to ensure good contact, and the linear recording speed is 15 i.p.s. But the effective recording speed obtained by the combined movements of heads and tape is over 100 feet per second, which is adequate for the video frequency bandwidth both in black and white and in colour. In addition a sound recording is made along one edge of the tape, the point of synchronization being eight frames ahead of the corresponding picture.

A simplified form of videotape recorder developed by both Philips and Sony uses one inch tape at a linear speed of $7\frac{1}{2}$ i.p.s. A single video record head is employed, rotating in a horizontal plane, and the tape is wrapped around the outside of the scanning drum.

Other videotape systems feature cartridge operation for recording and playing back colour programmes, which can be viewed by connection to a normal television receiver.

Tape Joining

The biggest virtue of magnetic recording is the ease with which tape can be cut and rejoined, thus permitting sound editing and general re-arrangement of recorded material. For example flawless musical performances can be achieved by the intercutting of several 'takes', and the removal of hesitations, fluffs, and other extraneous noises associated with the spoken word is possible. It is also easy to transpose material which has been recorded out of sequence, assembling each item in the order required.

Accurate tape joins demand some form of jointing block to hold the tape securely during the joining process. The normal method is to trim both ends of the tape simultaneously at an angle of 45°, using an Ever-Ready type of razor blade or a pair of non-magnetic scissors. Special jointing tape is then applied and pressed into position over the join. Surplus tape must be trimmed with a slightly bowed-in edge to prevent any over-width tape attempting to pass through the tape channel of a recorder. Normal adhesive tape is not suitable for tape joins, since the adhesive oozes at the edges after a short period of time, causing several layers of tape to stick together.

Some of the frustration in using a simple jointing block can be eliminated by a semi-automatic splicer, where the tape ends are inserted and held securely by two spring clamps. A central cutting has two positions marked *cut* and *trim*. The handle is first lowered in the cut position to make the diagonal cut across both tape ends. Jointing tape is applied, and the handle set to trim. Lowering the handle produces a neat join with the edges slightly bowed. This inward curve is a feature of several tape joining devices, and although its effect passes un-noticed on a full-track or twin-track recording, it can sometimes be detected on the outside track of a four-track recording.

A more permanent type of join can be made by overlapping the tape ends and cementing them together with a special *jointing fluid*. This fluid temporarily loosens the lacquer binding holding the oxide coating to the base, and permits a welded join to be made which sets quite rapidly. These fluids are of a thin consistency and must be used sparingly; otherwise they flow over the tape beyond the area of the join, dissolving the oxide layer in the process. At slow tape speeds cemented joins are inclined to become noticeable due to a slight buckling of the tape base, and are not considered as satisfactory as joins made with adhesive tape. All cartridge tapes have welded joins, since these are considerably stronger.

CHAPTER IV
Disc Recording and Reproduction

THE ADVENT of an efficient and practical magnetic recording system has in no way eclipsed the older disc method of sound recording. In fact the major record companies take full advantage of magnetic tape during their initial recording sessions, usually making several takes of the same item. Selected takes are often intercut to produce a flawless mastertape, and only then is the recording actually transferred on to a master disc. Modern gramophone records offer a very high standard of sound reproduction, often indistinguishable from the original master tape when played on high grade equipment.

At one time a hard *wax platter* was used for recording, varying from one to two inches in thickness and with a diameter of thirteen inches. It had a fine and homogeneous texture which was shaved before use to produce a highly polished surface, and all recording had to take place under controlled temperature conditions. Modern practice is to use a thin aluminium disc coated with a cellulose acetate lacquer, which remains much more stable. But it is important that any *lacquer disc* used for making a master recording, from which copies will subsequently be obtained, is fresh and free from hard patches or any other blemishes and surface defects. Any roughness in the walls of the recorded groove will introduce extraneous noise in the reproduced sound. Acetate discs which are not destined for further copying may be replayed immediately if required. But the acetate surface is rather delicate and will not last indefinitely.

All *monophonic* records are made from *lateral cut* discs, meaning that modulations cause a lateral displacement of the spiral groove. The *hill and dale* system, with the modulations varying the depth of the groove, was pursued for a few years; but it was eventually abandoned in favour of the lateral cut which produced a more satisfactory recording. But all *stereophonic* records use a combination of both principles, resulting in two channels of information being traced out in a single spiral groove. The original method was to record the information from one channel by a lateral cut, and the information from the second channel by a hill and dale cut. Thus the two sets of modulations were in effect recorded at 90° to each other. This system has been rotated through 45° on all modern records so that two hill and dale patterns are made with a *cutting stylus* having an angle of 90° between its two faces. One waveform is impressed on the left-hand side of the groove at an angle of 45° from the vertical, and the other waveform in a similar position on the right-hand side of the groove. This is known loosely as a 45/45 cut.

Recording Machine

The function of a disc recording machine is to receive audio power from the output of an amplifier and use it to modulate a spiral groove which is being cut in an acetate disc. The basis of a modern recording machine is actually a high grade lathe. The disc must be rotated at a constant speed past the recording stylus used for cutting the groove, whilst a worm gear tracks the stylus across the disc from outside to inside. A substantial turntable is fitted which has an effective flywheel action, and its drive is taken through an oil-damped mechanical filter to eliminate vibrations and rumble from the motor and reduction gearing. These recording machines are necessarily very expensive and beyond the range of domestic users.

The tracking mechanism which moves the stylus radially across the surface of the disc comprises a *lead-screw* and *half-nut*. The recording head is mounted on a bracket attached to the half-nut, and rotation of the lead-screw traverses the complete assembly across the disc. The groove spacing is determined by the speed of the lead-screw in relation to the speed of the turntable, both of which are powered by the same motor.

The standard recording speeds of $33\frac{1}{3}$, 45, and 78 r.p.m. do not all contain the same groove spacing. The 78 standard has a coarse groove spacing of 96 to the inch, which means that a 10 inch (250 mm) diameter record will play for 3 minutes and a 12 inch (300 mm) diameter record will play for just over 4 minutes. The $33\frac{1}{3}$ and 45 standards contain a groove spacing of 250 to the inch, which means that a 12 inch (300 mm) diameter disc will play for 25 minutes. In addition an even slower speed of $16\frac{2}{3}$ r.p.m. has been adopted to give an extra long playing time for specific purposes, although this is not widely used.

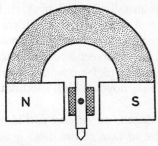

Fig. 4.1. Simplified drawing of moving coil type cutter head.

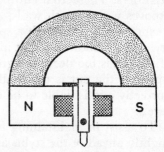

Fig. 4.2. Simplified drawing of moving iron type cutter head.

Recording Head

A recording head is designed to drive the stylus in a lateral direction on a *mono* recording at the required amplitude without distortion, and without introducing mechanical resonances within the recorded frequency range. The two types of recording head, or *cutter head*, currently in use are the *moving coil* and the *moving iron*. The construction of a moving coil head is shown by the simplified drawing in Fig. 4.1. The stylus is rigidly attached to a former carrying a speech coil, positioned between the pole faces of a permanent magnet and pivoted about its centre. The audio signals produce a varying magnetic flux in the gap between the pole faces, causing the stylus to vibrate from side to side. The stylus assembly is suitably damped with rubber to provide a restoring force.

In the moving iron head the speech coil is wound on a former inside the magnet pole pieces, as shown by the simplified drawing in Fig. 4.2. The stylus is mounted on a steel armature, one end of which is free to vibrate between the pole faces. Due to its construction this type of head is more likely to contain mechanical resonances, but these can either be arranged to fall outside the recorded frequency range or rendered ineffective by means of the rubber damping which provides the restoring force.

In both types of recording head the dimensions of the gap between the pole faces are quite critical, since the sensitivity of the head is considerably lowered as the width of the gap is increased. The size of the magnet also has an effect on sensitivity, although modern alloys can produce a large magnetic flux with a magnet of small dimensions.

Cutting Stylus

The actual cutting of the spiral groove is accomplished by means of a sapphire *cutting stylus*, although a steel stylus was not unknown on portable recorders. The actual cutting edges must be sharp and clean to produce grooves with smooth walls, and the stylus is usually heated by high frequency a.c. fed through a special auxiliary coil. The extent to which the stylus tip is allowed to cut into the acetate coating is carefully controlled. If the cut is too deep, the groove width will be incorrect and the spacing upset; if the cut is too shallow, the reproducing pick-up will not track correctly and is liable to be thrown out of the groove at high modulation levels.

To assist in maintaining an even groove depth, an *advance ball* is used slightly ahead of the stylus and resting on the surface of the disc. A more comprehensive design incorporates a servo mechanism which enables the depth of the groove to be accurately controlled and adjusted whilst the disc is being cut. On all professional recorders a microscope with a calibrated graticule is used so that a watch may be kept on the groove dimensions and groove spacing.

As the cutting proceeds a waste material is formed called *swarf* which with an acetate lacquer disc is highly inflammable. Steps are taken for the instantaneous removal of swarf by air suction down a pipe placed adjacent to the cutting stylus. A more economical method is to use a rotating felt pad to merely collect the swarf, although there is always the danger of a loose piece of swarf becoming entangled with the stylus and lifting the tip from the disc.

Groove Dimensions

The recorded groove consists of one continuous spiral, usually cut from the outside diameter of the disc to the inside, although the reverse is sometimes the case. Adjacent grooves must be spaced far enough apart to prevent overlapping of modulations on loud passages, yet close enough to make full use of the available space and achieve a reasonable playing time. There are two standards for groove dimensions, one for the coarse groove 78 r.p.m. records and another for the slower speed microgroove records.

The 78 r.p.m. standard follows very closely the standard used by Bell Telephone Laboratories in America over 40 years ago, and is illustrated in Fig. 4.3. The width of the groove at the surface of the disc is approximately 0·006 in. (0·15 mm), and the pitch of the spiral at 96 grooves per inch

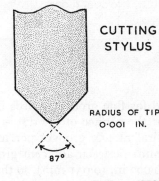

CUTTING
STYLUS

RADIUS OF TIP
0·001 IN.

87°

Fig. 4.3. Cutting stylus and recorded groove dimensions for 78 r.p.m. coarse groove discs.

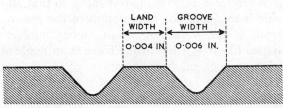

LAND
WIDTH

GROOVE
WIDTH

0·004 IN.

0·006 IN.

(25 mm) allows a space of 0·01 in. (0·25 mm) between adjacent groove centres. The space between each groove, called land, is approximately 0·004 in. (0·1 mm); which means that there is an area 0·002 in. (0·05 mm) wide available for modulation of the groove. To produce the desired depth of cut, usually 0·0025 in. (0·062 mm), the cutting stylus must be shaped like a V with cutting faces at an angle of 87°, the radius at the tip being 0·001 in. (0·025 mm).

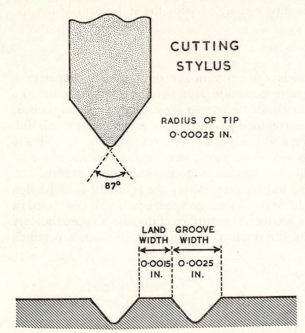

CUTTING
STYLUS

RADIUS OF TIP
0·00025 IN.

87°

LAND   GROOVE
WIDTH   WIDTH

0·0015   0·0025
IN.   IN.

Fig. 4.4. Cutting stylus and recorded groove dimensions for L.P. fine groove discs.

The standard for fine groove records is shown in Fig. 4.4. The width of the groove at the surface of the disc is 0·0002 in. (0·051 mm), and the pitch of the spiral at 250 grooves per inch (25 mm) allows a space of 0·004 in. (0·1 mm) between adjacent groove centres. The land between each groove is 0·002 in. (0·051 mm), so that an area 0·001 in. (0·025 mm) wide is available for modulation of the groove. To produce the desired depth of cut, usually 0·001 in. (0·025 mm), the cutting stylus must be shaped like a V with cutting faces at an angle of 87°, the radius at the tip being 0·00025 in. (0·0062 mm).

On quite a large number of microgroove recordings, the land width between adjacent grooves is varied according to the depth of modulation.

In order to record loud passages satisfactorily, the grooves are automatically spaced further apart; whilst during quiet passages the grooves are brought closer together to retain the maximum playing time of the record.

Standard cutting procedure is that all discs should start with at least one turn of an unmodulated groove, followed by a *lead-in groove* which is greater in pitch than the normal recorded groove pitch. The portion of the disc carrying the recording is called the *recorded surface*, and the portion of the disc where the groove pitch is increased to denote the separation of two recorded bands is called the *marker space*. After the final recorded surface there should be a *lead-out groove* which is greater in pitch than the normal recorded groove pitch, and finally a *finishing groove* which consists of a plain circular groove to arrest the reproducing stylus. Sometimes the finishing groove is concentric, but on all 78 r.p.m. discs the finishing groove is eccentric.

Radius Compensation

The linear speed at which a stylus cuts a groove depends on the radius of the disc and the recording speed. A 12 inch disc at 78 r.p.m. has a linear speed of 3 ft. per second on the outside, yet only about 8 inches on the inside where the radius is reduced to 2 inches or less. This causes a progressive reduction in the capability of the cutting stylus (and reproducing stylus) to trace high frequencies in the centre of the disc, a phenomenon known as *pinch effect* which happens with both mono and stereo.

To overcome this problem with 78 r.p.m. records, *radius compensation* is sometimes used, actuated by the recorder tracking mechanism. This is merely a tone control which automatically raises the volume level of high frequencies as the stylus nears the centre of the disc. But if too much compensation is made, a waveform will be presented to the recording head which is impossible for the stylus to reproduce with any accuracy. Radius compensation is not strictly necessary with fine groove recordings, since the groove does not extend so far into the centre of the disc.

Recording Frequency Response

The aim of a disc recording and reproducing chain is to re-create an exact copy of the original sound waveform, both in frequency and amplitude. Numerous electrical and mechanical links are involved in this chain, and they do not all possess a level frequency response: therefore deficiencies in one link must be made good in other links. For example the frequency response of the signal fed into the record head is far from flat, due to the behaviour of the cutting stylus at different frequencies,

If the volume level at the recording head is set so that the amplitude of a 250 Hz tone produces a fully modulated groove, the amplitude of very low frequencies (assuming a flat response) will be too great for the cutting stylus to trace in the space available. In other words the stylus will make a large lateral movement which cannot be contained within the normal groove spacing. To restrict this effect without having to reduce the volume level, a reduction of bass frequencies must be made with a suitable filter circuit.

Assuming full modulation of the groove at 250 Hz, the amplitude of the waveform traced by the stylus will become smaller as the frequency of the signal increases. This is due to the small amount of energy available at high frequencies, and at 10 kHz the modulated groove will only occupy approximately one twentieth of the available space. It is therefore common practice to increase the amplitude of high frequencies in the recording amplifier in order to utilize this space more fully.

All lateral cut discs are recorded with a frequency response which gives a constant amplitude to the recorded groove at frequencies below approximately 500 Hz or 600 Hz, and a stylus velocity which is proportional to frequencies above this figure. When reproducing a disc, the amplitude of the bass frequencies is restored and the high frequencies de-emphasized, usually by means of filter circuits following the pick-up. This produces a flat frequency response, and at the same time effects a considerable improvement in the signal-to-noise ratio. Noise energy increases with frequency due to the nature of the vinyl material used for commercial pressings, and the shape of the reproducing curve is a distinct advantage.

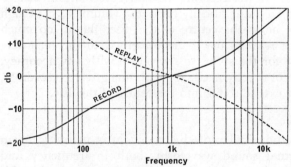

Fig. 4.5. Record and replay frequency response for fine groove discs.

Standard Recording Characteristic

In order to eliminate the different curves which have been used by various disc companies, the Record Industry Association of America (RIAA) have recommended standard recording characteristics for fine groove and

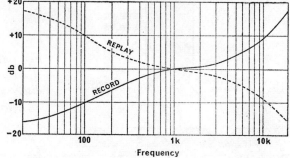

Fig. 4.6. Record and replay frequency response for coarse groove discs.

coarse groove records. These are illustrated in Fig. 4.5 and Fig. 4.6, together with the corresponding frequency corrections required for reproduction.

Instead of two entirely separate frequency corrections being made at the high and low ends of the frequency scale, with a flat middle section, a response curve has been evolved which is the combination of three separate curves with the following time constants.

	Fine Groove	Coarse Groove
Treble	75 μs	50 μs
Middle	318 μs	450 μs
Bass	3180 μs	3180 μs

Discs should be recorded with a smooth characteristic over a frequency range of 50 Hz to 12 kHz, with a tolerance of $\pm$ 2 db taking as a reference point the value at 1 kHz. In some countries the fine groove characteristic is used for coarse groove records, but the majority of manufacturers adhere to the RIAA standards.

Cutting a Stereo Disc

The recording and reproducing characteristics for a stereo disc are identical to those for a fine groove mono disc, and any difference between the two channels of a stereo disc should lie within the same tolerances. The groove dimensions also follow those of fine groove mono discs, although the cutting stylus must be capable of tracing a waveform which is the sum of information received from left hand and right hand channels (Fig. 4.7). The left hand channel corresponds to information recorded on the inside wall of the groove, and the right hand channel corresponds to information recorded on the outside wall of the groove.

A typical recorder used for cutting stereo discs is the Ortofon SV8/S, which features push-button control of all drive motor and cutter head movements. A stereo moving coil cutter head is used, with a swarf suction

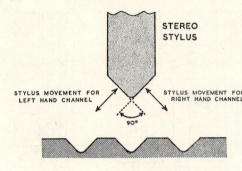

Fig. 4.7. Movement of cutting stylus when recording a stereophonic disc.

pipe located immediately behind the heated stylus. The turntable is a 75 lb. brass flywheel, and uses suction through a number of concentric grooves to hold the disc flat and prevent distortion of its surface. All movements of the cutter head are controlled by a separate motor, and variable contacts on top of the lead-screw permit automatic lowering of the stylus in a suitable position for any given disc size.

The groove spacing can be varied from 180 to 365 grooves per in. (25 mm), and adjustment is made automatically by the modulation on the magnetic tape. An additional replay head, in advance of the main head, scans the information on the bottom half of the tape. The signal is amplified and rectified for feeding into a thyratron which controls the relative speed of the lead-screw. The depth of groove can also be varied according to the amount of tape modulation, and a continuous watch on groove dimensions is kept by examining the disc surface through a microscope.

Certain types of programme material containing high level high frequency sounds can cause problems with amplifier overload, cutter head overheating, or stylus tracing distortion—especially on discs with small diameter centres. One solution is to use an amplifier which has a high frequency limiting circuit to restrain signal peaks, but the method frequently employed is to cut the disc at half speed which permits a high modulation level to be maintained at all frequencies.

Processing

Recordings made on acetate lacquered discs should not be replayed if the disc is intended to be used for making copies by processing. Even a single playing can cause damage or wear to the groove. Furthermore a disc used for copying purposes must be at least one inch wider than the finished article, so that it may be held securely in the processing machinery.

The first stage in processing is to wash the lacquer disc thoroughly to remove all dust particles, and then deposit a layer of silver to render it electrically conductive. The disc is then able to accept layers of nickel and copper in two electro-plating baths, and an impression of the recorded groove is built up. The whole of the plating is then stripped away from the original disc, which is usually destroyed in the process. If the stripping is successful, the nickel and copper plating becomes the metal *master disc*. If the stripping is unsuccessful, a new acetate disc must be recorded.

If only a few pressings are required, these can be made direct from the master disc; in fact a test pressing is often made at this stage for checking purposes. But the master would not stand up to the wear and tear of making a large number of pressings, so a further electro-plating process is carried out to produce a *mother*, which is a hard metal copy of the lacquer original. A series of *stampers* are produced from the mother, also by electro-plating, and it is these stampers which are used to produce the final pressings. The time required to complete all processing is seven days.

Successive plating operations do not cause any deterioration in the quality of the final pressing, although failures can occur at any stage. Producing a number of mothers protects the original copper master, and enables numerous stampers to be made. Each stamper is capable of producing several hundred pressings before it is discarded, and the master is retained in its original condition.

Disc Pressings

Two stampers mounted on copper backing plates are placed in position on the pressing machine, with labels already attached. The press is steam heated to raise the temperature of the stampers, and a wedge of thermoplastic material inserted. Closing the press forces this material to assume the contours of the two stampers, and the introduction of cold water allows the pressing to harden in two minutes. The pressing is removed and the stampers re-heated immediately.

The actual material used for pressings is a polyvinyl resin to which has been added some carbon colouring, and this gives a very smooth pliable disc. Vinyl has a tendency to attract dust particles into the grooves through static charges, so pressings must be protected in a jacket of polythene or paper.

Turntable Units

The first item of equipment to be considered for disc reproduction is a *turntable unit*, comprising turntable, motor drive, and speed selector. Modern turntables are constructed as a steel pressing or an alloy casting, the latter often being called a *transcription* turntable. The pressed steel table has the attraction of being fairly inexpensive, and is fitted to the majority of domestic record players and radiograms. The transcription table is considerably heavier which promotes a good flywheel effect at slow speeds, and is therefore more suitable for studio use or high quality domestic installations.

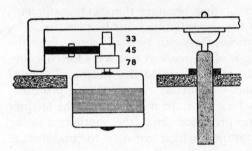

Fig. 4.8. Principle of three-speed turntable drive, using a stepped boss on the motor shaft.

The motive power is provided by an a.c. asynchronous motor, whose speed is determined by the frequency of the mains supply, or an a.c. induction motor which can vary in speed according to the load applied to it. The drive is transmitted to the turntable on its inside rim via a rubber tyred pulley, and a stepped boss on the vertical motor shaft provides a simple speed control (Fig. 4.8). This method enables the motor to run continuously at its normal speed, and it is always, therefore, developing full power. When the turntable is at rest the pulley becomes dis-engaged automatically to prevent the formation of 'flats' on the surface of the rubber tyre. Some transcription units are also fitted with a vernier speed control called an *eddy current brake*, which is an aluminium disc on the motor shaft passing between the poles of a small magnet. By moving the magnet towards or away from the disc, a limited speed control is introduced.

Other refinements include automatic change mechanisms operated by the main drive motor, turntable clutch systems for disc cueing, and automatic pick-up lowering devices. Belt driven turntables are now in vogue on some of the more expensive transcription types, also models with electronic speed control.

Stroboscope Disc

The precise speed of a turntable can be checked with a *stroboscope disc* illuminated by a neon lamp. A suitable disc for turntables would contain a set of black and white bars of equal dimensions for each speed required. To determine the exact number of bars, one divides the number of light fluctuations per second by the number of turntable revolutions per second. For example a 50 Hz mains supply will give 100 fluctuations per second to a neon lamp, and at 78 r.p.m. a turntable will rotate 1·3 times per second. So the number of bars required will be 100 divided by 1·3, which equals 77 (to the nearest full bar). Other turntable speeds require the following stroboscope bars.

Mains Supply	16⅔ r.p.m.	33⅓ r.p.m.	45 r.p.m.	78 r.p.m.
50 Hz	320	180	133	77
60 Hz	432	216	160	92

If the turntable speed is slow, the bars on the stroboscope disc will appear to be moving backwards, and if the turntable is running fast, the bars will appear to be moving forwards. The speed of the reproducing turntable must always match the speed of the recording turntable, so that the reproduced sound will be heard at exactly the same pitch as the original sound. Some transcription turntables have built-in stroboscopes, often illuminated, so that a continuous speed check can be made.

Pick-up Arms

During recording the cutter head is traversed across the disc exactly at right angles to the direction of rotation, cutting a continuous spiral groove. During reproduction the pick-up stylus must meet each groove at a true tangent, so that the effect of groove curvature is almost nil. The stylus and its cartridge are mounted in a specially shaped *pick-up arm*, usually straight with an off-set head, so that tangential errors are kept to a minimum.

The geometry of pick-up arms has a considerable influence over sound quality, since tracking errors can result in distortion especially at the innermost grooves. In addition all pick-up arms have a natural resonance which must be kept well outside the range of audible frequencies. This is achieved by a light-weight rigid construction from materials such as afrormosia wood, extruded duraluminium section, or a combination of both. The *trackability* of a pick-up cartridge, meaning the ability of the stylus to trace the modulated groove accurately, depends on the design and shape of the tone arm, and arms are generally supplied by the cartridge manufacturers themselves. Specialist manufacturers also produce high grade pick-up arms with shells for attaching a standard cartridge, since the international standard for fixing cartridges is by two holes with their centres half an inch (12·5 mm) apart.

When tracking the grooves of a disc, the pick-up arm tends to swing in towards the centre which imposes an extra load on the inside wall of each groove. This is known as *skating* and produces unnecessary friction with an increase in record wear. This skating tendency can be balanced out by means of a *bias compensator* consisting of a light spring or a cord and bob-weight. The tension is made variable so that it can be adjusted in relation to the weight of the cartridge and the stylus pressure on the groove. The stylus pressure necessary to give accurate tracing of the groove also depends on the amount of friction in the pick-up arm bearings, either vertical or horizontal. It is for the reduction of friction and record wear that special tone arms are manufactured.

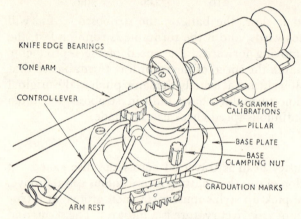

KNIFE EDGE BEARINGS

TONE ARM

CONTROL LEVER

½ GRAMME CALIBRATIONS

PILLAR

BASE PLATE

BASE CLAMPING NUT

GRADUATION MARKS

ARM REST

Fig. 4.9. Construction details of the S.M.E. precision pick-up arm.

The construction of a typical arm is shown in Fig. 4.9. Knife edge bearings are used for holding the circular pick-up arm, and an adjustable counterweight permits the required stylus pressure to be obtained. The pillar bearings contain totally enclosed ball-races to give a smooth lateral movement, and graduation marks in the base allow for movement of the pillar to accommodate different pick-up cartridges. A refinement is a built-in control lever for gently lowering the stylus into the groove of the disc.

Reproducing Stylus

The stylus used for disc reproduction is manufactured from either a sapphire or a diamond, and must be handled with care since it will chip easily. The stylus is tailor-made to line up with the angle of the groove wall, with a rounded tip of sufficient radius to prevent it touching the groove bottom. Since different groove dimensions are used for coarse groove 78 r.p.m. discs and long playing microgroove discs, different stylii are required for each type of groove as illustrated in Fig. 4.10. It will be noticed that the angle of the stylus face which makes contact with the groove wall is the same as the recording stylus in each case: but the radius of the tip is approximately double that of the recording stylus. The stylus

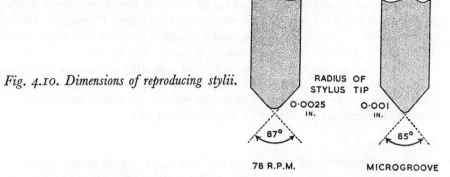

Fig. 4.10. Dimensions of reproducing stylii.

RADIUS OF
STYLUS TIP

0·0025
IN.

0·00I
IN.

87°

85°

78 R.P.M.

MICROGROOVE

surface should always be smooth and highly polished to minimize friction and reduce wear in the groove walls. In this way several hundred playings may be obtained with a sapphire stylus, and several thousand with a diamond stylus.

In addition to the circular stylus described, some cartridges are fitted with an *elliptical stylus*, with the wider cross-section positioned across the groove and the smaller cross-section in line with the groove. The elliptical stylus was developed to reduce the effects of *tracing distortion*, which occurs when the cartridge produces a different waveform from that recorded on the disc. Due to its reduced mass, an elliptical stylus follows the groove modulations much more faithfully than a circular stylus, especially at high frequencies. It also shows up record wear.

Tracing distortion is further reduced by tilting the stylus slightly forward of the vertical line, thus producing a trailing action at the tip. The standard angle for this is $15°$ which is adhered to by most cartridge manufacturers, although in practice any angle between $0°$ and $25°$ may be encountered.

Stylus Pressure

Modern pick-up arms are very light in weight and free in movement. They are also comparatively small in mass, even when fitted with a pick-up cartridge. Therefore the whole balance of the pick-up arm becomes critical, and the *stylus pressure* (also called *tracking force*) assumes importance. Obviously there must be a certain amount of downwards pressure to enable the stylus to trace the modulations in the groove; but there comes a point where any increase in pressure does not render the pick-up more efficient, and merely serves to increase friction and cause unnecessary wear to both stylus and disc.

The usual stylus pressure for coarse groove 78 r.p.m. discs is from 5 to

8 grammes measured at the stylus tip. The usual stylus pressure for fine groove recordings is from $\frac{1}{2}$ to 2 grammes with modern cartridges. These figures are only meant as a guide, and the actual pressure will depend on the maker's recommendations supplied with the pick-up concerned. Numerous pick-up arms today are equipped with fully adjustable counter-weights, so that the correct stylus pressure can be achieved by the user. A *stylus pressure gauge* is used to assist in this operation, which consists of an accurate spring balance directly calibrated in grammes.

Pick-up Cartridges

The reproducing stylus is part of an armature arrangement inside a pick-up cartridge, and is coupled to an element for converting mechanical vibrations into an electrical output. The main types in use today are the *crystal, ceramic,* and *variable reluctance* cartridges, although *moving coil* and *moving iron* types are still in evidence, with photo-cell and semi-conductor types available at a high price.

Crystal and *ceramic* elements are the most popular types due to their suitability for mass production at low cost. The crystal contains a bi-morph strip of rochelle salt which exhibits piezo-electric characteristics, and the ceramic uses a man made material which has the same properties. The lever action of the stylus and armature causes a slight bending of the bi-morph element, so that a voltage occurs across its surface. The maximum voltage obtained varies from 100 mV to 1V according to the type of element. This cartridge has a frequency response which follows the disc replay curve very closely, so that it may be directly connected to an amplifier. However the output impedance is high, and the following circuit should never present a load of less than 1 megohm to prevent low frequency losses.

Variable reluctance cartridges use a small armature which varies the dimensions of an air gap between magnet pole faces, and the flux which exists across that gap. This causes a voltage change to be induced into a coil wound around (or inside) the pole pieces. This type of cartridge gives the best possible quality due to the extremely small mass of the only moving part—the armature. The output voltage is low, the maximum between different makes varies from 2 mV to 15 mV, and the impedance is usually between 5 K/ohms and 25 K/ohms. The frequency response of the output must be corrected to provide the necessary disc replay curve, and filter details are given by the cartridge manufacturers.

Moving coil pick-ups also contain a stylus attached to a very small armature, but the coil of wire is wound directly on to the armature and the whole assembly is mounted between two magnet pole faces. To minimize any troublesome resonances the armature and coil are made as light as possible, calling for a coil with only a very few turns. This gives a low output at a low impedance, and an impedance matching transformer must be used before connection to an amplifier. The main virtue of a moving coil pick-up is that its output voltage can be made to correspond to the stylus velocity over a wide frequency range, thus producing an accurate electrical equivalent of the recorded waveform. This type of pick-up is not available in cartridge form.

Moving iron pick-ups—now obsolete—contain a comparatively large armature suspended in a magnetic field by being pivoted at the top (unbalanced) or in the middle (balanced). In another type a steel needle itself forms the armature. The coil is wound on a former inside the pole faces, and an impedance matching transformer is also required. Moving iron pick-ups suffer from resonances and frequency distortion, causing the output voltage to be non-linear to the armature velocity.

Semi-Conductor Cartridge

A radical departure from accepted design principles is a pick-up cartridge which has silicon semi-conductor (transistor) elements to convert the mechanical vibrations of the stylus into electrical terms. Most pick-up cartridges are voltage generators, but semi-conductor elements act as modulators with current supplied from an external power source. The American *Miniconic* cartridge currently available requires an operating voltage of 14 volts d.c., and a two channel pre-amplifier is incorporated into the power unit to give a high level output of 0·4 volts (equalized to the RIAA characteristic) or a low level output of 8 mV (unequalized). The wide frequency response of 30 Hz to 20 kHz, and low distortion figures, contribute towards a clean and crisp sound quality.

Photocell Cartridge

Another pick-up cartridge which is being given a new lease of life is the photo-cell type which picks up reflections from the recorded groove. This principle was employed many years ago, but it was never popular because of its poor reproduction due to the photo-electric cells available at the time. The signal-to-noise ratio was extremely low due to light reflected from other parts of the record groove which was not part of the modulations. However, with the modern photo-transistors and solar cells now available, this type of cartridge is being manufactured by Trio and Toshiba in Japan. It is an expensive cartridge, and has to be tracked very accurately across the record so that the light cell is centered exactly above the record groove.

Stereo Pick-ups

In order to reproduce the two 45° waveforms of a stereophonic disc, the stylus must be capable of tracing the sum of the two waveforms simultaneously, whilst inducing two separate voltages into two pick-up elements. The variable reluctance design is easily adapted for stereo work, and the armature itself is magnetized to be of opposite polarity to four pole pieces which surround it. The varying flux caused by movement of the armature induces voltages into two sets of coils, and these are connected so as to produce the information from the left-hand and right-hand channels.

Two crystal elements (or ceramic elements) can also be used for inexpensive stereo cartridges. The usual arrangement is for the elements to be attached to two links of a parallelogram lever system, the top point being fixed and the bottom point connected to the stylus. Movement of the stylus in one direction energizes one crystal by a slight twisting motion, and in the other direction the second crystal is similarly energized.

It is worthy of note that there is a standard colour code for the identification of channels in a stereo pick-up lead.

Lead	Left Channel	Right Channel	Ground
3 wire	White	Red	Black
4 wire	White and Blue*	Red and Green*	—
5 wire	White and Blue*	Red and Green*	Black

* Blue and green are 'earthy' connections.

Stereo pick-ups which have the right compliance and mechanical impedance are equally suitable for the reproduction of mono discs with a suitable stylus, but only *compatible mono* cartridges should be used for single channel reproduction of stereo discs. The older type of mono cartridge is incapable of tracing a stereo disc, and will usually cause irreparable damage to the groove walls.

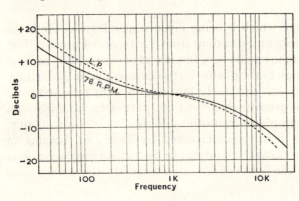

Fig. 4.11. Standard replay characteristic for L.P. and 78 r.p.m. discs.

Frequency Correction

Good quality magnetic pick-ups give an electrical output which is approximately proportional to the velocity of the stylus, meaning that they will reproduce the waveform recorded on the disc. Therefore a fixed amount of *frequency correction* must be provided which will be the exact inverse of the recording characteristic. For convenience the disc reproducing curve is again shown in Fig. 4.11, and a frequency correction circuit must be used between the pick-up and the amplifier, or within the amplifier itself. Crystal pick-ups operate on a different principle and do not require any frequency correction unless specified by the manufacturer.

No further frequency corrections should be necessary for playing discs which have been recorded to the standard characteristic, but listening conditions often dictate further alteration to compensate for room acoustics or to satisfy the preferences of the listener. These adjustments are usually made by continuously variable *tone controls*, which either raise or lower the bass or treble end of the frequency spectrum. The response curve of a typical tone control unit is shown in Fig. 4.12, and the degree of adjustment amounts to about 15 db or 20 db in relation to the middle frequency of 800 Hz or 1 kHz.

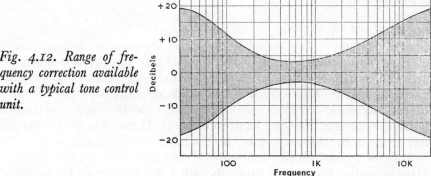

Fig. 4.12. Range of frequency correction available with a typical tone control unit.

Low Pass Filter

To prevent an excessive amount of high frequencies being reproduced in the form of hiss or other background noise, an improvement can be made by the insertion of a *low pass filter* rather than by the use of the treble tone control. Such a filter takes the form of a resistor/capacitor network which can be tuned to produce a fairly sharp cut-off at any desired frequency. Common figures are 12 kHz, 10 kHz, 8 kHz, and 6 kHz, which are selected by means of a rotary switch. The reproduction of old 78 r.p.m. records can be improved in this way, since their high surface noise is due to the fact that early pressings were made of shellac. Low pass filters should be removed when reproducing modern fine groove recordings.

Rumble Filter

Turntable units produce a certain amount of vibration when they are running, the amount varying according to the nature of the turntable used. This vibration is transmitted from the disc to the reproducing stylus, and also from the pick-up base if this is mounted on the motor board. The result is a low-frequency rumble in the loudspeaker.

This rumble may not be serious when using a system with a limited frequency range, but with a high fidelity system the rumble can be loud enough to become objectionable. It may also be the cause of intermodulation distortion, due to large movements of the loudspeaker cone at low frequencies which bear no relation to the recorded waveform.

The cure is a *rumble filter*, which is a form of *high pass filter*, built into the amplifier system to limit the response at low frequencies. The cut-off is usually around 20 Hz or 30 Hz, with a rapid attenuation below this figure. Such a filter does not interfere with the bass content of any programme material, which would be the case if the bass were reduced with a tone control unit.

Frequency Test Discs

The overall frequency response of a disc reproducing system can be checked with special *frequency test discs* which have been prepared in accordance with the RIAA recording characteristic. These discs contain a series of spot frequencies recorded in bands, covering the entire recording range. Each band carries an announcement for identification, and contains a run over groove from one band to the next. Correction figures showing any errors in the disc are printed on the label (see Appendix).

Another type of test disc contains a gliding tone from approximately 15 kHz, to 30 Hz, stopping at intervals with a marker groove for frequency identification. This gliding tone assists in seeking any peaks or dips in the frequency response which might be missed when using the spot frequency disc. Both these discs can be used to identify unwanted resonances in loudspeaker cabinets, etc.

Record Wear

Record wear is a direct result of mechanical friction between the wall of the groove and the reproducing stylus. The problem of minimizing this friction on fine groove records demands attention, since sapphire and diamond stylii are highly polished like the groove itself. The actual design of the pick-up arm can contribute to record wear, as well as incorrect stylus pressure. But the main cause of record wear is dust and dirt in the grooves, and there is a need for a scientific approach to the problem of record cleaning.

Long-playing microgroove records have no abrasive nature in their composition, but their surfaces are so highly polished that static charges are induced which cause dust to collect. Modern light-weight pick-ups do not push this dust out of the way; they ride over dust particles and cause 'clicks' and 'bangs' in the process, spoiling the otherwise silent background of a vinyl pressing. Any attempt to rub the surface of the record or brush off the dust generates a static charge which attracts more dust, and it is the smallest particles which are the greatest nuisance. Although some records are being produced in materials with a reduced capacity for holding static charges, all records require some form of treatment sooner or later.

The removal of dust and dirt is not difficult with the aid of suitable accessories. A simple device called the *Dust Bug* consists of a small nylon brush and plush pad suspended over the record on a perspex arm. It actually removes dust and static from record grooves at the moment of playing. The plush pad is cleaned and re-charged with an *anti-static fluid* after each playing. Another device for use with records in new condition is the *Disc Preener*, a small velvet covered drum which collects dust from record grooves without anti-static agents.

Records which have been neglected may require a more severe treatment to restore them to their prime condition. A suitable device is the *Parastat* which consists of a nylon brush held in a metal clamp between two velvet pads. These are primed with an anti-static fluid before being manually swept over the recorded area of a disc, preferably on a slowly rotating turntable. The bristles are capable of dislodging all foreign matter from the bottom of the groove, which is collected by the pads without any damage to the record surface.

Records which have become contaminated with greasy dirt that does not respond to normal cleaning may be washed in warm water with a few drops of washing-up liquid. When dry, the Preener or Parastat may be used. Records which have been previously treated with impregnated cloths or tissues may have to have the residue in the grooves softened or dissolved by alcohol, or a 50/50 mixture of alcohol and distilled water, before being given any further anti-static treatment and cleaning.

Separate cleaning devices should be kept for 78 r.p.m. records, especially shellac pressings which are highly abrasive.

CHAPTER V

Microphones

SOUND WAVES consist of changes in air pressure, which cause vibration of air particles as explained on page 12. The sole purpose of a microphone is to convert these vibrations into electrical energy, a task which can be accomplished by several familiar methods. However we should first consider the five essential characteristics of a microphone which is to be used for sound recording.

1. The conversion of energy should be equally efficient at all frequencies within the working range, so that the microphone will possess a flat frequency response.

2. The microphone must have a good sensitivity so that it will respond to sounds of low intensity.

3. The sensitivity of the microphone to sounds arriving from different angles (see Polar Distribution on page 88) should be the same at all frequencies.

4. The electrical output must be high to maintain a good signal-to-noise ratio.

5. The microphone must be robust, of a reasonable size, and not too heavy.

Basically a small diaphragm is suspended in the path of the sound waves, and the changes in air pressure cause it to vibrate. The diaphragm movements are then converted into electrical voltages. The five main types of microphone element used for energy conversion are carbon, crystal, condenser, dynamic (or moving coil), and ribbon.

Pressure Operation

The majority of microphones are described as being pressure operated since sound waves only impinge on the front of the diaphragm, the rear surface being enclosed in a small cavity, (Fig. 5.1).

If any kind of cavity is introduced between the front of the diaphragm and the sound wave, the air pressure tends to rise at the resonant frequency of the cavity, causing a peak in the high frequency response. Although steps are taken to avoid unnecessary cavities in the design of the microphone case, cavities are sometimes deliberately introduced (see Lavalier microphones on page 103) to obtain a particular response. All other resonances of the microphone case are only allowed to occur either above or below the frequency range for which the microphone is designed.

The performance of a pressure operated microphone depends largely

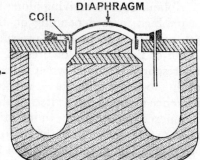

Fig. 5.1. Construction of a dynamic micro-phone.

on the construction of its diaphragm, which has to withstand extremes of temperature and humidity and be capable of handling shock sounds such as gunfire without deterioration. Diaphragms are usually made from a circular wafer of aluminium or metallized polyester, and have a long life with normal use. An exception here is the ribbon microphone (Fig. 5.2) whose diaphragm takes the form of a thin strip of aluminium, corrugated for strength. Since this ribbon diaphragm is exposed on both sides and vibrates in free air, it is not entirely pressure operated.

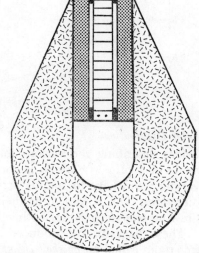

Fig. 5.2. Construction of a ribbon microphone.

Pressure Gradient Operation

The precise movement of the ribbon is determined by a difference in pressure which exists between sound waves arriving in front of and behind the ribbon. Sounds arriving along both paths impinge on the ribbon with a combined force depending on their phase difference, which increases with frequency to produce pressure gradient operation.

One of the features of pressure gradient operation is the increase in bass response obtained when working close, known as *bass tip-up*. This is not due to phase differences, which are small at low frequencies, but to a difference in sound intensities. As the microphone distance is reduced there is an increasing difference in intensity on either side of the ribbon, and this causes extra movement of the ribbon at low frequencies. The general effect is shown in Fig. 5.3, where it will be seen that frequencies below 200 Hz are the ones most seriously affected. The result on close speech is an unnatural voice quality. At high frequencies the phase difference assumes more importance than the intensity difference, and the close microphone distance has no effect. This feature is also called the *proximity effect*.

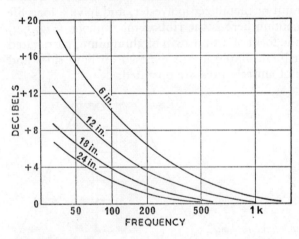

Fig. 5.3. Bass tip-up which occurs when speaking close to a pressure gradient microphone.

Polar Distribution

Before describing the various microphone elements mention should be made of a property which is common to all of them, and that is their varying sensitivity to sounds arriving at the diaphragm from different directions. This is known as their *polar distribution*, and is illustrated by drawing *polar diagrams* for both vertical and horizontal planes.

These diagrams are produced by checking the microphone in an echo free room called an *anechoic chamber*. This type of room ensures that there is no reverberation or unwanted ambient noise present to distort measurements. The output from an audio oscillator is fed into a loudspeaker, and the microphone positioned on axis about 6 feet away. The output level from the microphone is established, and then the microphone is rotated

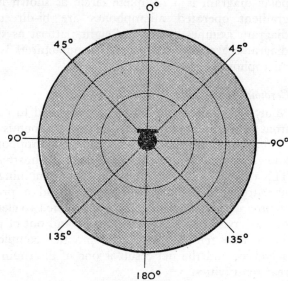

Fig. 5.4. Polar diagram
for a pressure operated
microphone.

through 360° whilst the changes in its output are tabulated. This procedure is repeated at spot frequencies throughout the working range of the microphone, and the results are plotted in diagram form.

Pressure operated microphones are omni-directional, therefore their

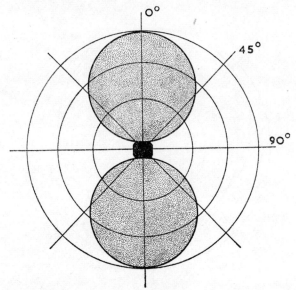

Fig. 5.5. Polar diagram
for a pressure gradient
operated microphone.

polar diagram is a complete circle as shown in Fig. 5.4. But pressure gradient operated microphones are bi-directional, and their polar diagram assumes a figure-of-eight pattern as shown in Fig. 5.5. Polar diagrams are supplied by the manufacturers with all professional type microphones.

Cardioid Microphones

Many situations occur when it is required to record sounds occurring in front of the microphone in preference to sounds from other directions. It is for this reason that uni-directional microphones were evolved, better known as *cardioid* microphones due to their heart shaped polar distribution. This cardioid pattern is obtained by combining the characteristics of a pressure element (omni-directional) and a pressure gradient element (figure of eight) as shown in Fig. 5.6. The two elements are in phase above the 90° axis and therefore additive, and out of phase below the 90° axis where they tend to cancel. In practice complete cancellation is never achieved, and the net result is one of discrimination between front and rear sensitivities.

The first cardioid microphone used two separate elements in a single case, a dynamic and a ribbon. This method has long been discontinued in favour of a single element, which gives an improved cardioid response at all frequencies. Dynamic, ribbon, and condenser microphones can all be

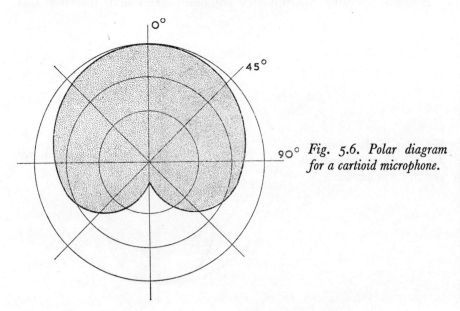

Fig. 5.6. Polar diagram for a cartioid microphone.

designed with cardioid characteristics, either by opening up a sound path to the rear face of a diaphragm or enclosing the sound path at the rear of a ribbon. With variations in design, any required degree of directivity can be produced.

Another feature of some cardioid microphones is a bass cut switch, often marked 'speech' or 'music'. For music the full bass response is always required, but for speech an attenuation of bass can improve intelligibility. The attenuation is usually effected by shunting a small inductance across the microphone output, or altering the design of the rear cavity. This facility is found mainly in microphones intended for amateur or semi-professional use, where quality control during recording is less likely to be available.

Carbon Microphones

These were the first type of microphone ever used for recording, since they were already in existence for telephony work. They are reasonably sensitive and easy to construct, but they are seldom used for recording today because they are not capable of very good quality. The diaphragm vibrations cause pressure changes on loosely packed carbon granules, thus varying a current flowing through them from a small battery. This produces a high background noise and a non-linear output, since the changes in pressure do not result in corresponding changes in the signal voltage obtained. A transformer is necessary to isolate the battery polarizing voltage (Fig. 5.7) and permit the transmission of the speech signal alone. This transformer also raises the impedance to the value required by the following circuit.

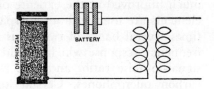

Fig. 5.7. Circuit for operating a carbon microphone.

Crystal Microphones

Certain varieties of crystalline structures, notably Rochelle Salt, contain the useful property of generating an electrical voltage when subjected to any mechanical stress. This is called the *piezo-electric* effect and is the principle of the crystal microphone. The same effect can be achieved with man-made ceramic materials. In practice a sandwich is made from two slices of a crystal of Rochelle Salt to give an improved output, and these slices are cemented together. This is known as a *bimorph* element, and is sealed with a protective coating against dampness. If a diaphragm is connected to one end of the element and the other end is fixed, a fairly large output voltage can be obtained as a result of the lever action (Fig. 5.8). The frequency response is fairly level, although it seldom reaches above 5 kHz due to the mechanical coupling.

DIAPHRAGM

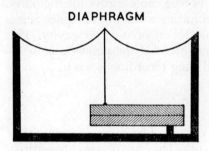

Fig. 5.8. Crystal microphone, diaphragm type.

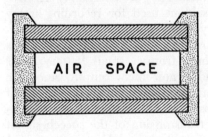

AIR   SPACE

Fig. 5.9. Crystal microphone, cell type.

Now if the sound waves themselves impinge directly on the bimorph element instead of on the diaphragm assembly, the frequency response is much improved at the expense of sensitivity. To increase sensitivity two elements are used with an air space between them (Fig. 5.9), and some-times several banks of two. This is called the sound cell type and has a frequency response which extends up to 10 kHz. All types have a good signal-to-noise ratio, and give a superior performance compared with carbon microphones. Crystal and ceramic microphones are pressure operated and have an omni-directional characteristic, that is they are sensitive to sound arriving from all angles. The resulting polar diagram is therefore a circle (Fig. 5.4).

These microphones are not favoured professionally since they possess a very high internal impedance, and prefer to work in a circuit of 5 megohms. There is also a limit to the length of cable which can be used successfully before the capacitance between leads introduces a shunting effect. This effect offers a shorter path for high frequencies than the input circuit of the amplifier, causing an apparent loss in the sensitivity of the microphone to high frequencies. The usual length of lead is about 10 ft. (3 metres), although this can be doubled with special low capacity cable. Crystal and ceramic microphones are extremely sensitive to hum pick up, and are normally housed in a metal container or liner which is connected to the screen of the microphone cable.

Dynamic Microphones

These are used extensively for recording by professionals and amateurs, since they are sensitive, have a wide frequency range, and are extremely robust. Due to their construction they are sometimes called moving coil microphones.

Dynamic microphones are pressure operated like the carbon and crystal types. A diaphragm with a coil of wire attached is accurately located between the poles of a permanent magnet where a high magnetic field exists. Sound waves cause movement of the diaphragm and induce an electrical current into the coil, normally referred to as the *speech coil*. The impedance of this coil is low, usually in the region of 30 to 50 ohms, which means that very long connecting cables can be used without any high frequency shunting effects due to capacity. A transformer is employed to match the impedance of the speech coil to the amplifier input circuit, and this also provides a step-up in the signal voltage.

A typical frequency response for a high quality dynamic microphone is 40 Hz to 16 kHz without any serious peaks or troughs; and because of this wide range dynamic microphones are also employed in work of a more scientific nature such as measurements and calibrations. Dynamic microphones are practically distortionless at all normal sound volume levels, although blasts of air due to explosive consonants, heavy breathing at close quarters, or wind as experienced out of doors, will upset the natural movement of the diaphragm.

The high frequency response is determined by the structure of the diaphragm and the tension under which it is clamped. The bass response depends on the design of the cavity or air space behind the diaphragm, which is often completely enclosed by a small circular magnet system. A small equalizing tube is sometimes fitted to relieve any back pressure and improve the bass response. Dynamic microphones are generally omnidirectional, but become slightly directional at high frequencies. This directional effect can be increased by fitting an *acoustic baffle* over the front of the microphone case. These baffles are from 2 to 2½ inches in diameter (5 to 7 cms) and usually made of metal or perspex. They also have the effect of giving a slightly rising response in the middle frequencies.

Certain types of dynamic microphones are manufactured with a special acoustic phase shifting network behind the diaphragm, open to free air, which renders the microphone almost uni-directional with a heart shaped polar distribution. This is known as a *cardioid* characteristic (see page 90), and is useful when recording in noisy surroundings to reduce unwanted sound approaching from the rear of the microphone. A good professional type of dynamic cardioid has a front to back discrimination of approximately 15 db, whilst some of the cheaper types only have a 6 to 8 db difference between front and rear sensitivities. Dynamic cardioids are partly pressure operated and partly pressure gradient operated, and suffer from bass tip-up when spoken into at very close quarters.

This 'proximity effect' has been overcome in some cardioid microphones which contain two dynamic elements in a single housing, one element for high frequencies and one element for low frequencies. These elements are coupled together with a cross-over network to give a smooth and extended frequency response, together with a highly directional characteristic over a wide frequency range. Such a microphone is the A.K.G. D.202, which is also fitted with a bass attenuator.

Ribbon Microphones

By its very nature the ribbon is essentially a studio microphone to be used indoors. It is eminently suitable for music recording and gives a faithful reproduction of transients. The transient response of a ribbon often surpasses that of a dynamic type, due to the extremely free undamped movement of the ribbon itself as compared to the rigidly held diaphragm of the dynamic. In fact the ribbon must be protected from strong currents of air which could blast it from its mounting.

Sound waves impinge directly on a thin strip of aluminium foil of very light mass, about 0·0001 in. (0·0025 mm) thick, which is clamped in the field of a magnet system (Fig. 5.2). A small electrical current is induced into the ribbon as it moves in the magnetic field, the amount of movement being almost directly proportional to the air particle velocity of the sound wave. This is why a ribbon is sometimes called a velocity microphone. As explained on page 87 it is pressure gradient operated. The actual impedance of the ribbon is extremely low—a fraction of an ohm—and an impedance matching transformer is usually built into the microphone case.

The polar distribution of a ribbon microphone assumes a figure-of-eight, for although it is equally sensitive at the front and the back it is relatively dead on either side. This is because any sound arriving at the side will reach both faces of the ribbon at exactly the same time, and in phase. So the sound will cancel itself out and theoretically the ribbon will not move. But in practice a little sound will always be heard from the side, although a ribbon is mainly bi-directional as shown by the polar diagram in Fig. 5.5. A ribbon can also be made uni-directional by means of an acoustic labyrinth or cavity enclosing the rear of the ribbon and fitted inside the microphone case. This prevents any direct sound from reaching the rear face and makes the ribbon act in the same manner as a diaphragm in a dynamic microphone, pressure operated. A uni-directional ribbon retains the bass emphasis when working close but gives an increased discrimination in a forward direction. This type of microphone is used extensively in film and television studios, where it is not always possible to position the microphone as close to the source of sound as one would wish.

A typical frequency response for a ribbon is 30 Hz to 18 kHz, although the output is usually a little below that of a dynamic. A well designed ribbon microphone has a large high flux magnet system, and sometimes two ribbon elements for increased output.

Condenser Microphones

These are the most suitable microphones for high quality recordings made under studio conditions, since they are extremely sensitive and have an extended frequency response. In its basic form the condenser is pressure operated, with a diaphragm forming one plate and the other being a fixed back plate. This unit is called a condenser *capsule*, and it requires a polarizing voltage of from 50 to 100 volts. Vibration of the diaphragm causes variations in the capacitance of the condenser, and a voltage change occurs across the capsule due to current variations through a load resistor.

The diaphragm and back plate are separated from each other by an air gap of approximately 0·001 in. (0·0254 mm) giving a capacitance of 50 picofarads (pf). Since this capacitance is low the impedance of the capsule to audio frequencies is high, between 10 and 15 megohms. It is impractical to transmit signals along a microphone cable at this impedance, so a small pre-amplifier is located inside the microphone body which enables a much lower output impedance to be obtained (Fig. 5.10). Line transformers are usually fitted so that a balanced output can be obtained at an impedance of 50 or 200 ohms.

A typical frequency response for a condenser microphone is from 20 Hz to 18 kHz, approximately the same as the human ear. In order to avoid any unwanted cavity resonances, the diaphragm is positioned very near to the microphone case, immediately behind a silk gauze screen. The diaphragm is also stretched very tight during manufacture so that its

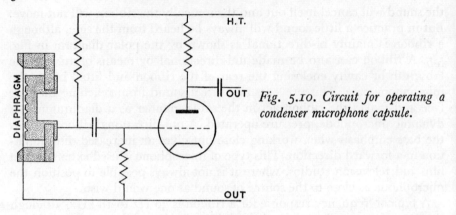

Fig. 5.10. Circuit for operating a condenser microphone capsule.

natural resonance occurs above the audible range. The rigid back plate has an appreciable effect on the stiffness and damping of the air behind the diaphragm, which causes a reduction in sensitivity at high frequencies. Since it is not practical to increase the distance between the diaphragm and back plate to ease the pressure, for this would reduce sensitivity still further, deep grooves are cut into the back plate as a compromise to improve the frequency response.

A condenser capsule as just described has an omni-directional characteristic; but making certain modifications can change this characteristic to bi-directional, or even cardioid. For example if holes are drilled in the back plate (in addition to the grooves), sound waves will impinge on both sides of the diaphragm. This gives a polar distribution in the shape of a figure-of-eight, and the capsule then acts as a pressure gradient microphone. Quite often a condenser capsule has a second diaphragm stretched across the other side of the back plate, both diaphragms being coupled together by the air space between them. Without polarizing the second

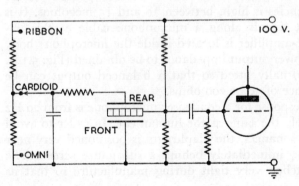

Fig. 5.11. Circuit for operating a double diaphragm capsule to obtain variable directivity.

diaphragm, such a capsule has a uni-directional or cardioid characteristic due to the combination of pressure and pressure gradient operation.

Once a polarizing voltage is applied to both diaphragms, an omni or bi-directional polar distribution can be obtained at will. This is the basis of condenser microphones with variable directivity controls, sometimes achieved by means of a slide switch on the microphone body or by remote control on a studio mixing console. Fig. 5.11 shows a circuit diagram for a double diaphragm capsule, and as many as nine different directivity patterns can be obtained by adjusting the polarizing supply. A multi-core cable connects the microphone to the special power unit, normally mains operated, which is located about 20 to 30 feet (6 to 9 metres) away.

The condenser microphones so far described are the conventional type with an audio frequency valve pre-amplifier. Transistor condenser microphones employ entirely different circuit techniques, and the condenser capsule is usually arranged to modulate a radio frequency oscillator of about 8 mHz. This oscillator is crystal controlled to reduce noise and improve stability. The output is demodulated, amplified by about 12 db, and passed through an r.f. filter—all inside the microphone body. The capsule itself has a low impedance at radio frequencies, which means that there is no need for a high polarizing voltage. This type of transistor circuit requires only a single low voltage supply, and draws very little current. The audio output impedance can be arranged to suit requirements, usually 50 or 200 ohms.

Mains or battery power systems for transistor condenser microphones are relatively simple, and use can be made of two wire screened cables which may already exist in some permanent installations. The positive supply to the microphone can be passed along one audio lead, and the negative supply passed through the cable screen. The audio signal returns through the second lead and cable screen to give an unbalanced output. But this method cannot be used where a system of balanced audio lines is employed, and there are two alternative solutions.

Fig. 5.12. Circuit diagram for phantom powering of transistor condenser microphone.

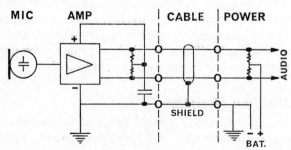

On long cable runs a system of *phantom powering* is used. The positive pole of a 50 volt supply is applied through two protective resistors to both audio leads, and the negative pole is applied to the cable shield or a third lead. Inside the microphone body the positive supply is obtained through a further two resistors, as shown in Fig. 5.12. With phantom powering the current consumption is low (less than 1 mA.) and the microphone will operate equally well if the audio leads are reversed. Furthermore other types of microphone, such as a dynamic or ribbon, may be directly connected without removing the power supply.

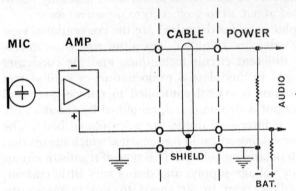

Fig. 5.13. Circuit diagram for modulation lead powering of transistor condenser microphone.

Another system for shorter cable runs is called *modulation lead powering*, where a supply of from 7 to 12 volts is connected across the audio lines through two resistors which together form the load of the microphone output transistor (Fig. 5.13). The balance of the audio signal is thus achieved at the power unit, and at no other point is the circuitry earthed. The current consumption is slightly higher, between 5 and 10 mA., and the microphone will not operate if there is a reversal in the audio leads. It is also more difficult for other types of microphone to be used with the same cable, and the power supply and load resistors must be removed.

Condenser microphones designed for phantom powering cannot be used with modulation lead powering, and vice versa. Some transistor condenser microphones are completely self contained, and are powered by internal mercury cells. These are designed mainly for portable use and are sometimes fitted with permanent windshields.

Directional Microphones

In addition to the normal range of microphones there are many special types manufactured for specific purposes. For example one particular application is for a highly directional microphone, where a sound pick up is required from a source at some considerable distance from the microphone—such as bird song. A simple arrangement consists of a parabolic reflector which will divert parallel sound waves to a point source, and a dynamic microphone mounted at or near the focal point—and facing the reflector. Sounds arriving along the axis provide additional in-phase signals to the microphone, thus giving an acoustic gain.

Directivity here is obtained at the expense of a restricted bass response, the latter being determined by the dimensions of the reflector. Theoretically the distance from the reflector to the microphone diaphragm should be half the wavelength of the lowest frequency it is desired to record. This implies that a 6 ft. (2 m) diameter reflector is necessary to record 200 Hz. But it is not always necessary to record bass frequencies at full sensitivity, and satisfactory recordings can be made with a reflector 3 ft. (1 m) in diameter, which provides an acoustic gain of 10 db. Parabolic microphones are not seriously troubled by wind, and may be hand-held or mounted on a tripod with a pan and tilt head.

In film and television work the requirement is often for a boom mounted directional microphone which will give good quality with music and voices. These are called *line* microphones and among the types currently favoured are a dynamic manufactured by Electrovoice in America and a condenser manufactured by Sennheiser in Germany. The dynamic, known as type 642, has a cardioid element with a tube one foot in length attached in front of the diaphragm. A one-eighth inch open slit is milled in

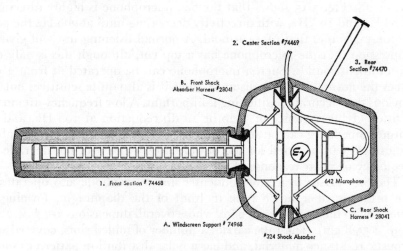

Fig. 5.14. Electro-Voice type 642 directional microphone.

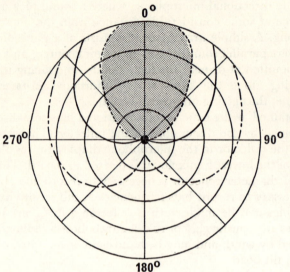

*Fig. 5.15. Diagram show-
ing the polar distribution
of Electro-Voice type 642
microphone. Shaded area
= 10 kHz, solid line =
1 kHz, and broken line =
200 Hz.*

the tube over its entire length, and the slit covered with a tapering acoustic resistance. This permits an uninterrupted passage to on-axis sounds, and proportionate delay networks to sounds approaching off-axis which cause their partial cancellation, especially at high frequencies.

The net result, assisted by the cardioid element, is a microphone with a frequency response of 30 Hz to 10 kHz whose acceptance angle varies with frequency. Fig. 5.15 shows that the 642 microphone is highly directional at 9 kHz and 10 kHz, with directivity decreasing until at 200 Hz the polar response assumes that of a cardioid. A normal listening test will give the impression that the microphone has a top cut, although this is only true with off-axis sounds. Such a microphone can be operated at from 2 to 3 times the normal working distance, since it is also quite sensitive, but it is obvious that accurate positioning is important. A low frequency attenuator is fitted giving a choice of 5 db or 10 db reduction at 100 Hz, and the output impedance can be adjusted to 50, 150, or 250 ohms. A foam rubber windshield can be fitted for use out of doors which will not degrade the frequency or polar response of the microphone.

The Sennheiser transistor condenser line microphone also operates on the principle of a single tube in front of the diaphragm, forming an extension to the microphone body whose overall dimensions are $\frac{3}{4} \times 22$ in. (1.9×55.8 cm). The tube carries a number of milled slots, covered with acoustic resistance material, and has a polar distribution pattern as shown by the diagram in Fig. 5.17. It has an extremely narrow front lobe, with

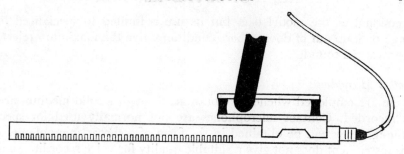

Fig. 5.16. Sennheiser model 805 directional microphone.

Fig. 5.17. Diagram show-
ing the polar distribution of
Sennheiser   model   805
microphone. Shaded area =
10 kHz, solid line = 1
kHz, and broken line =
200 Hz.

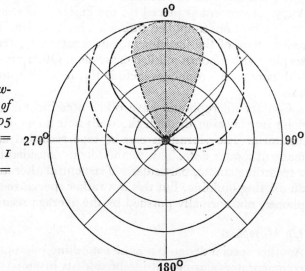

a high front to back (and side) discrimination. Being a condenser element
the frequency response is wide, and extends from 50 Hz to 20 kHz. The
internal noise level is low, and the construction renders the condenser
element impervious to wind and mechanical vibrations. Nevertheless a
pistol grip or boom fitting shock mount is available, also a plastic mesh
windshield supported on a metal frame. Model 804 is directly powered by
an external 9 volt battery, and has an unbalanced output designed to work
into a circuit of 2 K/ohms impedance. Model 805 is modulation line
powered from a 10 volt supply, and has a balanced output designed to
work into a circuit of 200 ohms impedance.

Another high directional microphone is the Electrovoice model 643,
which is approximately 7 ft. (2 m) in length. This makes it 5 times as

directional as the model 642, but its use is limited to specialized long range pick up out of doors where conditions give the maximum rejection of unwanted sound.

Contact Microphones

These are employed whenever vibrations through a solid medium are to be recorded. Contact microphones are not normally used for speech, although they can be obtained in the form of a throat microphone. But this instrument does not give a suitable quality for voice recording, and is therefore mainly of academic interest.

A good example of a contact microphone is seen in an electric guitar. A crystal element is placed on the guitar case near the bridge, and the string vibrations amplified through a loudspeaker. This alters the characteristic tone of the instrument, but creates an intensified sound more in keeping with modern musical expression. Other musical instruments fitted with contact microphones include the accordion, harmonica, and double bass.

Contact microphones have other uses including the measurement of noise transmission through the walls and floors of recording studios and auditoria. The vibrations can be tape recorded and a detailed analysis made at a later date. This method helps considerably in the designing of a recording studio, particularly if structural alterations are to be made to an existing building. But this is a rather specialized use of contact microphones, not normally pursued by the average recording engineer.

Lip Microphone

Another special design is a noise cancelling microphone, as used by sports commentators during outside broadcasts in noisy surroundings. Called a *lip microphone* it consists of a cardioid element, dynamic or ribbon, which has its bass response considerably reduced. By holding the microphone extremely close to the mouth, a flat response can be obtained from the voice. Naturally when speaking close there is a good deal of breath noise from the mouth and nostrils, which creates a disturbing blasting effect on the microphone diaphragm or ribbon. So breath shields are usually fitted consisting of silk for the mouth and a felt pad for the nostrils. A mouth-guard is included in the design so that the speaker's mouth is always at the correct distance from the microphone. Lip microphones are not unduly affected by wind, although a separate windshield is usually available.

Fig. 5.18 shows the frequency response of a noise cancelling ribbon microphone type 4104, manufactured by Standard Telephones and Cables Ltd. The shaded area shows the discrimination between a close speaking voice and random sounds, and the dotted line in between shows the sensitivity of the microphone to distant sounds on the same axis as the speaker. Distant sounds are mainly comprised of low frequencies, which are attenuated in the microphone and account for the good discrimination between these sounds and the close speaking voice.

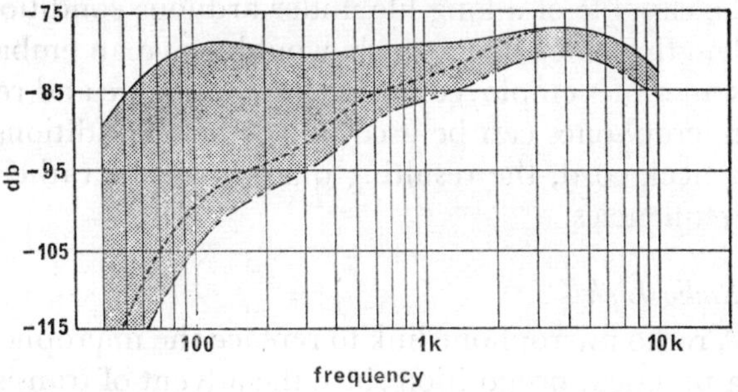

Fig. 5.18. Frequency response of type 4104 noise cancelling microphone.

Lavalier Microphones

These are a special type of high quality dynamic microphone, designed for correct speech balance when worn on a cord around the neck. They are used for film and television interviews, and for other recording applications where it is impossible to position a normal microphone. Since the human voice has pronounced directional characteristics, with high frequencies being emitted in a narrow angle from the mouth, poor quality will result if a microphone with a flat frequency response is worn against the chest. Lavalier microphones are designed to give the crispness of normal speech when worn in this position.

It has been found that the most natural voice quality was obtained when the microphone response was equalized to show a dip at 700 Hz, thus reducing the effect of chest cavity resonance. In addition the response curve usually shows a high frequency emphasis between 2 kHz and 7 kHz, with a peak of about 7 db at 5 kHz, to compensate for the lack of high frequencies in the area below the mouth, and to some extent the masking effect of clothing. One particular microphone, the A.K.G. D109, has its lavalier cord attached to a wide circular clip which holds the microphone body. If the clip is level with the top of the microphone, the response is flat. If the clip is raised above the top of the microphone, a cavity is formed which provides high frequency emphasis between 3 kHz and 5 kHz due to resonance.

All lavalier microphones are fairly small and can easily be concealed behind a neck tie. But if the microphone is concealed beneath layers of clothing there will be a severe loss of high frequencies, since the instrument is designed to be worn on the surface. A further problem with lavalier microphones is the interference from the rustle of clothing caused by the microphone body rubbing against the wearer's clothes. To reduce this effect the dynamic element should be insulated from the microphone body.

The screened connecting cable should be extremely flexible, and it must be capable of a long life under arduous conditions. On occasions where a lengthy microphone cable would prove an embarrassment, a radio link is sometimes employed between microphone and recorder. Although lavalier microphones can be used in free field conditions instead of hanging from a neck cord, the resulting quality will be rather thin and lacking in bass frequencies.

Radio Link

A radio microphone link to replace the microphone cable has only become a practical proposition since the advent of transistors, which have enabled miniature V.H.F. transmitters to be designed with conservative power requirements. Frequency modulation was chosen in preference to amplitude modulation due to the superior signal-to-noise ratio obtainable, especially with pre-emphasis of high frequencies in the transmitter and de-emphasis in the receiver. The amount of emphasis used corresponds to a time constant of 50 micro-seconds. A typical signal-to-noise ratio is 55 db, with an overall frequency response of 30 Hz to 15 kHz ($\pm$ 2 db). The output power from the transmitter is only about 20 mW, which is considered sufficient to give an adequate performance within normal camera range.

The pocket sized transmitters of a modern radio link system are crystal controlled for stability, and operate from an internal battery, such as the P.P.3 or its equivalent, which gives about 4 hours of continuous use. The P.P.3 was chosen because it is obtainable anywhere in the world, although it does have a very short shelf life of about 6 weeks. Any type of dynamic or ribbon microphone up to 600 ohms impedance may be used, but conditions usually dictate a dynamic microphone of the lavalier type.

Each country usually allocates V.H.F. bands for radio microphone operation, usually between 30 mHz and 175 mHz, according to local conditions. The use of radio links in the United Kingdom is governed by Post Office regulations, and a G.P.O. licence must be obtained. The frequency allotted in the United Kingdom is 174·8 mHz, which has proved to be very suitable and free from interference. Most other countries allocated frequencies below 50 mHz, which are more prone to interference from electric motors and car ignition. Also when transmitters are used in an enclosed area, the lower frequencies suffer from standing waves which cause partial cancellation of the received signal. This in turn means a high background noise.

The frequency band chosen also dictates the size of the aerial, since for maximum efficiency the length of the aerial should not be less than one quarter of a wavelength. At 50 mHz this is 5 ft. (1·5 m) which is too long to be worn by an artiste. At the English frequency of 174·8 mHz, the aerial is only 16 in. (0·41 m) long and can easily be concealed in clothing.

The receiver is also crystal controlled, and contains a tuning indicator and signal strength meter so that its performance can be visually checked. Tuning should stay constant over long periods of time, which makes such a radio link easy to use without an additional operator. Since re-tuning on some units is a workshop operation, no attempt at adjustment should be made in the field. Up to 5 radio links can be operated around 175 mHz without interaction, their tuning being spaced 1 mHz apart. When more than 5 channels are operated simultaneously, it is virtually impossible to avoid a whistle on one channel.

It is convenient if the audio output is a balanced line at microphone level and impedance, so that the signal can be fed directly into a conventional microphone mixing unit. Alternative outputs can be made available such as zero level at 600 ohms, or an unbalanced line for a tape recorder. A separate headphone monitoring outlet is usually included on the commercially available radio links. There is really no restriction on the size of the receiver, but it is beneficial if it is fairly compact and lightweight. It may often have to be hand-held so that its whip aerial is in line of sight with the transmitter. V.H.F. signals will easily be reflected from solid surfaces, but will become greatly attenuated if too many people or objects come between the receiver and transmitter aerials.

Microphone Loading

The electrical energy obtained from the movement of a microphone diaphragm is extremely small, and it must be transferred to the following amplifier circuit with the minimum loss of signal voltage. Since speech signals consist of an alternating voltage they do not follow Ohm's law of resistance; they also become affected by inductance and capacitance which, together with resistance, determine impedance. Impedance values vary with frequency, and unless otherwise stated impedances given in connection with sound recording are in relation to a signal of 1 kHz.

When placed in the path of sound waves, a microphone which is not connected to any item of equipment will nevertheless have an output voltage across its terminals. This is known as its open circuit output voltage, and is the condition the microphone manufacturer refers to when output level and frequency response are specified. With valve operated equipment these specifications hold good since the microphone is usually unloaded. It is connected to a matching transformer which raises the microphone impedance to 50 K/ohms, and the secondary winding is connected to the control grid of a valve—which is virtually an open circuit.

Transistor equipment is usually designed with an impedance match between the microphone and amplifier input stage, which loads the microphone so that its performance differs from that of an open circuit condition. If the load impedance is mainly resistive, there will be a drop in the microphone output level but no change in the frequency response. But if the load impedance is capacitive or inductive it will vary its value with frequency, and may cause a change in the frequency response of the microphone. An example of this is capacitance due to a very long microphone cable, causing a top loss.

The most noticeable effect occurs when bi-directional or cardioid microphones are operated with a resistive load equal to their own impedance. Under these conditions there will be a drop in output together with a reduction in the bass response below 500 Hz, amounting to about 5 db at 100 Hz. This change in response would not be heard as a severe degradation of quality, but rather as a colouration of the sound quality. To avoid these effects bi-directional and cardioid microphones should always be operated in an open circuit condition, or at least be connected to a circuit which is several times their own impedance.

In theory the connection of two items of equipment with unequal impedances represents a mis-match, which should produce a voltage loss. But a voltage loss only becomes serious when the mis-match ratio is more than about 3 to 1. A 50 ohm microphone fed into a circuit of 150 ohms impedance gives a 5 db loss, and the same microphone fed into a circuit of 250 ohms impedance gives a 7 db loss. Whether this is important or not depends on the output of the microphone and the signal-to-noise ratio of the recording system. A more disturbing effect occurs when feeding a microphone into a circuit of lower impedance than that for which it was intended, such as a 250 ohm microphone into a 50 ohm input. Although there is a 7 db rise in output from the microphone, there is a noticeable loss in the frequency response at both the bass and treble ends of the range.

Microphone Sensitivity

The output signal obtainable from a microphone is nearly always proportional to the pressure of sound waves on the diaphragm or ribbon. Due to their different construction, the various types of microphone elements produce different outputs from the same sound pressure. This pressure is measured in *dynes per square centimetre*. A person speaking in a normal voice 1 ft. (0·3 m) away from a microphone produces a sound pressure of 1 dyne/cm², whilst a shout produces 10 dynes/cm² and a whisper produces 0·1 dyne/cm².

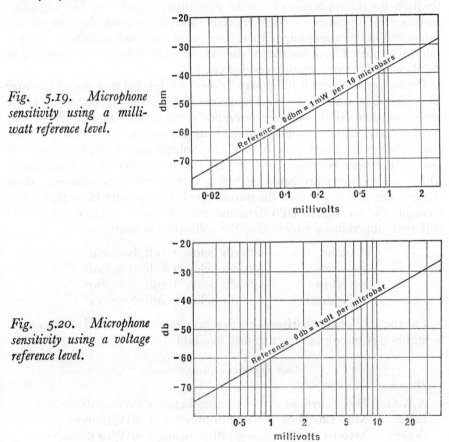

Fig. 5.19. Microphone sensitivity using a milliwatt reference level.

Fig. 5.20. Microphone sensitivity using a voltage reference level.

The sensitivity of a microphone is rated in terms of voltage output for a given sound pressure, and is expressed in millivolts per *microbar*. A microbar is a unit of air pressure corresponding to 1 dyne/cm². A high output microphone may give as much as 5 mV per microbar, and a low output microphone only 0·1 mV per microbar. The output level can also be expressed as so many decibels below a certain reference level, and the sensitivity ratings supplied by the microphone manufacturers can be converted into decibels by using the accompanying graphs. For low impedance microphones a power reference level is usually specified which does not change when the circuit impedance is transformed into a higher value at the amplifier input. The usual reference is o dbm = 1 mW per 10 microbars, and Fig. 5.19 shows the relationship between millivolts and decibels for microphones of 200 to 250 ohms impedance. For high impedance microphones a voltage reference level is specified, since we are not interested in changing impedance. The usual reference is o db = 1 V per microbar, and Fig. 5.20 shows the relationship between millivolts and decibels under open circuit conditions.

Confusion can arise if the power reference is related to a sound pressure of 1 microbar, since this would make the microphone appear to be 20 db more sensitive. If the voltage reference is related to 10 microbars, this would make the microphone appear to be 20 db less sensitive. Some microphones are rated directly in V.U.s (volume units) which are units of power, the zero reference level being 1 mW at 600 ohms impedance. Other microphones are rated against a voltage reference whatever their impedance, and in this case the output level changes with impedance. For example the Grampian DP8 dynamic microphone is available in several different impedances which give the following outputs:

25 ohms	—86 db below 1 volt/dyne/cm²
200 ohms	—75 db below 1 volt/dyne/cm²
600 ohms	—70 db below 1 volt/dyne/cm²
50 K/ohms	—52 db below 1 volt/dyne/cm²

For the sake of comparison here is a list showing the relative outputs of a number of microphones currently available:

Low Impedance (200 ohms)

Dynamic

A.K.G.	D25	Cardioid	—50 dbm below 1 mW/10 dynes/cm²
Beyer	M88	Cardioid	—49 dbm below 1 mW/10 dynes/cm²
Beyer	M100	Omni	—58 dbm below 1 mW/10 dynes/cm²
Beyer	M110	Lavalier	—58 dbm below 1 mW/10 dynes/cm²
Electrovoice	642		—48 dbm below 1 mW/10 dynes/cm²
Electrovoice	RE15		—56 dbm below 1 mW/10 dynes/cm²
Electrovoice	668		—51 dbm below 1 mW/10 dynes/cm²
R.C.A. BK6		Lavalier	—67 dbm below 1 mW/10 dynes/cm²
Sennheiser	MD 211N		—56 dbm below 1 mW/10 dynes/cm²
Sennheiser	MD 21		—52 dbm below 1 mW/10 dynes/cm²
Shure 546		Unidyne	—56 dbm below 1 mW/10 dynes/cm²

Ribbon

Beyer	M130	—59 dbm below 1 mW/10 dynes/cm^2
S.T. & C.	4038 (studio)	—65 dbm below 1 mW/10 dynes/cm^2
S.T. & C.	4104 (lip)	—62 dbm below 1 mW/10 dynes/cm^2
R.C.A.	10,001	—60 dbm below 1 mW/10 dynes/cm^2
Shure	300	—59 dbm below 1 mW/10 dynes/cm^2

Condenser

Fi-Cord	FC600	Omni	—54 dbm below 1 mW/10 dynes/cm^2
Fi-Cord	FC800	Omni	—52 dbm below 1 mW/10 dynes/cm^2
Neuman	U 77	Variable	—24 dbm below 1 mW/10 dynes/cm^2
Neuman	U 87	Variable	—60 dbm below 1 mW/10 dynes/cm^2
Sennheiser	105	Omni	—27 dbm below 1 mW/10 dynes/cm^2
Sennheiser	405	Cardioid	—27 dbm below 1 mW/10 dynes/cm^2
Sennheiser	805	Directional	—21 dbm below 1 mW/10 dynes/cm^2

High Impedance (50 K/ohms or more)

Crystal

Acos	Mic 39/1 Omni	—62 db below 1 V/dyne/cm^2
Shure	777 Omni	—62 db below 1 V/dyne/cm^2

Dynamic

Grampian	DP8 Omni	—52 db below 1 V/dyne/cm^2
Shure Unidyne	III	—55 db below 1 V/dyne/cm^2

The microphone sensitivity rating determines the output voltage at only one sound pressure, but since all quality microphones are linear over their working range, the output voltage is a direct function of sound pressure on the diaphragm. If the sound pressure is increased by a factor of 10, then the microphone's output voltage will also be increased by 10. Thus if the sensitivity is known and the sound pressure is known, the output voltage can be determined, also the amplifier input characteristics.

Microphone Cables

Since the output level from a microphone is rather low, a considerable amount of amplification must take place before a useable voltage is obtained. High amplification means that any electrical interference or hum picked up in the microphone cable itself will be increased in volume, as well as the audio signal. This is the main reason why all microphone cables are screened by a braided metal electrostatic shield, placed between the conductors and the outer cover. This shield prevents interference from reaching the conductors and also gives a certain amount of protection from accidental damage, without appreciably increasing the stiffness of the cable.

In the early days of telegraphy only a single line existed between the sending and receiving stations, the circuit being completed by an earth connection at either end. This method of transmission is called an *unbalanced* line, a term still used when one conductor is at earth potential. An unbalanced microphone cable having a single conductor and an outer metal shield is quite satisfactory over a distance of 15 to 20 feet (4 to 6 metres), the outer shield providing adequate screening against the electrical fields of motors, transformers, and house wiring with a.c. mains. The shield is used as the other signal line and is connected to the amplifier chassis and earth. If the microphone has a metal case, this is also earthed through the metal shield to eliminate an effect known as *hand capacity* (caused by handling the microphone) which introduces a hum.

When using long microphone cables, two conductors are better than one providing they are connected as a *balanced* line. The amount of interference picked up in each conductor is always equal and in phase. So by terminating the line with a centre-tapped transformer, the centre tapping only is connected to earth and the interference balanced out. The usual microphone line impedance used in sound recording today is 200 ohms, and for other transmission lines 600 ohms. The distance between microphone and transformer can be two or three hundred feet, that is, up to about 100 metres, without any noticeable loss in signal level or frequency response. But long microphone cables cannot be used at high impedances due to cable capacitance, so that there is no point in using a balanced line with a crystal microphone.

All microphone transformers are enclosed in a mu-metal case, mu-metal having the property of shielding against all magnetic fields. The case must also be earthed to effectively eliminate interference and hum. Transformers without a centre-tapped primary winding can be used for balanced lines by introducing an artificial centre tap. Two resistors are connected across the primary winding with their centre point earthed, their values being several times the microphone impedance to prevent any loading effects. The output from the transformer secondary is always unbalanced when feeding directly into a valve or transistor amplifier, although it may be centre-tapped for connection to a further transmission line. Transformers can also be used with unbalanced microphone cables, but it is not advisable over distances greater than 20 ft. (6 m).

In practice there is often a slight amount of 'unbalance' in the interference pattern which could be troublesome. Damp weather is also liable to increase interference from nearby motors and generators, and conditions which function quite well in dry weather can prove impossible in the rain. An efficient earth connection is not always an effective cure, and could actually increase the interference. Strong a.c. fields can also penetrate screened cables which only have a screen of twisted wire strands around the conductors. In general it is advisable to use only braided screened cable, and to keep microphone cables away from other wiring.

CHAPTER VI

Amplifiers and Filters

THE BASIC function of an amplifier is to convert a small amount of energy applied to the input into a large amount of energy appearing at the output, with sufficient power to operate a loudspeaker, recording machine, or some other item of sound equipment. Speech signals in their electrical form constitute an a.c. voltage of varying frequency, and the small amount of electrical energy obtained from a microphone can be conveniently amplified by using the properties of thermionic valves or transistors in a unit containing one or more stages of amplification. These units are known as *audio amplifiers*, and they are designed to cover a wide variety of applications within the audible frequency range of 20 Hz to 20 kHz. They are sometimes constructed in a single unit for hi-fi installations and tape recorders, or divided into several units to form the amplifier chain of a professional recording or broadcast studio.

The performance of an audio amplifier is judged by its overall gain in decibels, its signal-to-noise ratio (also expressed in decibels), the available output in watts, and the percentage of harmonic distortion. Harmonic distortion is always present to some extent, and it is essential that only a negligible amount should be introduced by any audio amplifier. The normally accepted value in professional equipment is 0·1 per cent or less, whilst domestic equipment may contain 1 per cent or more at full output. Audio amplifiers should also possess a flat frequency response within the audible range, as well as a reserve of power at normal operating conditions. The signal-to-noise ratio should be as high as possible, and figures of between 60 db and 80 db are quite common.

Voltage Amplifier

The front part of any audio amplifier can conveniently be described as a *voltage amplifier*. This may consist of one, two, or more stages of amplification, each one coupled to the next by means of a resistor-capacitor coupling as shown in Fig. 6.1. Resistor coupled amplifiers are simple to construct, have a wide frequency response, and have a good signal-to-noise level when low noise resistors are used. Valve operated voltage amplifiers use high gain triodes and pentodes, the latter type giving greater amplification per stage. Harmonic distortion is inclined to be higher with a pentode, but this can be minimized in circuit design with feedback loops.

Valve amplifiers have a high input impedance, up to 10 megohms, which enables microphones to work into what is virtually an open circuit.

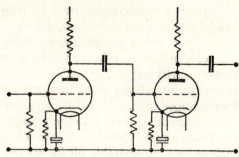

Fig. 6.1. Circuit of voltage amplifier showing resistor-capacitor coupling between two triode stages.

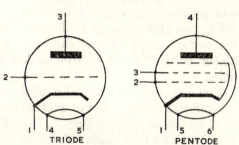

Fig. 6.2. Valves used in voltage and power amplifiers.

Triode: (1) Cathode, (2) Signal Grid, (3) Anode, (4) Heater, (5) Heater.

Pentode: (1) Cathode, (2) Signal Grid, (3) Screen Grid, (4) Anode, (5) Heater, (6) Heater.

TRIODE   PENTODE

Consider the case of a triode valve consisting of heater, anode, cathode, and grid elements. Such a valve will amplify because changes in grid potential cause a correspondingly greater change in the anode potential. The signal to be amplified is applied between grid and cathode elements, and the varying voltage of this signal causes an alteration in the current passing from anode to cathode. A 1 volt change at the grid can produce a 20 volt change at the anode, as measured across the anode load resistor, and this voltage is then passed on to the next valve stage for further amplification if required.

Voltage amplifiers are designed to have a frequency range of 10 Hz to 20 kHz and above, without distortion of any kind. But it is not possible to employ the same type of valve successfully in every stage of an amplifier, as it is essential that each valve will handle its input signal voltage, called the *grid swing*, without overloading. Distortion will occur if the input signal is greater than the grid *bias voltage*. This bias voltage becomes necessary to allow the input signal to swing the grid either side of the central point of the valve's operating characteristic. In practice the cathode is made positive with respect to chassis and ground by means of a low value bias resistor connected in series with the cathode. This bias resistor is normally shunted by a high value capacitor to maintain a good bass response.

Voltage amplifiers are used in conjunction with microphones, tape heads, and pick-up cartridges, since the actual voltage generated by these items is very small indeed. Typical values are 0·5 mV to 5 mV for a microphone, 5 mV to 10 mV for a tape head, 3 mV to 10 mV for a magnetic pick-up cartridge, and 150 mV to 500 mV for a crystal or ceramic pick-up cartridge. Sometimes an input transformer is used with items having a low source impedance, such as microphones and tape heads, so as to provide a better impedance match to the amplifier input. Frequency compensation is also introduced deliberately into voltage amplifiers as and when required, such as bass cut or treble lift for microphones, and bass lift for tape heads and pick-up cartridges. Control of volume is seldom made within a voltage amplifier, except in domestic equipment, but at a point between the voltage amplifier and the main amplifier where the signal is at a higher level. Volume controls in low level circuits generally introduce noise.

Voltage amplifiers are also used to raise the signal voltage before transmission along a line to another part of an installation, and they are then known as *line amplifiers*. It is preferable to send audio signals over long lines at a fairly high volume level, usually 0 db. or zero level (0·775 volts) in a line of 600 ohms impedance. This minimizes the possibility of hum and noise being picked up en route, and the signal can always be attenuated at the other end of the line if necessary. Line amplifiers must have a level frequency response, with input and output transformers matched to the line impedance. The input of a line amplifier can also be arranged for a *bridging* condition, which means raising the impedance to 10 times the line impedance, to enable connection across an existing line without a reduction of signal level. No frequency correction is normally used in a line or bridging amplifier, although there is sometimes an adjustment for overall amplification.

Power Amplifiers

The purpose of a power amplifier is to convert the amplified signal supplied by the voltage amplifier into power, thereby providing sufficient voltage and current to suit the impedance of the loudspeaker system or recording machine modulator. The design of any power amplifier commences with its output stage, since this determines how the remainder of the amplifier is constructed.

The type of output stage employed depends on the volume of sound required, bearing in mind that the amplifier must be capable of handling several times the average (or R.M.S.) power requirements to reproduce transient signal peaks without distortion. No amplifier will operate at its best when forced to work at maximum gain. The normal power output from a single small pentode is about 3 to 4 watts. This is quite sufficient for domestic listening conditions where the volume required is no greater than normal speech levels. For greater output power a pair of pentodes are operated in a push-pull circuit, in which balanced components work in phase opposition to cancel or reduce 2nd harmonic distortion.

Since the signal voltages applied to the grid of each push-pull output valve must be 180° out of phase with each other, all push-pull stages are preceded by a *phase splitter* network similar to the one shown in Fig. 6.3. One of the signal voltages is obtained from the anode of the phase splitter valve at X, and the other signal from the cathode of the same valve at Y. The two signal voltages are brought back into phase again in an output transformer which has a centre-tapped primary winding, and it is here that a cancellation of magnetic flux reduces distortion. Such a circuit can deliver from 10 to 50 watts or more, depending on the size and the number of valves used in push-pull.

There are three basic methods of obtaining push-pull operation, depending on which part of the valve's grid characteristic is used. If each valve is biased to the centre of the straight portion of its operating characteristic, the circuit is referred to as class 'A'. The peak signal voltage must then be limited to a value which does not exceed the bias voltage, and anode current flows at all times. Harmonic distortion is low, which makes class 'A' circuits suitable for high quality recording and reproducing systems. Higher power output can be achieved if each valve is over-biased, causing a greater variation in anode current, and this type of circuit is known as class 'AB'. A third method known as class 'B' requires each output valve to be biased to a point at or near cut-off, which means

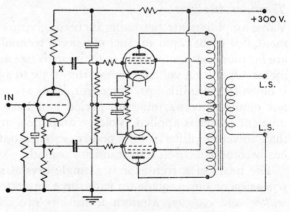

Fig. 6.3. Power amplifier with ultra-linear output stage, operating in class AB push-pull.

that no anode current will flow at all when no input signal is applied. Under these conditions the positive and negative portions of the audio signal are amplified separately by each valve. Class 'AB' is the one usually encountered.

In class 'AB' and 'B' circuits, harmonic distortion can be reduced and frequency response flattened by incorporating a *negative feedback* loop. This circuit permits a small proportion of the amplifier output to be fed back into the input. Since the feedback signal is arranged to be 180° out of phase with the input signal, the overall gain of the amplifier is reduced and must be taken into account. Yet another form of feedback is contained in an *Ultra-Linear* push-pull stage, where the screen supply voltage is obtained from a tapping on the primary of the output transformer. This arrangement permits pentode valves to be operated with the low distortion normally associated with triode valves, even at full output. In practice it is found that the maximum undistorted output is obtained when the output transformer primary impedance is twice the valve's internal impedance.

To permit maximum power to be transferred from the amplifier to loudspeaker, or recording machine modulator, the ratio between primary and secondary windings of the output transformer must be chosen so that the secondary impedance accurately matches whatever item of equipment is connected to it. The simple formula for calculating the turns ratio is:

$$\text{Turns Ratio} = \sqrt{\text{Impedance Ratio}}$$

For example a push-pull output stage with a combined anode to anode impedance of 13,500 ohms has to feed a loudspeaker whose impedance is 15 ohms. The impedance ratio is 13,500 divided by 15, which equals 900. The square root of 900 is 30, which is the turns ratio required.

Transistor Amplifiers

Valve amplifiers are becoming increasingly rare in modern sound equipment, due to the rapid advance of *transitor* technology. Transistor amplifiers are far more satisfactory due to their small size and modest power requirements. Operating voltages range from 1·5 v to 45 v d.c., and consumption is measured in milliamps. Since transistors are solid state devices, they do not require any warming up period and become operational from the moment power is applied. Voltage amplifiers are always easier to design than power amplifiers, and a poorly designed output stage can cause what has become known as the 'transistor' sound.

The heart of a transistor is a single crystal of a *semiconductor*, usually *germanium* or *silicon*, made up with three separate elements called the *base*, *emitter*, and *collector*. Modern transistors are encapsulated in plastic or

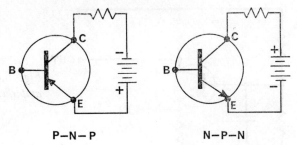

Fig. 6.4. Junction transistor symbols. Note reversed polarity for N.P.N. and P.N.P. types.

P–N–P   N–P–N

epoxy resin, also metal and glass, and those used in audio amplifiers are called *junction* transistors, since the emitter and the collector are joined to the base by one of several processes. There are also two types of junction transistors, the *P.N.P.* and the *N.P.N.* The P.N.P. is operated with a positive earth, and the N.P.N. with a negative earth, to suit the direction of the emitter current flow. The N.P.N. type is rapidly becoming standarized, and can be likened to a triode valve in that the base resembles the grid, the emitter the cathode, and the collector the anode.

Amplification with a transistor is achieved through an actual current gain, as well as an impedance difference, which exists between the elements used for the input and output circuits. The performance of a transistor is considerably altered according to which element is grounded, meaning that the element in question is common to both input and output circuits.

Basic Transistor Configurations

Grounded Element	Amplifier Gain	Input Impedance	Output Impedance
Base	Voltage	10 to 100 ohms	10,000's ohms
Emitter	Current	1k/ohms to 40k/ohms	1000's ohms
Collector	Current	100 k/ohms	100's ohms

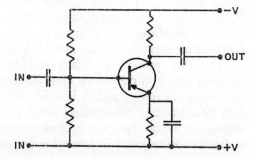

Fig. 6.5. Grounded emitter voltage amplifier, using P.N.P. transistor.

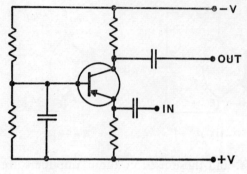

Fig. 6.6. *Grounded base voltage, amplifier, using P.N.P. transistor.*

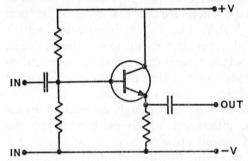

Fig. 6.7. *Grounded collector or emitter follower, using N.P.N. transistor.*

In practice it is the emitter which is normally grounded in an audio amplifier, the input being applied between base and emitter whilst the output is taken from the emitter and the collector. Such a circuit is illustrated in Fig. 6.5, and is suitable as a voltage amplifier with capacitor coupling to the next stage. The grounded base configuration is less frequently used due to the low input impedance, although this arrangement is satisfactory for a low impedance microphone as shown in Fig. 6.6. The grounded collector circuit, or emitter follower, is most useful as a buffer stage to isolate two circuits (Fig. 6.7) or for impedance matching. It cannot have a voltage gain greater than unity, but it does give a power gain like all transistors. A small signal current into the base results in a large signal current into the emitter load.

Transistor power amplifiers usually have push-pull output stages, working either in class A or class B. Class B is much favoured due to its increased efficiency, and it is used with negative feedback as shown in Fig. 6.8. All class B amplifiers suffer from *crossover distortion* as the signal waveform swings from one half of the push-pull circuit to the other. This is due to non-linearity in transistor (or valve) transfer characteristics, and

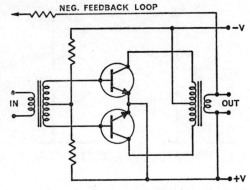

Fig. 6.8. Push-pull output stage operating in class B, with bias resistors to reduce cross-over distortion (see text) and negative feedback.

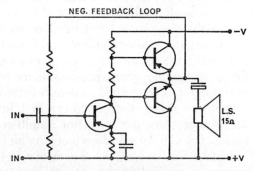

Fig. 6.9. Transformerless output stage using common emitter circuit with negative feedback loop.

is most noticeable at low signal levels. An improved performance is obtained when a small amount of *quiescent bias* is introduced via the two resistors in Fig. 6.8. The resulting current flow operates the transistors on a more linear part of their characteristic. The majority of modern power amplifiers have a transformerless output stage, with a pair of transistors operating as common emitter amplifiers. Fig. 6.9 shows a typical circuit for a transformerless output stage, using one P.N.P. and one N.P.N. transistor, together with a grounded emitter phase splitter and negative feedback loop. To prevent transistor damage if the loudspeaker leads are accidentally shorted, a suitable fuse should be incorporated in the power supply.

Field Effect Transistor

An important semiconductor device is the *field effect transistor*, called an f.e.t., which is a low noise transistor with a very high input impedance. The f.e.t. has three terminals known as the *gate*, the *source*, and the *drain*, which correspond to the base, emitter, and collector of a conventional

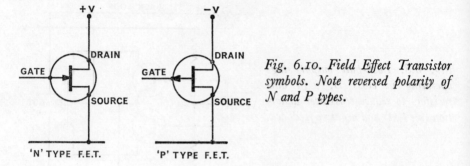

Fig. 6.10. Field Effect Transistor symbols. Note reversed polarity of N and P types.

transistor. They are manufactured in both N and P versions with reversed polarity, as shown in Fig. 6.10, and they can be used as audio amplifiers in any of the three basic configurations mentioned on page 117, now called common gate, common source, and common drain. Since the input impedance using the common gate configuration can be as high as 10 megohms, f.e.t.s are employed in pre-amplifiers within the body of a condenser microphone. They provide a convenient method of obtaining the necessary impedance change for matching a high impedance condenser capsule into an ordinary junction transistor amplifier. For the same reason they are sometimes used in pre-amplifiers for high impedance pick-up cartridges.

Field effect transistors are sensitive to breakdown if an excessive signal voltage is applied to the gate, so they are only used in low level audio circuits where the input signal is no greater than about 500 mV. But they are suitable for a wide variety of electronic timing circuits, and for an f.e.t. voltmeter with a high impedance input. The usual working voltage required by f.e.t.s is from 9 v to 18 v.

Photo Transistor

In assembly all germanium transistors are encapsulated in epoxy, glass, metal, or plastic. The outside of a glass envelope is always painted black because the germanium crystal inside is sensitive to light. This feature makes germanium junction transistors adaptable as *photo transistors* and *photo diodes*, merely by scraping off a small section of paint. In practice the transistor envelope also contains a small lens system to direct light on to the germanium element. This generates a minute current which can be amplified, and provides an alternative to the more familiar photo-electric cell. Photo transistors are used mainly for relay operation and similar applications, since their frequency response is not entirely suitable for sound film reproduction. Their greatest sensitivity is to infra-red light.

Compression and Limiting

One of the prime duties of a recording engineer is to ensure that quiet sounds are recorded within the dynamic range of the recording system, and that loud signals do not overload. Whilst this can be achieved by manual volume control, and very often is, the task is simplified by employing electronic aids such as *compression* amplifiers and *limiter* amplifiers. The gain of these amplifiers is automatically adjusted by a d.c. control voltage derived from the audio signal, which is obtained in practice by rectifying part of the amplifier output. The control voltage is fed back into an earlier stage to give the amplifier its required characteristic. All amplifiers contain the following features:

    (a) Attack Time —Time taken to reduce gain, usually 1 or 2 milliseconds.

    (b) Release Time—Time taken to restore gain to normal, usually 0·1 to 1 second or more, variable in steps.

    (c) Threshold   —Signal level at which compression or limiting action commences.

Limiting reduces the amplifier gain as the signal level approaches 100 per cent modulation, so that unexpected signal peaks will not exceed 100 per cent by more than 1 db or 2 db. The threshold is set at 1 db or 2 db below 100 per cent, and a high ratio of gain reduction is employed—usually 10 to 1. Limiting is used for music recording where the volume range accepted by the microphone is greater than the recording system can tolerate.

Compression is similar to limiting but the threshold is set at a predetermined level below 100 per cent modulation, usually 6 db or 10 db. This is called the *break-away point*, and signal levels above this point are compressed at a ratio of 2 to 1, a lower ratio than that used for limiting. This means that a 20 db rise in signal level can be compressed into the last 10 db before 100 per cent modulation, a condition known as '20 into 10'. Other ratios used are '12 into 6' where the break-away point is 6 db below 100 per cent, and '8 into 4' where the break-away point is 4 db below 100 per cent. Compression raises the average signal level whilst reducing signal peaks to manageable proportions, and is used a great deal in speech recording to even out variations in volume level. It is especially useful to improve intelligibility, and for singers who modulate their voice unevenly.

Fig. 6.11 shows the input/output characteristic of a limiter/compressor amplifier, and clearly illustrates how much automatic gain control is introduced. It is also obvious how much overload *might* occur with manual

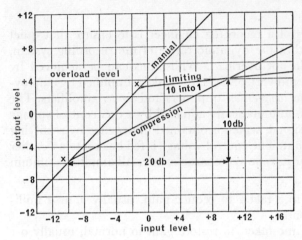

Fig. 6.11. Level diagram showing effects of limiting and compression, with X being the breakaway point from linear operation.

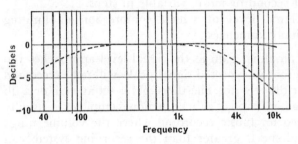

Fig. 6.12. Frequency response of compressor amplifier (solid line) and restricted response with 'de-esser' in circuit (broken line).

control. The main differences between limiting and compression are (1) the threshold or break-away point at which the limiting or compression action takes place, and (2) the amount of d.c. control voltage used to provide the desired ratio.

Compression amplifiers usually contain a filter circuit known as a *de-esser*, which reduces high frequencies to remove excessive sibilants. This filter is necessary because the voltage levels of S's in the region of 5 kHz to 6 kHz are less than the lower speech frequencies, so they are not reduced in gain by the same amount and are left to predominate. Also any high frequency pre-emphasis inserted ahead of the compressor amplifier tends to aggravate the problem. Fig. 6.12 shows a typical de-esser response with high frequencies reduced by 9 db at 10 kHz and the bass frequencies reduced by 4 db at 40 Hz to compensate. With the de-esser circuit switched out, the compressor amplifier should have a perfectly flat frequency characteristic.

Some limiter/compressor amplifiers are power amplifiers, and so are not suitable for insertion into a low level signal line in a mixing console. The

Fairchild compact compressor overcomes this problem with photo-electric principles, using a light sensitive cell and a lamp activated by a transistor sensing amplifier, which can be inserted into an audio line of 600 ohms impedance. Only the light cell is inserted in the audio line, and accounts for a 2 db or 3 db insertion loss. The audio signal is fed into the sensing amplifier, which is in a bridging condition, and the output used to illuminate the lamp. This action affects the resistance of the light cell, thus achieving a form of compression. The attack time depends on the characteristic of the lamp, and with high speed lamps having a thin filament an attack time of 1 millisecond is possible. The threshold and the release time are both variable by controls on the front panel, and the light cell does not introduce any distortion or noise.

No compression or limiting need be used when original dialogue recording is made on tape or film, although limiting is sometimes favoured to guard against unexpected signal peaks. Compression should be employed when re-recording dialogue for films, and for certain types of percussive effects such as jangling keys or breaking glass. Compression is seldom used for music recording as it spoils the musical dynamics, but limiting is often employed as a ceiling level control. Compression and limiting are sometimes used together on difficult material, the former to raise the average signal level and the latter to prevent overload.

Noise Reduction System

In order to obtain the maximum signal-to-noise ratio from magnetic recording, the usual practice is to record as high a signal level as possible without causing audible distortion. Most studios rely on compression and limiting to contain high level signal peaks, whilst raising low level signals manually to keep them above the background noise of the system. Further improvements in the signal-to-noise ratio can be achieved with a compressor/expander circuit, which compresses on record and expands on replay to restore the original dynamic range. A few expanders have been available in the past, but generally speaking they were not always 100 per cent successful. Some of them actually introduced signal degradation and distortion due to over-complicated valve circuitry.

A comparatively recent introduction is the solid state *Dolby Audio Noise Reduction System*, described as a signal-to-noise stretcher, which can be added to any type of recording system. Basically the Dolby system raises low level signals by 10 db during recording, and lowers these signals again during replay without any distortion or other defects. In doing this the Dolby unit reduces *tape hiss*, *modulation noise*, stereo *crosstalk*, and *print-through*. The main body of the signal remains virtually unaltered. The reduction of tape hiss is possible because hiss is added in recording after the programme material has passed through the Dolby unit, and print-through is similarly reduced during replay whether it has occurred immediately after recording or six months later.

Tapes which have been recorded with the Dolby unit may be copied directly using two normal recorders. But the tapes should not be mixed, equalized, or compressed whilst in their treated condition, and should be passed through a Dolby unit before an audible replay. The overall effect is to greatly improve the clarity and noise content of magnetic recordings, and also in any subsequent disc transfers. Furthermore magnetic transfers made with treated master tapes retain the characteristics of original recordings.

Printed Circuits

The modern method of amplifier construction eliminates most of the wiring between components by using a *printed circuit*. There are numerous ways of manufacturing printed circuit boards, but the one most generally used contains the complete wiring for an amplifier in copper, supported on a base material of high insulation such as paxolin.

The circuit is first drawn on paper with indian ink, from which an ordinary printers line block is made. This block is used to print the circuit on to a copper covered paxolin board with an acid proof ink, so that the area of copper not printed can be etched away in an acid bath. A series of holes are then drilled for mounting the various components, such as capacitors and resistors, and the soldering process carried out by dipping the completed circuit board in a tray of molten solder. An accurately wired amplifier is thus produced in a relatively short time, and is a far more reliable method of construction than an amplifier with separate hand soldered joints.

Completed circuit boards are often lacquered prior to installation as a protection against excessive humidity since this could cause a breakdown due to shorting between adjacent circuits. Servicing of printed circuit boards can sometimes prove difficult with many miniature components packed tightly together, but faults due to the printed circuit itself are less likely to develop.

Integrated Circuits

A more recent development is the *integrated circuit* in which a complete amplifier or some other transistor device is encapsulated within a single solid circuit block. Conventional components are discarded and replaced by microscopic pieces of material representing transistors, resistors, and capacitors. Integrated circuits, known as I.C.s, have become possible due to the minute size of the working parts of a transistor, and the feasibility of printing resistors and capacitors as part of the circuit. The only external wiring required is usually input, output, and power supply.

Integrated circuits may be found in modern recording equipment, where they form the basis of *operational amplifiers* (known as op amps). Their advantages include extremely low noise, high output, low distortion, stable characteristics, and extreme miniaturization. Their applications include microphone pre-amplifiers, line amplifiers, equalized pre-amplifiers for specific purposes, and combining amplifiers in mixing circuits. Their actual amplification is fixed, but their effective amplification may be accurately controlled by feedback loops and series or shunt resistors. A typical operational amplifier will have a high input impedance, a gain of 100 db., a low output impedance, and a power consumption of approximately 30 mA at 20 volts DC. The use of such a unit, which is usually designed as a simple plug-in module, reduces maintenance and service costs—the module being merely discarded in the event of a breakdown.

Filters

When setting up a recording channel it is customary to commence with a flat frequency characteristic, so that recordings can be made which are an exact copy of the original waveform. The response of any item in the chain is then further adjusted to suit a particular situation, so that quality control can be exercised at the discretion of the recording engineer.

The circuits used for quality control are called *filters* or *equalizers*. Their design varies from simple combinations of resistors, inductors, and capacitors in *passive networks* without amplifying stages, to *active networks* which contain an integral amplifier to restore the loss of gain which frequency compensation entails. Passive networks which give a boost to selected frequencies always have a certain *insertion loss* when introduced into an audio circuit, the actual loss being roughly equal to the amount of boost. This means that some adjustment to volume must be made each time passive filters are used, whilst active filters are usually designed to have no insertion loss.

Before connecting any filter or equalizer into a recording or reproducing system, its effect should be measured to ensure that it is actually providing the desired amount of frequency correction. It should be remembered that the frequency response of a filter depends on the impedance of the line or circuit in which it is used, since capacitors and inductors change their value with impedance as well as frequency. It is not proposed to dwell on the general design of filter circuits, but it is as well to know the various types one is likely to meet and their respective functions.

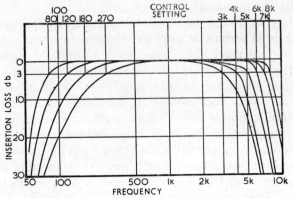

Fig. 6.13. Frequency response obtained by introducing various high pass and low pass filters.

High Pass Filter

This is the term given to a filter which restricts the low frequency response of an amplifier system. As its name implies, it permits signals of high frequency to pass, whilst attenuating all frequencies below a pre-determined value, usually below 100 Hz or 200 Hz. This can be useful in removing motor and machine rumble in film recording, also troublesome wind noise.

Low Pass Filter

This is the term given to a filter which restricts the high frequency response of an amplifier system. Some low pass filters are designed for one particular frequency, whilst others are made variable from 3 kHz to 10 kHz or 12 kHz. They are used mainly to restrict frequency response when handling low range material on a wide range system, and vice versa, thus preventing any unnecessary noise and distortion from becoming audible. Both high and low pass filters can be designed for either a sharp or gradual cut-off or slope, and they are used extensively both for recording and re-recording.

Hi-Lo Equalizer

This is a rather specialized filter which is capable of raising or lowering both bass and treble frequencies, and for boosting or reducing selected frequencies within the audible range. It is used during recording to compensate for studio acoustics or a microphone deficiency, also during

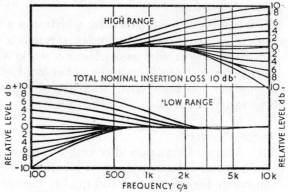

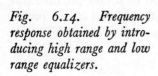

Fig. 6.14. Frequency response obtained by introducing high range and low range equalizers.

re-recording for making some deliberate alteration to the frequency response of an original recording.

Band Stop Filter

This consists of a combination of high and low pass filter sections, each one designed to have a sharp cut-off without overlapping so as to suppress a narrow band of frequencies. The filter sections are tunable to enable the required frequency band to be selected for suppression, although the degree of tuning is limited by the variable capacitor employed. Separate filter sections are switched to deal with high, medium, or low frequencies within the audible spectrum. This type of filter enables objectionable noise to be removed from a signal line, or from a recording, without completely destroying the average signal quality. Typical noises requiring suppression include picture camera noise, arc lamps, etc.

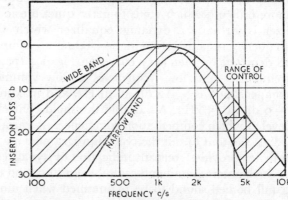

Fig. 6.15. Frequency response obtained by introducing a telephone simulator.

Telephone Simulator

This is a form of band pass filter which uses a simple resonant circuit to simulate dialogue quality as heard through a telephone ear-piece. It is used extensively in film and television work, also in sound broadcasting where it is sometimes known as a *distort box*. Fig. 6.15 shows the frequency response curve of the Westrex telephone simulator, and gives an indication of the range of control within the unit.

Dialogue Equalizer

This is a form of high pass filter with a very gentle slope, and is sometimes called a low frequency reducer or low frequency roll-off. It is designed to compensate for voice effort and quality control in dialogue recording by attenuating the bass response below 250 Hz or 350 Hz. This becomes necessary to improve intelligibility when a dialogue recording is going to be replayed at a higher volume level than the original sound, as in a cinema auditorium.

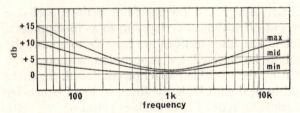

Fig. 6.16. Frequency response of Dynalizer control unit.

Dynalizer

The apparent loudness of programme material depends on frequency distribution as well as human auditory perception. As listening levels are reduced, the perception of high and low frequencies becomes more and more difficult, which tends to make quiet music sound 'thin'. The Dynalizer is virtually a dynamic equalizer which automatically adjusts the frequency response of an audio channel to compensate for hearing losses, as depicted by Fletcher's curves in Fig. 1.4 (page 18), boosting the high frequencies and low frequencies at low volume levels. Maximum 'lo' compensation is + 12 db at 40 Hz, and maximum 'hi' compensation is + 9 db at 15 kHz. A variable threshold control determines the volume level at which compensation commences. A variable h.f. control is fitted to adjust the unit to suit the type of programme material being handled, and a meter provides constant indication of dynalizer action.

Such a unit is eminently suitable for films and television, since it enables a full bodied sound to be maintained when music is faded down under dialogue or narration. In fact the Dynalizer can be installed in all types of sound reproducing systems to provide a more balanced sound level. Low level music always sounds louder to the ear after frequency compensation has been added to restore listening losses, and a *loudness control* for this purpose is sometimes included in high quality domestic amplifiers.

Film Loss Equalizer

This is a special correction circuit used only with photographic sound recording, and it is designed to compensate for high frequency losses in optical systems and film processing. Film equalizers give a high frequency pre-emphasis between 1 kHz and 6 kHz, which is applied to the audio signal before it reaches the modulator in the recording camera. The amount of pre-emphasis is adjusted to give a flat replay characteristic from a print of the sound negative.

Presence Equalizer

This is a circuit which raises the response in the middle of the audible frequency range, between 1 kHz and 3 kHz, and it is also known as a *mid-range equalizer*. It is used to improve the intelligibility of dialogue and to correct for deficiencies in microphone response, or in room or studio acoustics. Raising the middle frequencies in this way improves the 'presence' of any recording, and imparts a life-like quality. Some music recordings are enhanced with a 'presence' equalizer, and here the frequency correction is usually between 3 kHz and 7 kHz.

Rumble Filter

This is virtually a high pass filter which attenuates the response below 20 Hz or 30 Hz. Its purpose is to eliminate low frequency rumble caused by mechanical vibration, usually from a gramophone turntable or film replay machine. Rumble filters are usually fixed at one frequency, and are seldom variable.

CHAPTER VII

Loudspeakers

THE MAIN PURPOSE of a loudspeaker is to provide a piston arrangement for setting up vibrations of air particles which correspond to the electrical energy applied to the loudspeaker. This conversion of energy from one medium to another should of course be performed without the addition of distortion in any of its various forms. It is relatively easy to construct a distortionless amplifier and select a good quality microphone, but unless the loudspeaker is entirely satisfactory the reproduced sound is likely to be disappointing to say the least.

It is not generally realized that the loudspeaker is usually the weakest link in the sound reproducing chain, which often results in the blame for inferior reproduction being unfairly placed on some other item of equipment. Frequently the only consideration given to a loudspeaker is that it must be of a given size to fit into a particular place, and it must be inexpensive. Sometimes a loudspeaker is chosen after a few simple listening tests, which is quite satisfactory if the loudspeaker is only to be used in the home. But if the loudspeaker is to be used as a monitor for the evaluation of programme material, its performance and response curve are of the utmost importance. The response must be smooth over a wide range, equivalent to the range of associated equipment, as well as distortion free. Loudspeaker designs are constantly being improved with new and better materials, so that a unit which was considered to give good reproduction ten years ago would not always compare favourably with a modern product.

Early Types

Greater progress has probably been made in perfecting loudspeakers than in any other item of sound equipment. Many early types were developed directly from existing telephone earpieces, the idea being to produce a loudspeaking telephone receiver. These were called electromagnetic speakers, and contained either a diaphragm or reed which vibrated in the field of an electromagnet. A metal horn, and later a cardboard one, was placed over the diaphragm or reed in an attempt to load it sufficiently to move a column of air. This was achieved to some extent, although such loudspeakers were extremely insensitive by modern standards. Their bass response was limited by the dimensions of the horn or cone, as well as the inability of the moving parts to respond to bass frequencies. The units also had pronounced natural resonances, usually in the middle of the audible frequency range, which gave the reproduced sound a decidedly 'tinny' quality.

Due to progress made with more powerful amplifiers, loudspeakers were required which could handle much greater power than was possible with these magnetic types. As a result they went out of fashion to be replaced with a then revolutionary design called a *moving coil*. This is the most widely used type of loudspeaker today, due to its comparatively simple construction and fairly low cost. Other loudspeaker elements are also in use, including ribbon and electrostatic types.

Moving Coil Loudspeakers

The principle of a moving coil loudspeaker is similar to the principle of a moving coil microphone. The same type of *speech* or *voice coil* is suspended in a strong magnetic field, and an audio signal passing through the coil causes it to move. Although the coil is sometimes connected to a diaphragm, it is more usually attached to a cone with a diameter of any-thing between 2 in. and 18 in. (11 cm and 45·7 cm). The larger the dia-meter of the cone the more sensitive the loudspeaker is to low frequencies. The larger the magnetic flux, the larger will be the power handling capacity of the loudspeaker.

Materials used for the loudspeaker cone have varied considerably over the past few years. It is obvious that to obtain low distortion the movement of a cone or diaphragm should resemble as accurately as possible the waveform of the audio signals applied to the speech coil. The ability of the cone to do this accurately depends on the lightness and stiffness of the cone material. Cones made from stiffened paper, impregnated cloth, plastic, or thin metal such as sheet aluminium, all suffer from a comparatively low stiffness—even though they are light in weight. The result is that cone vibrations are set up which are not as a result of signals in the speech coil, causing the 'hangover' of transient sounds (called ringing), amplitude distortion (uneven frequency response), and intermodulation (lack of clarity).

In an attempt to minimize these defects, one manufacturer has produced a cone material consisting of a sandwich of expanded plastic between stiff aluminium skins, which has resulted in a lightweight material of extreme rigidity. Another manufacturer has tackled the problem by developing an oval shaped polystyrene diaphragm, also with the same result. Other materials including fibre-glass laminates and titanium metal are also in current use.

All cones are suspended in a frame which allows freedom of movement backwards and forwards, and they are fixed at the speech coil end by a flexible coupling. This coupling is used to centre the speech coil in the gap between the magnet pole faces where there is very little clearance. This gap must be as small as possible if the sensitivity of the loudspeaker is to be maintained.

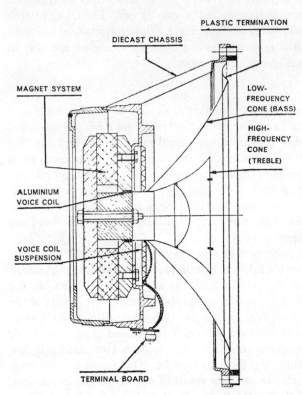

PLASTIC TERMINATION

DIECAST CHASSIS

MAGNET SYSTEM

LOW-FREQUENCY CONE (BASS)

HIGH-FREQUENCY CONE (TREBLE)

ALUMINIUM VOICE COIL

VOICE COIL SUSPENSION

TERMINAL BOARD

Fig. 7.1. Cross sectional drawing of a modern moving coil loudspeaker unit.

The efficiency of any moving coil loudspeaker depends on the size of the magnet and the density of the magnetic flux in the air gap between the pole faces, as well as the size of the speech coil and the current passing through it. It is a little known fact that only about 8 per cent or 10 per cent of the electrical energy fed into the coil is reproduced as audible sound! If only a small magnet is fitted, the unit will not only be less sensitive but require more power to operate it. Then there is the danger of currents in the speech coil producing a magnetic flux which is larger than the flux from the magnet, which results in the coil and cone assembly over-riding their normal limits and introducing distortion instead of louder sound.

Confusion may arise over the apparent smallness of some magnets fitted to modern loudspeakers. The truth is that the magnetic alloys in use today permit a much larger flux to be obtained from a given size than was considered possible a short while ago. However it should be made apparent that a small, cheap type of unit cannot be efficient, even if the quality sounds impressive for a short while. A bad loudspeaker will cause listening fatigue at longer sessions, which is enough reason to choose a good loudspeaker in the first place.

A glance through manufacturers' leaflets will reveal a large number of moving coil loudspeakers with various sized cones, all quoted as having a frequency response of 40 Hz to 16 kHz. The fact is that these units offer the basis of a compatible loudspeaker system where economy is the deciding factor, and are sensitive enough to give a fair reproduction over the quoted frequency range. The extended high frequency response is achieved by special attention to cone design, and winding the speech coil with aluminium wire or ribbon to save weight. A reduction in weight means a greater excursion of the cone at high frequencies.

It is difficult to design a single moving coil loudspeaker which is equally sensitive at all frequencies. A large diameter cone is considered necessary for the propagation of bass frequencies, but high frequencies propagated by the same cone tend to suffer from *intermodulation*. This is because large excursions of the cone at low frequencies limit the cone's capabilities of moving quickly at the same time to reproduce high frequencies; and it is the high frequencies which suffer. The usual remedy for intermodulation is to use two loudspeaker units, a woofer for frequencies below 1 kHz and a tweeter for frequencies above 1 kHz. They are fed through a *frequency dividing network* which is described on page 138. All professional monitoring loudspeaker systems use two separate units, also many high fidelity systems for use in the home. A large diameter cone is used for propagating the bass end of the spectrum, and a smaller unit for the treble. Dual loudspeakers are always to be preferred for the most natural sound reproduction.

All these moving coil units must be correctly installed in a suitable enclosure before they can be correctly called a loudspeaker system, and the quoted response figures obtained. Since a loudspeaker is required to set up a satisfactory wave motion at all frequencies, it must be of the requisite dimensions and compare favourably with the wavelength of the lowest frequency it is desired to reproduce. The speech coil cannot be made very large so it is 'loaded' by a cone which is capable of moving a larger column of air. The cone is in turn 'loaded' by being installed in an enclosure (see page 140).

Horn Loudspeakers

A moving coil element is also utilized in the *horn* type of loudspeaker, where the cone is replaced by a small diaphragm no larger than the diameter of the speech coil. This diaphragm is constructed of very thin aluminium, slightly curved to maintain rigidity, which is loaded with a column of air when attached to a flared horn. The horn acts as a coupling device, receiving energy from the small diameter diaphragm and distributing it over a much wider area. The coupling between horn and diaphragm must be tight to maintain a good high frequency response. These loudspeakers are more efficient than the cone type, due to the loading effect of the horn, and efficiency figures of up to 20 per cent are quite usual.

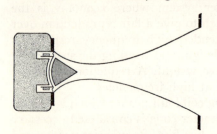

Fig. 7.2. *Construction of a horn type loudspeaker.*

Since the dimensions of the horn govern the response of the loudspeaker to low frequencies, a full range loudspeaker using these principles would be impossibly large. Horn loudspeakers are therefore more suitable for the reproduction of frequencies above 1 kHz, and are used indoors almost exclusively as tweeters. The speech coil itself is normally made of aluminium ribbon, wound 'edge on' and insulated with a coating of shellac. Such a coil can be made to very close tolerances which results in only a narrow gap being required between it and the magnet pole faces. With all horn loudspeakers which have been designed as tweeters, the passage of low frequency signals through the speech coil must be avoided; otherwise the diaphragm will be severely damaged.

When used in conjunction with a cone loudspeaker for handling the bass frequencies, it is important to ensure that both speech coils are connected the same way round, or that they are 'in phase'. This means that a signal applied to both coils will cause the cone and diaphragm to start moving an air column in the same direction. If this condition is not met, a phase displacement of 180° would take place at certain frequencies, causing phase distortion. For this reason speech coil terminals are usually designated + and − on all high quality loudspeaker units. It is equally important to have both tweeter and woofer placed as close together as possible, so that high and low frequencies appear to be radiating from the same point source. This minimizes any displacement in the phase relationship between various frequencies. The result of using a horn loudspeaker as a tweeter is a general clarity of high frequencies due to the small mass of the moving parts, which also gives an apparent smoothness to the overall response. Distortion due to intermodulation is also eliminated.

Fig. 7.3. A horn unit with a cellular flared opening to give an even sound distribution.

The front of the horn is usually of cellular construction which disperses the sound waves effectively over the desired listening area. Large cellular horns powered by several units are used in cinema installations, and improve the distribution of high frequencies over a large area. In fact horn loudspeakers are often used out of doors or in noisy surroundings, due to their high directivity, and not only as tweeters. No horn unit should ever be operated with the horn itself removed, as without the loading effect of the horn the diaphragm is liable to be blown from its mounting by the passage of normal speech currents.

Re-entrant Horn

This merely describes a horn which has been folded back within itself to retain the advantages of a large horn in a small space. Re-entrant horns are mainly confined to public address work, and they have no value in the field of sound recording. They are quite efficient although they give a rather harsh quality, the main criterion in public address work being intelligibility.

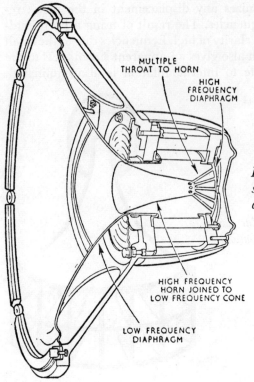

Fig. 7.4. Cross sectional drawing showing construction of dual concentric loudspeaker unit.

MULTIPLE
THROAT TO HORN

HIGH
FREQUENCY
DIAPHRAGM

HIGH FREQUENCY
HORN JOINED TO
LOW FREQUENCY CONE

LOW FREQUENCY
DIAPHRAGM

Dual Concentric Loudspeaker

This is a comparatively modern development, a combination of a cone loudspeaker and a horn loudspeaker both using the same magnet system. This loudspeaker is called *dual concentric* since the horn unit is contained within the centre pole piece of the cone unit. This design represents the nearest approach to a single source radiator with a corresponding reduction of phasing problems, but the more complicated design and construction renders them more expensive.

Cone diameters vary from 8 in. to 15 in. (19·3 cm to 38·1 cm), and the overall frequency response with the horn unit adequately covers the entire audible range. The correct balance between high and low frequencies is achieved by a special attenuator attached to the horn unit and supplied by the manufacturer. This is normally set by a listening test after the loudspeaker has been correctly installed. Due to the very small diameter of the diaphragm in the horn unit, the crossover frequency is usually around 5 kHz. A suitable frequency dividing network is attached to the loudspeaker frame. An added refinement is a short cone of stiffened plastic which has a free outer edge, its purpose being to assist the response of the main cone at middle frequencies. Fig. 7.4 shows the internal construction of a typical dual concentric loudspeaker, which is a favourite unit in many monitoring rooms.

Electrostatic Loudspeaker

Loudspeakers which operate in the reverse manner to a condenser microphone are called *electrostatic* loudspeakers. Several of these have appeared as tweeter units from time to time, suitable for handling high frequencies only. The main difficulty is to design an electrostatic element which has sufficient freedom of movement to generate a large wave motion at low frequencies, whilst remaining fairly sensitive. At least one manufacturer has achieved this as a commercial proposition, although it is still less sensitive than a moving coil loudspeaker and consequently less popular. It is also more expensive.

Basically it consists of one large diaphragm with an area of just over 6 square feet (0·6 square metres), insulated by a plastic covering and supported between two perforated fixed plates. This gives a figure-of-eight radiation pattern, equal at the front and the rear. A d.c. polarizing voltage is required between the diaphragm and the fixed plates, as in a condenser microphone. No baffle board or other form of coupling is necessary as the diaphragm itself is sufficient to excite the requisite volume of air. The frequency range is from 45 Hz to 18 kHz, and the unit is quite sensitive to high frequencies. This causes a noticeable improvement in transient response compared with other types of loudspeaker, due to the nature of the electrostatic element.

Even when mounted on a suitable wooden framework, electrostatic loudspeakers are extremely thin and take up very little space. But they must not be placed in a position near a wall, as their performance is liable to be upset by reflections of sound waves into the rear of the unit. Not every power amplifier takes kindly to a capacitive load, and these loudspeakers should be used with the amplifiers for which they were designed.

Impedance Matching

In order to maintain maximum efficiency and power transfer, it is important that a loudspeaker should have its impedance matched to the output of its associated amplifier. The loudspeaker represents a load across the amplifier output, and following normal power theory a loss will be incurred with a mis-match. Valve and transistor amplifiers are rated at a certain number of watts at a specified impedance, usually 12 to 15 ohms in professional equipment and 3 to 7 ohms in domestic equipment. Electrostatic loudspeakers constitute a much higher impedance and usually contain their own matching arrangements.

Another important factor which is a direct result of mismatching is the introduction of harmonic distortion. This is caused by valves and transistors being non-linear devices at all frequencies, causing the signal fed to the amplifier output to be frequency selective. The amount of distortion introduced is not always serious, and since there is no difficulty in achieving a correct impedance match, problems associated with distortion and power loss need never arise.

Frequency Dividing Networks

The function of a *frequency dividing network* is to separate the high frequency content of an audio signal from the low frequency content, passing both bands of frequencies on to their respective loudspeaker units. This is achieved by using the frequency selective properties of capacitors and inductors. A capacitor offers a certain impedance to a.c. signals which *decreases* as the signal frequency rises. An inductor offers an impedance to a.c. signals which *increases* as the signal frequency rises. So if a tweeter has an inductor shunted across its terminals, and the bass unit a capacitor, the desired frequency separation can theoretically be achieved.

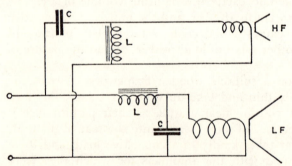

Fig. 7.5. Circuit of frequency dividing network.

In practice the more usual arrangement employed is a double half section filter, the circuit of which is shown in Fig. 7.5, which will be recognized as a simple type of combined high and low pass filter. Both a capacitor and an inductor are used in conjunction with each loudspeaker unit to give a sharper cut-off at the crossover point, which prevents any doubling up of frequencies handled by both units. The actual crossover frequency where one unit takes over from the other is usually between 800

Hz and 1·5 kHz, depending on the size and make of loudspeaker employed. There is always a slight overlap to avoid a dip in the overall frequency characteristic.

Loudspeaker manufacturers generally recommend the exact crossover frequency for their products, and even supply the frequency dividing network. Obviously the correct values for L and C in Fig. 7.5 will vary enormously according to the impedance of the loudspeaker circuit in which they are to be used. As a guide for readers who wish to experiment, the following table shows some of the values which have been selected in the past for various crossover frequencies and impedances.

Ohms Impedance	Crossover Frequency	Capacitor	Inductor
15	800 Hz	10 mfd	4·0 mH
15	1000 Hz	8 mfd	3·5 mH
15	1250 Hz	6 mfd	2·7 mH
15	1500 Hz	5 mfd	2·2 mH
7	800 Hz	20 mfd	2·0 mH
7	1000 Hz	16 mfd	1·8 mH
7	1250 Hz	12 mfd	1·4 mH
7	1500 Hz	10 mfd	1·1 mH
3	800 Hz	40 mfd	1·0 mH
3	1000 Hz	32 mfd	0·9 mH
3	1250 Hz	24 mfd	0·7 mH
3	1500 Hz	20 mfd	0·5 mH

Another method of improving loudspeaker performance is to use three separate units with a triple frequency dividing network. In this case the two crossover frequencies may be 800 Hz and 5 kHz. A moving coil cone unit is used as a bass radiator, with two horn types or one cone and one horn for the middle and treble loudspeakers. An attenuator is included in the dividing network to provide a means of h.f. control. This assists in attaining a flat overall frequency response, and enables the complete loudspeaker system to be quickly adjusted to suit the listening conditions in any particular room.

A simple method sometimes used to improve the h.f. response of an existing loudspeaker is to connect a small diameter tweeter across the

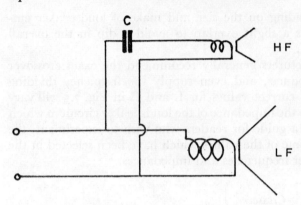

Fig. 7.6. Circuit for improving the h.f. response of an existing moving coil loudspeaker.

speech coil, with a capacitor in series to reject low frequencies. This method is inexpensive and can give sufficient improvement under certain conditions. What it does not do is to remove any intermodulation occurring in the main loudspeaker, as the operation of this unit is in no way affected. But the intermodulation tends to be hidden under the extra h.f. response supplied by the tweeter. This can be a small diameter cone type with an aluminium speech coil, or one of the special horn units designed for use as a tweeter. The value of the capacitor required would be 4 mfd for a 15 ohm circuit, 8 mfd for a 7 ohm circuit, and 16 mfd for a 3 ohm circuit.

Loudspeaker Enclosures

All moving coil loudspeaker units with a cone or diaphragm type radiator will set up sound waves in two directions, backwards and forwards. These waves will be 180° out of phase with each other, since an area of compression in front of the cone corresponds to an area of rarefaction at the rear. If no precautions are taken these two sets of waves will meet and cancel out, especially at low frequencies. To reduce this cancellation effect the loudspeaker unit can be mounted on an open baffle board (Fig. 7.7), but the bass response will only be improved down to a frequency which is comparable in wavelength to the size of the baffle board. Even when calculating with half wavelengths, the amount of space required by a plain baffle to reproduce very low frequencies is an obvious drawback.

There are several types of enclosures which can be used to obtain the correct loading of the loudspeaker cone, so that the full frequency range of which the unit is capable can be heard. The three main types are the *bass reflex cabinet*, the *folded horn*, and the *infinite baffle*. The optimum design for these enclosures is constantly changing as manufacturers seek further improvements from new shapes and materials.

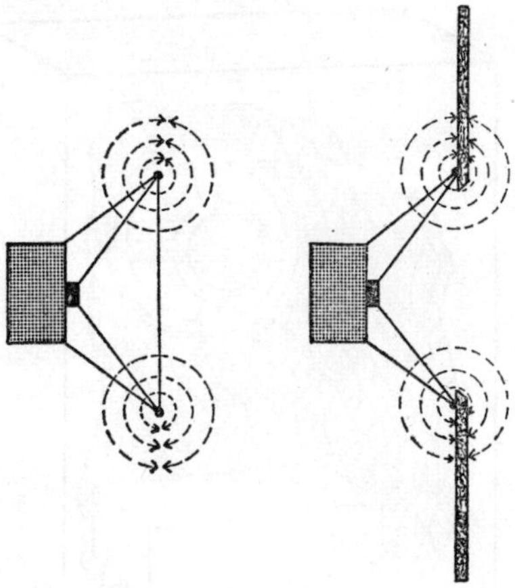

Fig. 7.7. Loudspeaker unit mounted on baffle board to prevent cancellation of bass frequencies.

The principle of a bass reflex cabinet is to totally enclose the loudspeaker except for a small opening near the bottom of the cabinet, which is called the *port*. The sound waves from the rear of the cone are slightly delayed inside the cabinet, and when they finally emerge through the port they are in phase with waves from the front of the cone, and therefore additive. The cabinet and port dimensions are fairly critical for an optimum performance, and the minimum volume for a cabinet housing a 12 in. unit is 9 cubic feet (0·3 cubic metres).

The usual material used for construction is plywood with a minimum thickness of $\frac{1}{2}$ inch (12 mm). Chipboard can be employed as an alternative, although this has a higher density and is somewhat stiffer and heavier. The amount of energy permitted to be lost due to vibration in the walls of the cabinet is open to debate. Experience has shown that it is quite in order to permit slight vibration without any distressing effects. The walls must be braced internally, and it is unwise to economize on the thickness of the timber used for the main structure, even with small enclosures.

Due to the fact that cone type loudspeakers have mass and weight, they also have a natural cone resonance between 20 Hz and 80 Hz. In order to reduce these and other resonances as much as possible, the internal walls of the cabinet are lined with sound absorbing material such as thick felt or mineral wool. This particularly avoids sound colouration due to cabinet resonances. Bass reflex cabinets are usually designed for one particular type of loudspeaker, and may not give the same results when used with a similar loudspeaker from another manufacturer. In general the dimensions furnished by each manufacturer should be adhered to.

Access to bass reflex cabinets is usually made through a small removable

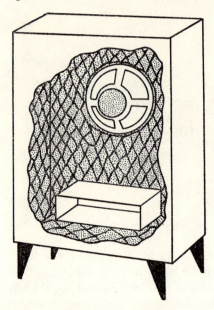

Fig. 7.8. Cut-away drawing to show construction of Bass Reflex cabinet.

panel at the rear, which is essential for loudspeaker installation and maintenance. The same cabinet can also house one or two tweeters by making suitable openings in front of the cabinet. If it is desired to use only one loudspeaker unit, adding the tweeters at a later date, the necessary holes can be drilled during the assembly of the cabinet and covered over until required.

The *folded horn* enclosure is the most efficient means of coupling the loudspeaker cone to the air, and it can easily be driven by an amplifier of modest output. The inside of the enclosure is partitioned off to provide a long, folded air path between the loudspeaker cone and the outside air. A careful design with non-parallel partitions will reduce resonances due to standing waves, but a folded horn enclosure must still be fairly large if it is to reproduce bass frequencies efficiently. The complex construction renders them rather more expensive than bass reflex cabinets, but they are not so boomy as the bass reflex type and a folded horn is more capable of reproducing good transients.

Apart from the rather large enclosures used professionally, there is a need for a much smaller loudspeaker system which will fit into the average domestic surroundings. The *infinite baffle* enclosure has been designed with this end in view, and permits a good bass response to be obtained with a very small size. Basically the loudspeaker unit is mounted in a totally enclosed cabinet without any ports. The inside is heavily damped to completely absorb the sound waves from the rear of the loudspeaker cone, which makes the sensitivity of the enclosure rather low—about half that of the other types. This effectively halves the amplifier output in terms of reproduced sound volume, and does give rather a false bass response.

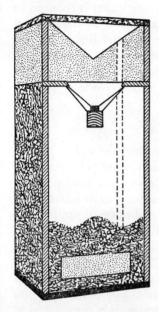

Fig. 7.9. Cut-away drawing to show construction of domestic loudspeaker system.

A Small Domestic Loudspeaker

Cone type loudspeaker units exhibit certain directional characteristics, and do not radiate all frequencies in all directions with equal strength. They tend to become extremely directional at high frequencies, radiating only in a direct line with the cone. Various designs of reflectors are sometimes fitted in an attempt to diffuse high frequencies over a wider area, usually with varying degrees of success. The cabinet illustrated in Fig. 7.9 contains a small 8 in, moving coil unit with an extended frequency response, mounted with its cone facing upwards. Beneath the top of the cabinet is a conical reflector which diffuses high frequencies throughout 360°. In this way a compromise is reached which makes for pleasant listening at home over a wide area. The small port which is an important part of the design has been placed at the rear of the cabinet for the sake of appearance.

Another type of domestic enclosure is a large, plain baffle, which fits closely into the corner of a room forming an air-tight seal with the walls. The walls themselves then complete the baffle area, and provide a more acceptable type of enclosure under some conditions.

Acoustical Resistance Unit

It has already been stated that the optimum dimensions for a bass reflex cabinet to suit a particular size and make of loudspeaker unit must be strictly adhered to. But if the normal port opening is fitted with an *acoustical resistance unit*, the cone resonance of the loudspeaker is reduced in both amplitude and frequency. This permits a cabinet to be constructed one half of the normal size. The special acoustic unit consists of a metal grill with a felt backing, supported by several wooden slats. This unit can be fitted in any of the enclosure walls, but the shortest distance between the unit and the loudspeaker (as measured over the outside of the enclosure) should not be less than 1 ft. (0·3 m).

Column Loudspeakers

Although not directly concerned with sound recording, the *column* type of loudspeaker is ideal as a means of sound reproduction in difficult situations. Column loudspeakers are sometimes known as *line source* loudspeakers, because they consist of a number of small diameter cone units mounted in line on a narrow baffle board. The area of distribution is quite wide horizontally, but is limited vertically almost to the height of the unit. This is due to the addition of the polar distribution of each individual cone unit.

It requires only two such units to cover the Royal Festival Hall as part of the sound reinforcement system, and two in one of the main departure halls at London Airport. Column loudspeakers are mainly directional at middle and high frequencies, and give better sound quality than the familiar horn type which is usually employed for public address systems.

Cinema Loudspeaker Systems

Cinema loudspeaker systems are required to handle from 20 to 80 watts of audio power, according to the size of the auditorium and its seating capacity. Separate bass and treble units are always employed, with a frequency dividing network. The bass units are moving coil loudspeakers with 15 or 18 in. (38 or 45 cm) diameter cones, usually mounted in pairs. They are built into a folded horn cabinet 6 ft. 6 in. (2 m) high, with inspection covers at the rear for repair work and making replacements.

These loudspeaker systems have been improving gradually both in sensitivity to high frequencies and their effective dispersal throughout the whole auditorium. This is no small problem in a large building, and with stereophonic sound an even greater degree of distribution is essential to achieve a good stereophonic effect. Obviously a horn type of loudspeaker unit is used for high frequencies, but these still have to be evenly dispersed.

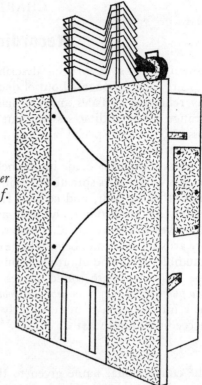

Fig. 7.10. Westrex cinema loudspeaker system incorporating a vane type h.f. radiator with an acoustic lens assembly.

Acoustic Lens

In an attempt to overcome this problem, an h.f. unit has been developed which incorporates the principle of an *acoustic lens*. This consists of a series of specially shaped perforated discs, equally spaced in front of the diaphragm of the moving coil horn unit. The diameter of the diaphragm in the Wextrex loudspeaker system is 4 inches (101 mm), and this, together with the acoustic lens assembly, provides a horizontal distribution angle of 50°.

In front of the acoustic lens is a series of slanting vanes or plates, and these provide a vertical distribution of 80°. The actual shape of the plates determines the angle of distribution, and the sides are kept open to prevent any unevenness in the overall frequency response. The effect of this type of h.f. assembly is a wider distribution over greater distances than was possible with the older type of cellular horn. The crossover frequency between h.f. and l.f. units is 500 Hz, with a 12 db per octave attenuation on both sides of this point.

CHAPTER VIII

Recording Studios

SOUND WAVES have been described in earlier chapters only as they appear when propagated out of doors, travelling in all directions without any reflecting surfaces and gradually fading away. It is not possible to arrange all recording sessions out of doors, and it is desirable, when possible, to use a special *recording studio* where the acoustic conditions can be controlled.

When a sound is made in an enclosed space such as an ordinary living room, sound waves spread in all directions and strike the interior surfaces such as walls, floor, and ceiling. If these surfaces are such that they are unable to absorb sound, and ordinary plaster walls absorb only 3 per cent, the waves will be reflected. These reflections will continue backwards and forwards several times before they eventually diminish, and finally become inaudible. If instead of ordinary building materials, such as plaster, wood, and concrete, these sound waves strike a material which has a high *absorption factor*, such as *asbestos wool* or *acoustic tiles*, they will diminish in their intensity much more quickly and leave the air particles clear for succeeding sound waves.

Reverberation

The conventional name given to the conditions causing reflected sound waves is *reverberation*. This is not the same as an *echo* although it is often spoken of as such. An echo is a single reflection of a particular sound wave whereas reverberation is a multiplicity of reflections.

When any sound ceases abruptly in a recording studio, the sound wave disappears in a definite period of time. This period is called the *reverberation time*, and its calculation is determined by the sound absorbing properties of that particular studio. The reverberation time for any studio or building is inclined to vary throughout the audible frequency range; but for all practical purposes the figures generally accepted are those based on the time taken for a sound wave with a frequency of 512 Hz to be reduced in intensity by 60 db. This frequency was chosen because it represented one octave above middle C on the musical scale, and is almost in the middle of the range of audible frequencies.

If the reverberation time of a recording studio is excessive, there will be a confusion of sound as in a public swimming pool destroying clarity and definition. On the other hand there can be too much absorption which results in dull and lifeless sound quality, often lacking in high frequency content as well. It follows that there must be an optimum condition for reverberation in every studio in order that the most pleasing results shall be achieved.

Conditions for Recording

It is not very satisfactory to attempt dialogue recording in rooms or studios having a long reverberation time. This causes intelligibility to be considerably impaired due to sound reflections and echoes. It has been found that echoes are not noticeable when they exist for less than one-fifteenth of a second, although the maximum echo permissible when making an acceptable speech recording is three quarters of a second.

A studio which feels slightly dead to the ear, due to sound absorbing materials on the walls, will undoubtedly provide the best acoustics for dialogue recording. It should be remembered that the reverberation time of the *monitor room* must be added to the reverberation time of the studio, which provides a good enough reason for avoiding rooms which are exceptionally 'live'. However, it is always possible to control difficult situations by either temporarily lining the walls with blankets or felt drapes, or permanently fitting acoustic tiles over the area suspected of producing unwanted reflections.

Music recordings are considerably improved by the presence of a certain amount of reverberation; in fact reflective surfaces are deliberately introduced into music recording studios. The reverberation time required is largely determined by the type of music to be recorded, large symphony orchestras requiring more reverberation than a quintet. Many experiments have been carried out to discover the ideal reverberation time for music and speech in studios of various sizes. For light music this time should not exceed 1 second, but for orchestral music of a heavier nature 1 or 2 seconds appears to be the ideal time. Pop music and speech recording studios should be of small dimensions with a short reverberation time. A section of a larger studio screened off with curtains may provide these conditions.

Sound Isolation

The first problem to be solved in constructing or adapting a recording studio is one of sound isolation; since it is essential that all sounds occurring outside the studio are prevented from coming inside if recording is to continue undisturbed. Two kinds of interference must be considered and reduced to a degree where they are no longer troublesome; *structure-borne sound*, causing vibration of the studio walls and generating a sound wave within the building, *and air-borne sound*, caused by leakage through doors and windows.

Insulation from structure-borne sound is obtained by breaking up the continuity of the structure by the use of insulating materials in the path of the sound. A double clad type of construction with an air space between the two walls produces the ideal studio, since air is a very good sound insulator. The air space can also be filled with a sound absorbing material such as compressed fibre board or cork chippings. One method of suppressing sound transmission through concrete floors is to introduce an insulating layer of rock wool and roofing felt, and then float a new floor surface on top.

Structure-borne sound can be much more difficult to eliminate than air borne sound because whatever method of construction is used no studio can be entirely separated from the main supports of the building. These may transmit sounds to the studio walls, floor or ceiling. There may be no complete cure for structure-borne sound. Careful selection of the studio site in the first place is vital. It is clearly unwise to site a sound studio where there is frequent vibration from such things as a railway or an airport.

Air-borne Sound

The elimination or reduction of air-borne sound is the more usual problem encountered, particularly when the studio is a conversion of an existing building. Doors and windows are the weakest spots, and demand a great deal of attention before they can be considered fully insulated. If the windows are to be retained and not bricked up, they should be covered with a sound absorbing material or double glazed with plate glass.

Recording studios are always fitted with double doors which are often called '*sound-traps*'. The doors themselves have an air space between them, sometimes several feet wide, and they must be a tight fit in their frames without any cracks or air leaks. Rubber or plastic sealing strips are normally fitted, similar in principle to a draught excluder, and a strong latch which holds the door firmly shut.

Air conditioning must also be carried out, but without the introduction of any noise from the plant. Ventilation is a science in itself and it is not proposed to venture into the subject in detail. Sufficient to say that the air ducts should be lined with sound absorbing materials, and fan motors insulated from the floor or roof of the building. Heating must also be installed, and can conveniently be combined with the ventilation plant. The more usual form of central heating with pipes running the length and breadth of the building is one sure way of introducing structure-borne noise, due to expansion and contraction of the pipes and steam traps.

Studio Acoustics

The whole problem of studio acoustics is one of controlled reverberation time, and this is affected by the size, shape, and nature of the studio walls. Due largely to the work of Professor Sabine in the early part of this century, it is possible to design a recording studio, cinema, theatre, or concert hall, and to fortell exactly what the acoustic treatment should be and the results to be expected from the building. The original *Sabine formula* for calculating reverberation time has now been written into every textbook dealing with acoustics:

$$T = \frac{0.05 \times V}{A}$$

T = the reverberation time in seconds of any room in which a sound
      of a standard intensity dies away to inaudibility;
V = the volume of the building interior in cubic feet;
A = the total number of *absorption units* present in the building.

Absorption units have been determined for practically all materials used for the interior structure and finishings of walls, floors, and ceilings, as well as furnishings, clothes, and people. Unity is taken as a surface of one square foot which absorbs all sound and reflects none, such as an open window. This is said to have an absorption coefficient of 1·0. All other surfaces are directly related to this standard, and a list of the more usual items is given in the table on page 150, together with their absorption coefficients.

The final value for A is calculated by measuring the areas of the various materials used inside the studio, multiplying these areas by their respective coefficients, and finally adding the products. Similar calculations are required for all studio furniture and fittings. By following the Sabine formula through, the reverberation time of any existing studio or room is easily discovered.

When designing a studio which will be satisfactory for a particular type of recording, the required reverberation time will already be known. The problem then is to arrange the decor of the studio so that it contains the correct number of absorption units according to the formula, and at the same time creates a pleasing appearance to the eye. One factor which must be taken into account is that some materials absorb more sound at certain frequencies than at others. Acoustic tiles for example absorb high frequencies more than low frequencies; but if these tiles are fixed away from the studio wall with a felt drape placed behind, the sound absorption will be more consistent at all frequencies.

TABLE OF SOUND ABSORPTION COEFFICIENTS FOR USE WITH THE
SABINE FORMULA. APPROXIMATELY CORRECT AT A
FREQUENCY OF 512 HZ.

Material	Coefficient per square foot	Coefficient per square metre
Open window	1·0	10·76
Brick, marble, glass, plaster	0·01 to 0·03	0·10 to 0·32
Solid wood, varnished	0·03 to 0·08	0·32 to 0·86
Wood panelling	0·1 to 0·2	1·07 to 2·15
Breeze blocks, untreated	0·4	4·30
Fibre-board panels, thin	0·2 to 0·3	2·15 to 3·22
Perforated panels, thick	0·4 to 0·7	4·30 to 7·51
Hardboard, plain	0·1 to 0·2	1·07 to 2·15
Hardboard, perforated	0·1 to 0·2	1·07 to 2·15
Cretonne curtains	0·15	1·61
Medium weight curtains	0·2 to 0·4	2·15 to 4·30
Velvet curtains in folds	0·5 to 1·0	5·38 to 10·7
Concrete floor	0·01 to 0·03	0·10 to 0·32
Wood floor	0·03 to 0·08	0·32 to 0·86
Linoleum or rubber tiles	0·1	1·07
Carpet	0·15	1·61
Heavy pile carpet on thick felt	0·3 to 0·5	3·22 to 5·38
Audience seated in auditorium	0·96	10·32
Acoustical plasters and tiles	0·2 to 0·35	2·15 to 3·76
Asbestos wool or felt, 1 in. (25·4 mm) thick	0·55 to 0·8	5·91 to 8·60
Felt with muslin cover	0·75	8·05
Felt with canvas cover (unpainted)	0·45	4·84
Fibre-board tiles, perforated or slotted	0·5 to 0·65	5·38 to 6·99
Wood seats or furnishings	0·1 to 0·2	1·07 to 2·15
Upholstered seats	1·0 to 2·0	10·76 to 21·52
Armchairs or settees	3·0	32·28
Audience, per person	4·7	50·55

Flutter Echoes

In any recording studio which has a 'live' acoustical characteristic there is a risk of obtaining *flutter echoes*. These can occur between two parallel walls with highly reflective surfaces. Sounds occurring between these two walls will set up a wave motion which is reflected backwards and forwards at speed, causing undesirable effects. Fortunately it is a relatively simple matter to cover one of the offending areas with sound absorbing material. When a flutter echo is discovered between floor and ceiling, this means laying a strip of carpet or placing some acoustic tiles overhead.

When recording away from the studio, flutter echoes are often found in large rooms in old buildings or in public halls. The remedy is to avoid any direct sound occurring in the troublesome area, and keep microphones well away. Flutter echoes are usually discovered somewhere in the centre of the building, and can play havoc with music. A well designed studio should be completely free of this defect.

Standing Waves

Another problem associated with the acoustics of a reverberant studio is the creation of *standing waves*. These are produced by reflections of sound from walls or ceiling which are in phase with the direct sound wave as heard at a particular point. Being in phase the amplitude of the two waves add together, producing a sound of louder than normal intensity. If the listening point is moved slightly, the two waves will become out of phase and tend to cancel each other.

The frequency at which standing waves are most likely to occur depends on the dimensions of the studio. In an ordinary living room the 9 kHz note from a television receiver can become alternatively audible and inaudible as one moves about the room. In a large room or studio it is frequencies below 500 Hz which usually cause standing waves, and this may influence microphone placement to a marked degree. The cure for standing waves is to fit sound absorption units to the studio walls, each unit being tuned to absorb a particular frequency. Standing waves will prove to be troublesome in a listening or monitoring room, where the sound source is a loudspeaker. Untreated parallel walls can also produce *eigentones*, which are unnatural room resonances.

Helmholtz Resonators

Since the majority of sound deadening materials are more effective at high frequencies, special treatment is necessary to absorb bass frequencies in an enclosed space. The treatment most frequently employed is the fitting of several *Helmholtz resonators*, which are boxes made of wood panels and lined with sound absorbing material. The size of each box can be varied so that it is tuned to any low frequency, and decorated to blend with the general scheme of the studio. The boxes are open at one end and absorb energy at their tuned frequency, due to sound waves resonating against the column of air inside.

Panel Absorbers

Another low frequency reducer commonly used consists of panels of hard-board or building board, supported on wood battens about 2 or 3 inches away from the studio walls. Low frequency sounds cause these panels to vibrate and absorb an appreciable amount of energy, their exact resonant frequency depending on the size of each panel. The main disadvantage of *panel absorbers* is re-radiation of their resonant frequency into the studio, causing an objectionable sound colouration. However if these panels are damped at the rear with felt or rock wool, re-radiation is very much reduced.

Membrane Absorbers

A third type of low frequency absorber which does not introduce re-radiation consists of rectangular wood boxes covered with roofing felt stretched across their open side. These are called *membrane absorbers* and are frequently used by the B.B.C. for the treatment of both small and large studios. The units give very efficient absorption at their resonant frequency, which is largely determined by the depth of each unit. Additional damping takes place if rock wool is introduced behind the felt, but if too much absorption occurs at high frequencies this can be reduced by covering the outside of the felt with perforated hardboard.

Reverberation Chambers

Although we are usually faced with the problem of avoiding unwanted resonances and reverberations there are occasions when we wish to create an echo deliberately. In fact, one of the most important rooms in a record-ing studio is the *reverberation chamber*. This is normally a brick-built structure without any parallel surfaces formed by its walls, floor, or ceiling. The walls are rendered smooth with cement or plaster, and a small sound-proof door permits access to the interior. The chamber can be further insulated by a brick-built shell on the outside, with an air space between, thus giving adequate protection against extraneous air-borne noise.

A typical design for a reverberation chamber is shown in Fig. 8.1. Such

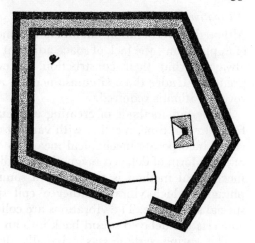

Fig. 8.1. Ground plan of brick built reverberation chamber.

a chamber will provide an almost unlimited number of reflected sound waves, upwards of 200 to 300, varying in their time delay according to the dimensions of the room. The sound waves originate from a loudspeaker, and the reflections are picked up by a microphone. It is necessary to experiment with the position of the microphone to obtain an optimum pick-up of reflected sound, and it is not desirable to place the microphone directly in front of the loudspeaker.

Another design enables an ordinary room of medium size to be used for reverberation purposes, without the necessity of building non-parallel walls. The design uses a number of cylindrical columns to obtain an infinite number of reflecting surfaces, the columns extending from floor to ceiling. Since the actual shape of the room is not critical, use can generally be made of any available space.

Once a reverberation chamber has been constructed, its reverberation time is usually fixed. It can be reduced temporarily by the introduction of a felt screen, but this upsets the correct working of the chamber. The frequency response of the loudspeaker system is not critical, and it is preferable if extreme bass frequencies are omitted. The microphone must also be suspended in such a way that it is insulated from structure-borne vibrations.

The output from a reverberation chamber is usually added to a recording when there is insufficient reverberation present in the studio, or to create a special effect such as the acoustics of a cathedral. Music frequently benefits from the addition of controlled reverberation, especially if the recording studio is not so 'live' as it should be.

Alternative Reverberation Units

Although reverberation chambers are most satisfactory for the majority of applications, the lack of space adjacent to the recording studio does not always permit their construction, or even the conversion of existing premises. Under these circumstances an alternative method of producing reverberation is required.

Numerous methods of creating artificial reverberation have appeared from time to time, meeting with varying degrees of success. Modern units either incorporate mechanical means to obtain the necessary time delay, or some form of delayed magnetic recording with a tape loop system. The mechanical method is to employ a sound modulator containing a diaphragm, which vibrates either a coil spring held under tension or a special steel plate. The vibrations are collected by a pick-up device which converts the delayed sound back into an electrical current.

The spring system was originally designed for use with electronic organs, and has certain applications in a small studio. A typical unit employs a pair of stretched helical springs, mounted in a floating framework to isolate them from external vibration. The two springs are mechanically different in order to promote multiple reflections, and have time delays of around 27 and 29 milliseconds. A transmitter is located at one end to excite the springs, and a receiver is located at the opposite end (Fig. 8.2). This arrangement gives an effect that is comparable to reflections from two pairs of hard surfaced parallel walls spaced approximately 32 and 41 feet (10 and 12½ metres) apart. The main criticism of the helical spring system is the dispersion of signals through the spring, the higher frequencies travelling faster than the lower frequencies. This is due to natural spring resonances, and if too much reverberation is used the result is not always a pleasing sound. Unwanted noise due to microphony of the springs is also introduced at high sound levels.

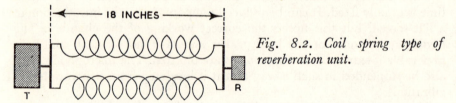

Fig. 8.2. Coil spring type of reverberation unit.

A more satisfactory system uses vibration of a steel plate, perforated to minimize mechanical resonances. The overall size of a typical plate unit is 8 ft. × 4½ ft. (2·40 m × 1·32 m), and the plate itself has a reverberation time which can be varied from ½ to 5 seconds. This is achieved by adjusting

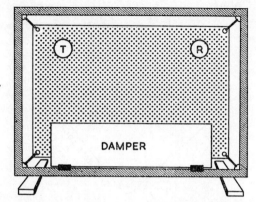

Fig. 8.3. Steel plate type of reverberation unit.

the distance between the reverberation plate and a special damping plate (Fig. 8.3). The damping device can be motorized for remote control, and a special indicator meter mounted alongside the recording engineer. Two adjacent push-buttons give more reverberation, or less reverberation, according to the proximity of the two plates. Even a steel plate is not entirely free of mechanical resonances at high sound levels, but they are very convenient to use and can meet the stringent demands of a professional recording or broadcast studio. A plate can also be used in a stereo system, with two receivers placed at different distances from the transmitter and picking up out of phase signals.

Magnetic recording provides a further system of obtaining delayed sound signals, signals which are of high quality and free from the resonances of mechanical systems. Magnetic reverberation units offer complete control over the number of echo or reflected waves it is desired to introduce, their intensity or volume, and their time delay. Furthermore it is possible to influence their time of decay, which is the time taken for each sound reflection to be reduced to inaudibility. By introducing a number of tape replay heads it is possible to have a number of delayed signals, each with a different time constant. The time constants will depend on the speed at which the tape is travelling, and the spacing between the record and replay heads (Fig. 8.4).

Ideally this system would employ a large number of replay heads in order to produce a smooth decay, since two or three heads would merely produce a decay consisting of a series of sharp reductions in volume level. However by careful adjustment of tape speed and head spacing, satisfactory results can be obtained from about 4 or 5 replay heads. The output from each successive head is made less than the previous head. The combined output from all these replay heads is fed back and added

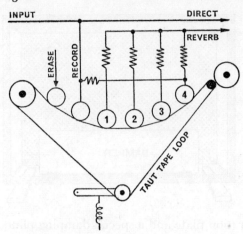

Fig. 8.4. Magnetic tape reverberation unit.

to the original sound source. This simulates the effect of an extended sound decay, or echo. A continuous loop of tape fitted into an endless cassette offers an ideal arrangement, since there will be no fear of the tape supply running out during a recording. A variable speed tape drive should be incorporated to control the time delay, which is easier than moving replay heads and achieves similar results.

Another type of magnetic reverberation unit employs a drum coated with an iron oxide laquer around its circumference. As the drum rotates it makes contact with an erase head, a record head, and several replay heads. Provision is made for adjusting the position of the replay heads, both individually and collectively. The individual controls determine the nature of the reverberation, and the collective control determines the time delay of the reverberation. All magnetic reverberation units should be installed with a tone control unit in their output line. This permits the use of treble and bass filter sections to adjust the frequency response of the reverberated signal before it is finally added to the original sound source.

Studio Lay-out

The general layout of a recording studio usually spreads over three or four rooms; for apart from the actual studio itself there is a monitoring room, recorder or apparatus room, reverberation chamber, workshop, and other necessary accommodation. A typical arrangement for a small studio is shown in Fig. 8.5. To enable the recording engineer to see what is going on in the studio, a plate glass window is fitted into the wall of the adjacent monitoring room. This window consists of two layers of glass, or occasionally three, with a small air space between them. This elaborate arrange-

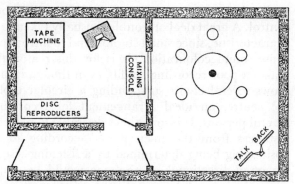

Fig. 8.5. Diagram show-
ing the lay-out of a small
B.B.C. studio.

ment is necessary to obtain sufficient sound insulation, since the amplification between microphone and monitoring loudspeaker is quite high.
Obviously if only headphone monitoring is employed the amount of sound
insulation required is much reduced. In fact the engineer can be located
in the studio itself, providing his headphones have close fitting rubber ear
pads to exclude any direct sound. Only sound picked up by the microphone should be audible. This system of monitoring is the one most
commonly used by film recordists when recording synchronous sound at
the same time as the picture is being shot, whether inside the studio or out
on location. For subsequent stages of recording and mixing film studios
require a proper monitoring room, as do television and sound broadcasting studios.

Double doors are usually required between the studio and the monitoring room, in addition to the normal sound trap arrangements between the
studio and the outside. This helps to keep the noise level in the monitoring
room as low as possible, especially in noisy surroundings. To maintain
communication with the studio, a *talk-back* microphone is fitted to the
control console. This has its own talkback amplifier, the output of which
is fed to a small loudspeaker in the studio. When this talk-back is in use the
monitoring loudspeaker is muted to prevent *feedback*.

In a small installation there is no reason why the recording equipment
should not be located in the monitoring room to save space. It should be
remembered that any generating plant or other noisy equipment in the
same building can cause structure-borne interference, and such equipment should be mounted on compressed cork pads or rubber 'silentbloc'
fittings.

A small studio need be no larger than the average sized living room,
suitably equipped with sound absorbing material set at a short distance
away from the walls. The air space formed provides additional damping

against structure-borne interference, as well as being a form of acoustical control. A great deal of trouble is usually taken to achieve a flat absorption characteristic, since small studios tend to introduce room resonances which cause sound colouration. It is for this reason that an untreated room makes a poor recording studio, even though it may be furnished. Fig. 8.5 shows several chairs surrounding a circular table with a microphone in the centre, an ideal arrangement for recording a discussion between several persons. It is sometimes desirable to place them at slightly different distances from the microphone according to their strength of voice, positioning being determined by a listening test in the monitoring room. An omni-directional microphone would be employed here, but if only two persons are taking part in the discussion a single ribbon microphone with its 'figure-of-eight' directional characteristic would be satisfactory.

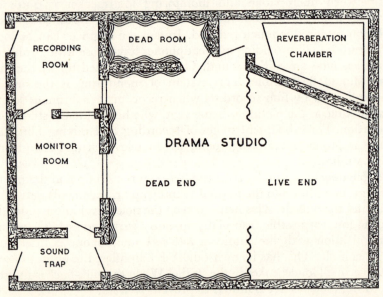

Fig. 8.6. Diagram showing the layout of a B.B.C. drama studio with various acoustic conditions.

Drama Studio

A studio suitable for recording or broadcasting a drama presentation is shown in Fig. 8.6. This is much larger than a discussion studio and possesses more facilities. Apart from being able to use several microphones, a drama studio has to provide several different acoustic conditions simultaneously. One end of the studio is made 'live' by having non-parallel plaster walls, and the other end has sound absorption materials fitted to reduce reverberation. A corner or alcove is sometimes completely screened off to provide the typical 'dead' acoustic as experienced in the open air. Curtains may be fitted to adjust the damping of the 'live' end, and if necessary shut this end off completely from the remainder of the studio.

The results obtained from any studio will depend considerably on the type of microphone used, due to their different polar distributions. Condenser and ribbon microphones are favoured for most studio recordings, with the dynamic reserved for recordings out of doors. Microphone positioning is carried out meticulously, and the result analysed over the monitoring loudspeaker. This subject is further discussed in Chapter 12, Microphone Techniques, on page 234.

Monitoring Room

The type of sound which is being recorded has quite a bearing on the required dimensions of the monitoring room. A small cubicle is quite large enough to listen to a few people engaged in conversation, or for listening to a commentator delivering a narration. Music and drama require much more spacious surroundings, and a room 10 ft. × 20 ft. (3 m × 6 m) is the minimum size which should be considered. The performance of orchestras can never be accurately appraised in cramped conditions, since it is desirable to sit well away from the monitoring loudspeaker which will be delivering a fairly loud volume level.

The acoustic conditions of a monitoring room must also be controlled to avoid colouration of bass frequencies, although reverberation can be slightly higher than in a general discussion studio. A reverberation time of $\frac{1}{2}$ or $\frac{1}{3}$ second would not be out of place, but a higher figure would be misleading as to the amount of reverberation actually being recorded. Soft furnishings and a carpet would not be out of place in a monitoring room; in fact these items will assist in simulating normal listening conditions where recordings are most likely to be heard. Parallel walls cannot always be avoided in a monitoring room, but good acoustics can be obtained with cylindrical surfaces to scatter standing waves and areas of acoustic tiles to control reverberation. The dividing wall between monitoring room and studio must always contain a double glazed window for viewing, with the mixing console situated immediately in front.

Mixing Consoles

Whatever the nature of the recording being made, the *mixing console* is the link between the microphones and the recording channel. There are many types of console currently in use, some simple, and some elaborate in construction and facilities provided. But their object is the same, which is to feed a balanced quality-corrected signal into the recording channel.

Apart from accepting the outputs from a number of microphones, using attenuators or faders to control the volume of each microphone individually, a mixing console also provides quality control by tone correction units and filters, either overall or on each input. For example if several different microphones were used, they may need different frequency correction to obtain a satisfactory sound balance, especially when recording dialogue. A special *dialogue equalizer* giving control of the lower frequencies is often incorporated into the console. Reverberation controls are also brought out to a convenient position, and consist of separate echo send or mixture controls for each input position (pre or post the input fader), and an overall echo return control. In this way the amount of signal from each input which is fed into the reverberation device can be individually controlled, and the overall balance between direct and reverberated signals adjusted on the echo return control—which is a single fader.

The actual faders themselves are of two types, rotary and sliding. Rotary faders have been the accepted style for many years, and still remain on some equipment. However the sliding type of fader is more popular and is to be found on the majority of new installations. The reason is one of convenience since a slider fader takes up far less room on the console; several can even be controlled by one hand by placing a single finger tip on each. A rotary fader requires one complete hand to operate it successfully, and although it is always possible to pre-set a number of rotary faders and combine their output through a single group fader (which is usual practice), the arrangement is not very flexible and ties up an additional control. As a general rule, sliding type faders are fitted to permanent installations; miniature rotary faders being reserved for small portable mixing units.

Sliding faders which move through an arc of a circle are termed *quadrant faders*. Other sliding controls which move in a straight line are known as *linear faders*. A typical quadrant fader element consists of a number of resistors wired in a T circuit, which is a circuit that maintains the same input and output impedance at all settings. The sliding control moves over a number of studs giving 16 steps of 1·5 db attenuation, and another 14 steps of increased attentuation giving an overall figure of 60 db. There is also an 'off' position. The fader control sometimes has a translucent scale engraved from 0 to 30, edge lit so that the position of the control can be seen in rooms with a low level of illumination. Groups of these faders can be mounted close together with only $\frac{3}{4}$ inch (19 mm) between centres, and they can easily be ganged for stereo operation. Some linear faders contain wirewound elements which give continuous attenuation without steps, and these are preferable for music recording and film re-recording.

Further refinements found in modern console design are master and sub-master faders, which are terms for group faders. Any number of channels can be switched or patched into a sub-master fader, from which a recording line can be taken or further routing arranged. Associated with the sub-masters will be adjustable high-pass and low-pass filters, and perhaps compressor amplifiers. A selection of sub-masters can be fed into master faders to provide overall control, or for distribution to other recorders or monitoring systems. Music mixing consoles will also incorporate a *foldback* facility so that the output from any microphone channel or number of channels can be fed back into the studio on headphones to the conductor, soloist, choir, or any member of the orchestra.

Volume Indicators

The most essential component of a mixing console is the *volume indicator*, which usually takes the form of a meter to establish the actual modulation level. This meter can be regarded as a visual form of monitor, in addition to the aural form of monitor such as a loudspeaker or a pair of headphones. The two forms of monitoring are closely related, and a comfortable listening level from the monitor should correspond to an average modulation as shown by the meter. Given these conditions it is possible to obtain settings for monitor volume and meter sensitivity, and these should remain unaltered for all normal recording.

Visual monitors are to be found in numerous forms, and may consist of a simple neon lamp, a magic eye, a meter, a beam of light from a galvanometer, or even a row of neon lamps adjusted to light up at different volume levels. However the volume indicating meter is the more robust and reliable method, and is more universally used.

There is no such thing as a standard volume indicating meter, although some types appear more often than others in recording equipment. A meter which is widely used because of its consistent accuracy over long periods of time is the Weston model 802 (Fig. 8.7), manufactured by the Weston Electrical Instrument Corp. It has a 4 inch (10 cms) scale calibrated in *Volume Units* (V.U.'s) and percentage modulation, and is designed to operate in a circuit of 600 ohms impedance. Zero level on the scale indicates a level of $+4$ db above the usual reference level of 1 mW, and to extend its range the meter is used with a variable attenuator having 2 db steps. The sensitivity of the movement does not

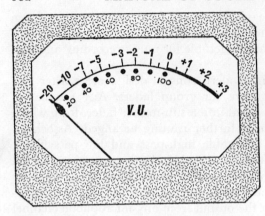

Fig. 8.7. A V.U. meter type 802, manufactured by Western Electrical Instrument Corp.

vary more than 0·5 db over the entire audible frequency range, which makes it eminently suitable for sound recording equipment and test gear.

A v.u. is a unit of volume similar to a decibel and possessing the same logarithmic properties. But v.u.'s can be used to express a definite power, since their zero reference level is always 4 db above 1 mW in a 600 ohm line. However, when expressing a power or voltage ratio between two different volume levels, it is preferable to use the decibel.

Another popular meter with an equally clear scale is the Westrex type 31832 shown in Fig. 8.8. The scale width is 3 inches (7.5 cm) and is calibrated from − 10 db. to + 2 db. Once again it is used in conjunction with an attenuator switch, variable in 2 db steps. A setting of the attenuator can be found which will enable zero level on the scale to coincide with 100 per cent modulation of the recording system, or to permit the meter sensitivity to be increased for a more accurate determination of low level

Fig. 8.8. A D.B. meter type 31832, manufactured for Westrex by Sifam Electrical Instrument Co. Ltd.

signals. Both meters show the mean or r.m.s. voltage of the sound signal, which makes their construction virtually the same as an a.c. voltmeter.

Another type of volume indicator is the *peak programme meter* or p.p.m., which gives an accurate indication of programme peaks instead of their r.m.s. value. This type of meter is favoured by the B.B.C. and a number of disc recording studios, since it provides a more accurate assessment of possible overload. A p.p.m. requires its own valve or transistor amplifier and shaping circuits to give a fast rise time to peak value and a slow decay, and the requisite circuitry is made available in module form for simple installation. It is quite possible that two sounds of different character, which sound different in loudness to the ear, give similar readings on a p.p.m. Therefore a p.p.m. is not a very satisfactory indicator of general sound volume, and it is frequently used in conjunction with a v.u. or db meter.

The movement of a db meter is usually much faster than a v.u. meter, and so gives a better indication of peak levels. This is important when recording under conditions which necessitate monitoring on headphones, although the final choice is really a matter of individual preference. Recording studios having loudspeaker monitoring systems prefer the v.u. meter with its slower movement, but they also use a p.p.m. alongside. A mirror galvanometer also operates as a p.p.m., and is fitted to disc recorders where the measurement of signal peaks is of great importance.

Monitor Loudspeaker Volume

In all sound recording it is most essential to listen to material over a high quality *monitor loudspeaker* system, since this is the only way to judge the quality of the signals being picked up by the microphone. The loudspeaker system may consist of two separate units for high and low frequencies, fed from a frequency dividing network as described on page 138, or a single dual-concentric unit. Power for the loudspeaker system is obtained from a separate monitor amplifier, and the combined frequency response of amplifier and loudspeaker should match the range of the recording system. Otherwise signals of low or high frequency can be recorded out of proportion to their volume level as heard in the monitoring room, or maybe without even being heard at all.

The sound level fed into the monitor amplifier is adjusted by the monitor volume control, which is incorporated into the mixing console or placed in a convenient position nearby. The correct setting of this control is purely arbitrary, determined by the preference of the user; but it must be set in conjunction with the attenuator on the volume indicator, in order to establish the relationship between the two forms of monitoring. As a general rule the sound volume being propagated by the loudspeaker should bear some resemblance to the sound volume being generated in the studio.

An exception to this rule occurs when recording certain low level sounds, which will eventually be re-recorded again. Such sounds are often recorded at a high level with a reduced monitor setting so as to make better use of the dynamic range of the recording system.

The importance of the sensitivity of the human ear to different intensity levels must not be overlooked. If the monitor volume is reduced, the bass and top frequencies will appear to decrease more than the middle frequencies leaving an impression of 'thin' sound. If the monitor volume is increased, the extreme bass and top frequencies will become more accentuated than the middle frequencies, and this is known as *attenuation distortion*. Since the balance of frequencies as heard by the ear depends on the setting of the monitor volume control, it is essential that material should be monitored at the same volume level as it will eventually be heard.

Since recording engineers tend to monitor at a higher sound intensity than that preferred by the average listener, it is suggested that frequent checks should be made during rehearsals at a lower sound intensity to ascertain the true balance. Monitoring should always be carried out in line with the main loudspeaker axis, because of the directional effect of high frequencies. Similarly, there should be no obstruction between the loudspeaker and the ears of the recording engineer. People are very efficient high frequency absorbers and so no one should stand between him and the speaker during a recording session.

Listening for prolonged periods at high volume levels soon produces listening fatigue, so that loud sounds appear to be of normal level. This could easily become a permanent condition, which may eventually lead to partial deafness.

CHAPTER IX

Music Recording

THE DIFFERENCE between recording music and recording dialogue is that music with its overtones has a far greater frequency range, which makes greater demands on equipment for faithful reproduction. There are two entirely different classes of music, one consisting of symphonic and light orchestral music, and the other comprising dance music and all forms of beat, 'pop', and jazz. Each class of music requires different studio acoustics, microphone placement, and orchestral balance. Pop music intended for disc release has its own special requirements, such as selective reverberation. Background music for films is not always composed like a normal orchestral score and sometimes calls for special treatment.

All musical instruments are designed to produce pleasing tones, some being easier to record than others. Musical tones are generated by bowing strings, blowing brass and woodwind, or by the vibrations of percussion instruments. The latter type can produce a waveform with very heavy transients as each note is struck, sometimes with a hard hammer, causing violent signal peaks which can easily go into distortion. This effect can prove disturbing, even though the peaks last only for a fraction of a second. The sound engineer himself need not be an accomplished musician to be able to record music, but he should have a working knowledge of musical theory, and an understanding of the various musical instruments which are likely to come his way.

String Instruments

The mainstay of any symphony orchestra is its string section, and the leader of the orchestra is always the principal violinist. The violin consists of a special shaped sound box and bridge, over which four strings are held taut and tuned by adjustable pegs. The fingers of the left hand are used to adjust the string lengths which between them give a fundamental range of four octaves. The strings are bowed close to the bridge to obtain a brilliant quality. Sometimes a *mute* is fitted to the strings to suppress resonance, and this produces a quieter and more mellow tone—not so rich in harmonics. Numerous variations of tone are possible, depending on the performer and his method of bowing. Instead of using the bow the strings may be plucked with the fingers, a method of playing called *pizzicato*.

Next comes the *viola* which is slightly longer, has heavier strings and is tuned to a lower pitch than the violin. Although a slightly larger instrument it is played like a violin and has a fundamental range of just over three octaves. The *'cello* is longer still and is tuned an octave lower than the viola, and has a fundamental range of just over three octaves. It is positioned between the performer's legs, and has an adjustable spike which raises the instrument to a convenient height. The *Double Bass* has four heavy strings, and occasionally a fifth string, and stands about 6 ft. (1·8 m) high. Its fundamental range is also about three octaves, and it is either plucked or played with a large bow.

The *Harp* contains 46 strings mounted on a roughly triangular frame, one side of which is designed as a sounding board. Seven foot-pedals are provided to adjust the pitch of the notes by a semitone or a full tone, with the result that the fundamental range of the instrument is six and a half octaves. The *Banjo*, *Guitar*, and *Mandolin* family contain any number of strings from four to twelve, and differ only in the type of sounding box used to amplify the strings in resonance—creating the harmonics which give each instrument its characteristic tone.

Woodwind Instruments

This group is so named because the instruments are made of wood and produce tones when an air column is vibrated inside them. This vibration can be set in motion either by *edge tones* or *reeds*. Edge tones are produced when an air stream is directed on to a solid lip or wedge, which is the working principle of the *Flute*. This instrument consists of a tube closed at one end, the air column inside being vibrated by blowing across a small hole. Various notes are produced by uncovering a series of holes along the length of the tube, which in theory alters its length. In early flutes these holes were placed in a convenient position for covering by the fingers, like Elizabethan *recorders*, but a modern flute has a series of pads operated by keys placed close together. It has a fundamental range of three octaves. A similar, but smaller instrument is the *Piccolo*, which is played like a flute but ranges an octave higher.

The *Clarinet* is probably the best known single reed instrument, and this has a fundamental range of just over three octaves. The holes in the tube are also covered by key operated pads, although the system is more complicated than that of the flute. There is also a *Bass Clarinet* which covers a range one octave lower than the clarinet. The *Oboe* is a double reed instrument with a small flared tube, key operated pads, and a range of three octaves. It is frequently used for tuning an orchestra by sounding an A note. A similar instrument is the *Cor Anglais*, or *English Horn*, whose tube ends in a spherical bulb. It has a slightly smaller range than the oboe. Another double reed instrument is the *Bassoon*, which has a long tube doubled back on itself to make it a convenient size. It plays two octaves lower than the oboe, and has the usual range of three octaves. There is also a *Contra-Bassoon*, much loved by some composers, which has a tube folded three or four times and plays one octave lower than the bassoon.

Wind Instruments

The most familiar wind instruments used for light music are those of the *Saxophone* family, consisting of soprano, alto, tenor, baritone, and bass. They are all single reed instruments ending in an upturned bell, except the soprano which is straight, having a brass tube which is wider than the clarinet. Each saxophone covers a range of two and a half octaves, and the fingering of the keys is almost identical to the clarinet. In practice the same performer will often 'double' on any of these instruments during a recording session.

Brass Instruments

A third method of causing a column of air to vibrate and produce different notes is by varying the performer's lip tension and blowing pressure. This is the principle by which all brass instruments are played, including the *Trumpet*, which has a cup-shaped mouthpiece and a tube six feet (nearly two metres) in length. Three valves, together with assistance from the performer, give a range of three octaves. Wood or metal *mutes* are sometimes fitted into the flared end of the tube, which give a change in quality at the expense of a drastically reduced output. The *Cornet* is a more compact instrument which covers a similar range, but it has a less brilliant tone.

The Trombone operates on a similar principle, and has a tube nine feet (nearly three metres) long with a telescopic section in the form of a large U. There are no valves, and tuning is accomplished by sliding the telescopic section—which makes *glissandos* possible. The *tenor* trombone has a range of two and a half octaves, and the *bass* trombone a range of three octaves. The *French Horn* consists of a tube twelve feet (nearly four metres) in length, coiled into a circle with a very wide flared opening. It contains three valves which effectively change the length of the tube, and the fundamental range is three octaves. The instrument is played with one hand inside the bell to adjust pitch, or to provide muted effects.

The *Tuba* and the *Sousaphone* are the big brothers of the brass family, each having a tube at least eighteen feet (five and a half metres) in length and a large flared bell. The tuba has its bell facing upwards, and the Sousaphone has its bell facing forwards with the instrument resting on the

performer's shoulders. Three or four valves are used which give a fundamental range of three octaves.

Percussion Instruments

In all percussion instruments the musical tones are generated when the
instruments are struck by drumsticks, hammers, or some other hard
object. The tones are caused by the resulting vibration of bars, bells,
chimes, drumskins, plates, or strings. Instruments like the *triangle, bass
drum, cymbals,* and *gongs* generate a very wide range of frequencies and
harmonics (overtones), so that they cannot be tuned in any way and are
said to possess an *indefinite pitch*.

Instruments like the *xylophone* (wood bars), *vibraphone* (metal bars with
vibrato effect), *marimba* (wood bars), *glockenspiel* (metal plates), *celeste*
(metal plates), *chimes* (metal tubes), and *tympani* (drumskins) are all
tunable and are said to possess a *definite pitch*. Technically speaking a
Piano is a percussion instrument, since it consists of steel strings hit by
hammers which are operated from a keyboard. Another string instrument
is the *Cymbalum*, originating from Hungary, which is rather like a harp on
its side and is played with small hammers.

A Music Studio

In the early days of sound recording, a studio with a *live* and a *dead* end
was often employed for music, the orchestra being situated in the live
section. Although the musicians themselves may be surrounded by conditions of high reverberation, reflections from the dead end will be notice-
ably absent. This gives the effect of an unnatural sound decay which is
not pleasing with orchestral music, although sometimes essential with jazz.
A symphony orchestra is normally heard in a fair-sized concert hall,
which probably has a reverberation time of at least two seconds. This
produces a certain balance in the ears of the listener between the direct
sound waves emanating from each instrument, and the reflected waves
from the interior surfaces of the hall. In order to record a symphony
orchestra successfully, these acoustic conditions must be simulated in the
music recording studio.

One of the first considerations in designing a music studio is to determine
the maximum number of musicians which are likely to be present at any
one time. Particular attention must be given to all the factors affecting
reverberation, and it has been found by experience that a minimum
volume of 2,000 cubic feet (75 cubic metres) per instrument is necessary
for a small-sized orchestra, and 3,000 cubic feet (111 cubic metres) per
instrument for a large-sized orchestra, to give satisfactory results. Any

reduction in these figures will naturally reduce the reverberation time, and a feeling of being 'cramped' can be experienced by the musicians themselves. Also music played in too small a studio will lose some of its tonal quality. But placing a small orchestra in a large studio is not nearly so objectionable, since it is always possible to position some *acoustic screens* around the musicians to cut off any excess reverberation. These screens contain sound absorbing material such as acoustic tiles mounted on substantial wooden frames which can be wheeled into any position.

The average symphony orchestra consists of some 60 or 70 musicians, and these will require a recording studio having a volume of 210,000 cubic feet (6,175 cubic metres). The optimum ratio for the dimensions of the studio should be length—4, width—2, and height—1. The reverberation time of such a studio will be 1·2 seconds at a frequency of 1 kHz. This is shown by the graph in Fig. 9.1, which illustrates the relationship between studio volume and reverberation time. It will also be noticed that the reverberation time increases as the frequency is lowered, which is one reason why bass frequencies should be absorbed fairly quickly.

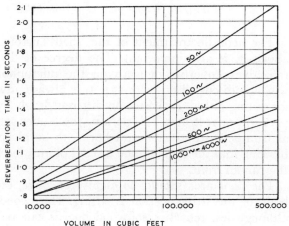

Fig. 9.1. Graph showing the reverberation of a music studio at various frequencies.

Acoustic Treatment

The distribution and type of sound absorbing and sound reflecting materials used for treating the interior surfaces of a music studio are quite important, and may even determine the final contours of the walls and ceiling. The layout of a large music recording studio is shown in Fig. 9.2. Cylindrical reflective splays are used at intervals along all walls to ensure enough sound diffusion to break up standing waves. The splays are constructed either of plaster or plywood, and are separated by areas of acoustic tiles. Plywood columns are more absorbant than plaster at low frequencies, and therefore provide a more pleasing tonal response within the studio.

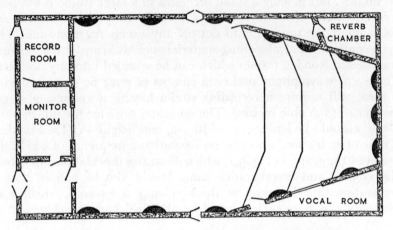

Fig. 9.2. Ground plan of typical music recording studio.

The acoustic treatment of the 'shell' surrounding the orchestra, and above it, is also important. The degree of 'liveness' required from its reflective properties depends on the microphone technique employed, which is discussed on page 174. It is always advisable to make provision for setting out an orchestra on different levels by means of a three-tiered platform or rostrum. This permits the louder sounding instruments, such as trumpets, trombones, and horns, to be placed at the rear while still blowing into the microphone instead of into the backs of the musicians in the row in front.

The floor area should be highly reflective, especially where the main body of the string section is sitting. Hardwood block flooring is ideal, although less reflective softwood boards can be overlaid with sheets of 'Laconite'—or similar hard surfaced material—if it is desired to increase the brilliance of the strings.

Vocal Room

In many cases the orchestra and vocalist require to be separated physically, so it is useful to have a vocal room which is acoustically isolated from the main studio. Since no direct sound must be heard in the vocal room from the studio, and vice versa, a double glass window is fitted into the partition wall for mutual observation. Such an arrangement means that the conductor of the orchestra must wear headphones with a feed from the vocal microphone, and the vocalist must wear headphones with a feed from the orchestra microphones—or listen to a monitor loudspeaker operating at a low volume level.

Orchestra and vocalist are frequently recorded on separate tracks contained on the same piece of tape or film, especially with pop music or when recording musical numbers for a film. In the case of films the music is frequently pre-recorded before the film is actually shot, and the music played back on a synchronized magnetic recorder whilst the cameras are turning. The vocalist is photographed mouthing the words in time with the playback. It is therefore difficult to determine a correct balance between orchestra and vocal and the correct mix is achieved at a later date whilst watching the completed picture on the screen.

The acoustic treatment of the vocal room should be fairly bright, with *membrane absorbers* on the walls covered with perforated hardboard and sufficient acoustic tiles to keep the reverberation time down to about half a second. A carpet on the floor will soon reduce any excess reverberation. It is a mistake to make a vocal room too small, since sound colouration will be apparent even with directional microphones.

Monitoring Room

The monitoring room should be adjacent to the recording room and easily accessible from the studio, although acoustically isolated and separated by a sound trap with double doors. A double clad glass window must be fitted into the front wall, large enough to give good visibility over the entire studio and vocal room. The acoustic treatment should resemble that of the vocal room, with some poly-cylindrical surfaces to break up standing waves and a reverberation time of half a second. A more reverberant monitoring room will give a false impression of the sound being picked up by the microphones, since the reverberation present will be heard as an addition to the reverberation in the studio.

A room of fairly large dimensions should be used for monitoring music, since there are usually a number of people present in addition to the sound engineer. A large room will avoid the necessity of having to sit close to the loudspeaker systems and being obliged to operate with too low a monitor volume setting. Low volume levels can give rise to a loss in the appreciation of *auditory perspective*, and in consequence the ability to obtain a good orchestral balance is impaired. A good position for the loudspeaker systems is on the front wall above the glass window, so that stereo effects and channel separation can be easily observed at the mixing console in relation to the orchestral lay-out. If the loudspeakers are too large to be hung and must rest on the floor, they can be positioned at one end of the monitoring room and the mixing console turned through 90° to face them.

Orchestral Combination

Before describing the actual lay-out of a symphony orchestra in a music studio it may help to mention the placing of the various instruments within the orchestra. The four main sections are strings, woodwind, brass and percussion, and each section contains instruments which cover almost the entire musical scale.

STRINGS   Violin, viola, 'cello, bass, harp.
WOODWIND   Piccolo, flute, clarinet, cor anglais, oboe, bassoon.
BRASS   Trumpet, trombone, french horn, tuba.
PERCUSSION Bells, chimes, cymbals, drums, triangle, tympani.

In addition there are numerous other instruments employed from time to time, such as the harpsichord, celeste, and of course the pianoforte. The celeste, which has a piano-type keyboard, is frequently used. It is situated near the piano and usually played by the same performer.

The *orchestral combination* is decided upon by the composer (or conductor) to give a fairly balanced output of sound from each section. Since the violin gives a relatively low output, it always exists in greater numbers than any other instrument. For example, a string section may contain eight first violins, six second violins, four violas, four 'celli, and two bass, a combination known as 8—6—4—4—2. Woodwind instruments are usually found in pairs, although musicians in this section frequently play more than one type of instrument, such as piccolo and flute or oboe and cor anglais. The size of the woodwind section depends on the size of the string section, but the size of the brass section depends on the type of music being played, and can vary from two to six instruments of any particular type.

In general an orchestra can be increased or decreased in size so long as a workable ratio exists between each section and each instrument. A string section of 6—4—3—2—1 would be practical, or for a large orchestra 12—8—6—4—2. In the latter case the woodwind section would probably be doubled with three or four of each instrument, and two harps employed instead of the usual one. The percussion section is manned by any number of musicians from two to ten, depending once again on the nature of the musical score and the general size of the orchestra.

Orchestral Lay-out

The lay-out of a symphony orchestra for recording purposes closely follows the normal concert arrangement, since the musicians always play

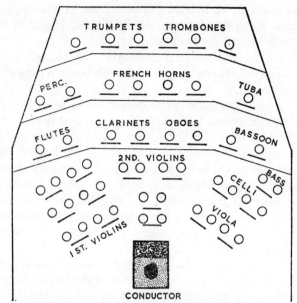

Fig. 9.3. Seating plan in a 'live' studio to obtain an internal orchestral balance.

best in close formation. At one time it was thought that better results could be obtained by splitting the orchestra into its individual sections of strings, woodwind, and brass, each with its own microphone. Although some recording studios operate in this way, it is not easy for members of the orchestra to hear each other when they are spread out, which results in untidy playing in spite of the efforts of the conductor and orchestra leader. Also, since balancing is carried out in the monitoring room, the conductor cannot accurately judge the results which are being obtained.

The final arrangement for the orchestral lay-out is left to the discretion of the recording engineer, who should produce a plan which is workable for himself and acceptable to the conductor. A suitable plan for close formation is shown in Fig. 9.3, an arrangement which has been used by the author many times with varying sized orchestras. It has been proved that perfectly acceptable results can be obtained with only a single microphone, provided its position is determined by experiment to secure the correct orchestral balance, and budding engineers are encouraged to follow this procedure.

Most symphony orchestras playing in close formation are arranged so as to have what is called an *internal balance*, which means that every instrument is so placed that the combined playing sounds correct, or balanced, to the ears of the conductor. A good microphone position in this case would be several feet above the conductor's head, enabling a sound pick-up to be obtained which is similar to that heard by the conductor. With very large orchestras it is wise to position the microphone further away to obtain a characteristic 'big' sound. This is achieved when the balance between direct and reverberated sound waves is correctly proportioned.

Apart from the main microphone, others may have to be placed at strategic points to cover any instrument playing a solo passage. This will increase the amount of direct sound pick-up, and prevent musicians from having to move towards the main microphone during the actual recording. On the other hand there is no reason why a complete piano concerto cannot be recorded successfully on one microphone, provided the piano is situated immediately in front of the conductor's rostrum, called a *podium*. In practice it is prudent to set up a close microphone on the piano as well, in case the main microphone does not prove effective on quiet passages.

The ratio between direct and reflected sound arriving at the microphone varies according to the distance of the microphone from the sound source. This has a pronounced effect on the apparent reverberation time of the studio, and definition will be lost if the microphone working distance is too great. It should be borne in mind that the microphone is a monophonic device, and requires to be considerably nearer to the sound source than a pair of ears in order to obtain similar definition. Generally speaking if the quietest instruments are positioned at the front, and the loudest instruments positioned at the rear, a good internal balance should not be hard to achieve.

Multi-Microphone Technique

In an effort to obtain the maximum definition from every instrument in the orchestra, it is frequently necessary to use a multi-microphone technique. This is achieved by spreading the orchestra out into sections, with each section having one or more microphones placed fairly close as in Fig. 9.4. Some orchestral lay-outs require as many as 20 to 25 microphones, and a satisfactory balance may be difficult to achieve. Under these conditions the conductor himself will wish to balance the orchestra in the monitoring room, in co-ordination with the recording engineer.

The selective pick-up of individual instruments by this method is only successful if the recording studio is not too 'live'. A highly reflective orchestral shell should be avoided when using this technique, thus preventing acoustic spill-over from one instrument or group of instruments to the next. If better separation is required, for example between strings and

MUSIC RECORDING 175

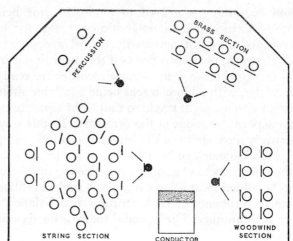

Fig. 9.4. Seating plan used with multi-microphone technique. Orchestral balance obtained in monitoring room.

brass instruments, an acoustic screen can be positioned so that the brass instruments do not blow into the microphone positioned above the strings. If any particular instrument sounds too 'dry', or lacking in reflected sound waves, the microphone can be positioned a little further away or artificial reverberation added from the chamber or plate unit.

The multi-microphone technique is normally employed when recording dance orchestras, 'pop' music, and small rhythm combinations. With this type of music every instrument has to be heard at fairly close range and at maximum clarity. Modern practice is to position microphones about 2 or 3 feet (0·9 m) away from each instrument or group, giving a sound pick-up consisting almost entirely of direct waves. In this way a 'dry' or 'tight' sound is obtained with good clarity. The exclusion of indirect sound waves reflected from the studio walls is relatively unimportant, since any large scale studio reverberation would spoil the definition of the music generally, especially when the orchestra is playing in fast tempo. Artificial reverberation can always be added if required.

Reverberation is not always added to all microphones. For example if a vocal number is being recorded, the orchestra may be left 'dry' and reverberation given only to the singer. Sometimes it is the reverse, and the string section gets the benefit of reverberation. There is no ready-made formula, and the treatment given depends on each individual orchestra or group and the effect it is desired to achieve. The final result, including the problem of orchestral balance, is entirely in the hands of the recording engineer.

At any music recording session the biggest expense is the musicians' fees, and everything is geared to minimize time being wasted on technical matters. In order to make things easier for himself, the professional recordist may not necessarily record a complete musical number on a single track, or on two tracks if the recording is in stereo. When he thinks in terms of using a four-track recorder he really means a four-channel recorder, with all four tracks being available simultaneously. The modern trend is to use eight tracks so that eight separate channels can be employed for separate sections of the orchestra. In this way the strings can be kept entirely separate from the brass, woodwind, and percussion, and the final artistic balance can be achieved at leisure by a tape transfer process after the musicians have gone. In practice the multi-track system enables vocals to be added in at a later date, and offers additional facilities for carrying out experiments in reverberation and balance to an already recorded musical number. The demand today is for sixteen or twenty-four channel recorders.

Orchestral Lay-out

Dance music does not need the same volume of studio space and long reverberation time as is required for symphonic music, and it can be recorded quite successfully in a studio half the size. A typical dance orchestra will contain rhythm, brass, woodwind, and string sections with the following instruments:

RHYTHM	Drums, double bass, guitar.
BRASS	Trumpet, trombone, saxophone.
WOODWIND	Flute, clarinet.
STRINGS	Violin, viola, cello.

In addition there are frequently a number of solo instruments, apart from the piano, and these include electric guitars, accordians, and mouth-organs. It will be noticed that the double bass is no longer attached to the string section, and is considered as part of the rhythm section. This is because the double bass is usually plucked with the fingers in a fairly fast rhythm, and the performer has to take his timing from the jazz drummer who must be positioned fairly close at hand.

The orchestral lay-out of a dance orchestra for recording purposes is seldom the neat arrangement seen when the same orchestra is performing in public. Conductors usually have their own preferred arrangement when constantly using one particular studio, and this is arrived at in consultation with the recording engineer. Figure 9.5 shows the fairly tight grouping of the B.B.C. Northern Dance Orchestra, with each section playing into its own microphone which is a pressure gradient type with a ribbon element.

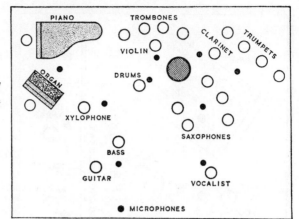

Fig. 9.5. Seating plan and microphone arrangement used for the B.B.C. Northern Dance Orchestra.

The saxophone section contains alto, soprano, tenor, and bass instruments, and this section changes over to clarinets when required.

Smaller combinations with only six or seven musicians may be encountered with traditional jazz. These combinations usually consist of only two sections, rhythm and front line. They usually contain the following instruments:

     RHYTHM   Drums, banjo or guitar, tuba or double bass.
     FRONT LINE Trumpet, trombone, clarinet.

A piano is also used occasionally, and unless it is featured prominently in a solo passage, very little is heard of it in competition with the remainder of the combination. Clarity is all important, with each instrument playing into its own microphone positioned fairly close. This produces a 'dry' sound and enables a good degree of separation between instruments to be obtained, even in a live studio. This method also permits the type of microphone to be selected which suits each particular instrument, although the condenser microphone remains the favourite in Europe.

A typical lay-out for a small jazz group is shown in Fig. 9.6, with the musicians arranged roughly in a circle with a radius of only 10 feet (3 metres). The acoustics are fairly 'dead', and a curtain is shown which screens off the remainder of the studio. Members of the rhythm section are also surrounded by low *acoustic screens* to increase separation, and the studio walls are fairly well damped. Artificial reverberation is seldom used, but it can be added to the signal from each individual microphone if required. One sure way of preventing the jazz drummer from being

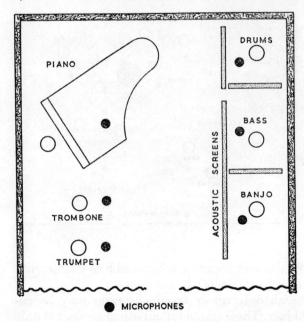

Fig. 9.6. Seating plan in fairly 'dead' studio for small jazz group.

picked up on the double bass microphone, thus giving a muddy sound, is to use a lavalier type microphone positioned in the bridge of the double bass, surrounded by a cushion of foam rubber or plastic. Quite apart from separation, this arrangement gives a good, clean sound to the double bass, so that each individual note is clearly heard.

Brass instruments produce sound waves of very great amplitude, rich in harmonics which can extend up to 15 kHz on a trumpet. This is why the brass section is normally placed at the rear of a symphony orchestra. But when recorded with the close microphone technique it requires a large amount of skill on the part of the recording engineer to keep the volume below overload point. He is helped to a large extent by a *limiter amplifier* (see page 121), whose gain is automatically limited by the volume of sound being fed into it. A limiter is sometimes included overall, but more often a line limiter is inserted in just the brass microphone lines.

Since a jazz or beat group creates a considerable volume level, a similar volume level must exist in the monitoring room during recording in order to obtain a precise appraisal of the group's performance, and the correct balance. This high monitor level is considerably louder than is considered comfortable listening level in the home, and should not be endured for very long periods or slight deafness will result.

Recording Choirs

Choral works are probably one of the most difficult items to record successfully. Quite apart from the performance of the choir, which should of course be beyond reproach, the definition of the singing depends on the studio acoustics and a reasonably close microphone position. A cardioid microphone does not always provide a uniform coverage at close range over a group of singers, so that persons in different positions within the general pick-up area of the microphone are heard with varying tonal quality and volume. The remedy is to use an omni-directional microphone, or a cardioid with an evenly distributed frequency response over the required pick-up area.

It is obviously impossible to work at close range with a large choir unless a number of microphones are used. The choir can be split up into groups containing contralto, soprano, tenor, baritone, and bass voices, and the multi-microphone technique employed. But a better performance will be given if the choir remains as a single group, and the minimum number of directional microphones used. The result will sound more like a large choir since the microphones will be a little further away.

The use of a vocal room is seldom satisfactory for a choir if quality is the main consideration. The best arrangement is to place them in the main studio in sight of the conductor and not too far away from the orchestra. If space permits, as in the B.B.C.'s Maida Vale Studio, tiered seating can be arranged on rostrums behind the orchestra and the choir assembled in its usual formation. If the studio is too small for both the orchestra and the choir, the orchestra can be recorded first and the choir recorded at a later session to an orchestral playback, using multi-track tape or film. This idea assumes that the particular musical work lends itself to such an arrangement.

Soloists usually require a microphone to themselves, so that a correct balance can be achieved between them and the remainder of the choir. Different microphone techniques are employed by classical and 'pop' singers. A trained classical singer will have a powerful voice and work further away from the microphone. In this case the singer will sound better if recorded under the same acoustic conditions as the orchestra, and the conductor will have a much better sense of integration if the singer is standing nearby.

Pop singers use an extremely close microphone position, and can easily be recorded in a separate vocal room. This will achieve complete separation of voice and orchestra which is often essential with a weak singer. To assist in maintaining a fairly even voice level, a certain amount of compression can be used to advantage which will avoid having to continually adjust the fader. Also rehearsals and takes are seldom the same for voice level, and even different takes produce different voice levels from some singers. This is just one reason why it is current practice to keep vocals on a separate track to the orchestra, and a satisfactory balance is made at the transfer stage.

One disadvantage of using a close working distance is the over-emphasizing of consonants, and in particular the letters P, S, and T, which tend to produce a blast of air which disturbs or 'pops' the microphone diaphragm. To avoid this effect a special *anti-pop shield* or *breath shield* is fitted which completely encloses the diaphragm without restricting the frequency response. Such a shield is also effective in preventing breathing noises being recorded, and is similar in construction to the usual type of wind shield used when recording out-of-doors (see page 243).

Organ Music

Apart from the small portable electronic organs, the large pipe organ is still to be found in concert halls, churches, and other auditoria. These organs are usually specially designed to suit the particular acoustics of the building in which they are to be installed, with the pipe arrangements varied to suit local conditions, and therefore each organ will present different problems in microphone placement to achieve a balanced result. Magnetic recording usually provides a sufficient volume range to capture the loud and soft passages of organ music, although quiet passages may have to be raised slightly in volume—preferably by the organist—to prevent them becoming lost in the background noise of the auditorium and the recording system.

In order to capture the full tonal quality of a pipe organ, and the best volume range, it may be necessary to employ more than one microphone. The main microphone can be either a condenser or a ribbon, and it should not be positioned too near the pipes in order to obtain a satisfactory balance between direct and indirect sound waves. At the same time it is never wise to select a microphone position near the centre of the auditorium, as this is the area most likely to contain *standing waves* of low frequency. Organ music contains plenty of low frequencies, in fact the foot pedals which control the lower diapasons will often cause frequencies to be emitted extending to the lower limit of the recording equipment and beyond. For this reason the microphone should be mounted in an anti-vibration suspension to prevent the natural movement of the diaphragm or ribbon from being disturbed, and to eliminate unnecessary rumblings on the recording.

Some organs may have their pipes spread out in such a fashion that a single microphone does not cover the direct waves from the entire range. In situations like this an additional microphone placed closer to, and in line with, the small pipes forming the top notes will be beneficial. There is always far less power delivered from small pipes, which is one reason why the top notes are among the first to be lost. However a close microphone position may also pick up a certain amount of mechanical noise from the foot pedals and stop mechanisms, as well as interference from the blower motor. Therefore a close microphone should only be used to obtain maximum definition on quiet passages, so as to prevent an excessive amount of auditorium noise being included in the recording.

Electronic Organs

Electronic organs are a different proposition, since the sound waves are generated electronically and propagated through a normal loudspeaker system. At first sight it would seem feasible to dispense with a microphone and feed the output from the amplifier in the organ straight into the recording system, via a suitable matching circuit. Technically speaking there is no objection to this procedure, and electronic organs have been recorded in this way. But the quality is rather 'dry' due to the total absence of room tone or natural reverberation.

A microphone placed in front of the organ's loudspeaker system is the preferred method, and the organist himself will be able to judge his performance more accurately. Artificial reverberation can also be added from a spring-type unit mounted inside the organ. Some loudspeaker units have forward facing bass radiators and upward facing tweeters, which may mean having to use two microphones to obtain a satisfactory balance.

Mechanical Organs

There is also the mechanical type of organ as used by street musicians in various parts of the world, some of which are operated by electricity or steam at most fairgrounds. It is seldom that the larger type of mechanical organ will find its way into a recording studio, and they are best recorded in their natural surroundings. The results should sound quite authentic if there is not too much extraneous noise present at the time of recording. It should be remembered that sound waves out of doors can be disturbed and attenuated by the wind and general air movements, so a reasonably close microphone position is to be preferred.

Electronic Music

Magnetic recording has made it possible for an entirely new form of music to be created consisting of synthetic and electronic sounds. Looking at a page of a normal music score we see that each note is carefully marked, together with signs indicating the strength and duration for which it is to be played, and the time relationship between it and the notes on either side. In addition there is usually some indication to show on which instrument the passage is to be played. The interpretation of this music, and consequently the final performance of it, depends on the musician.

With electronic music the composer has complete control over the entire composition from its conception to its performance, since the component parts usually exist only on pieces of magnetic tape and are not written down on paper. Conventional musical notation contains intervals of one octave, the highest note being twice the frequency of the lowest. If these two notes are played together they are said to be 'in tune', because the second harmonic of the low note corresponds in frequency to the fundamental of the high note. With electronic music a new and different relationship can be established between each note, depending on the desire and skill of the composer. Each note can be recorded individually, and the harmonics added later on as required, so that there would be no feeling of discord if there were as many as 10 or 12 notes in an octave. Once a few bars of music have been constructed, it is only necessary to re-record and produce several copies for extending the composition. Each bar does not have to be constructed every time. Magnetic recording also permits cutting, editing, speed doubling, and other transformations of original sounds not possible with any other method. It is therefore the composer who is responsible for the performance of electronic music, which is in the form of a completed tape.

The tools for manufacturing such musical sounds are all electronic instruments, such as an *audio oscillator*, a *white noise generator*, a *multivibrator*, and various circuits for shaping and transforming the generated tones such as a *gating amplifier* and a *ring modulator*.

WHITE NOISE GENERATOR—An expensive device for producing a background noise of multiple frequency. White noise must be passed through a band pass filter before use to select the frequency required. White noise can also be purchased already recorded on tape, and filtered for various frequencies.

MULTIVIBRATOR—This is a primary tone source consisting of an oscillatory circuit which produces a sound very rich in harmonics. It generates a square waveform and can be designed to cover any frequency in the entire audible range.

GATING AMPLIFIER—A circuit used to alter the characteristics of primary tones generated by an audio oscillator or multivibrator. Sounds can be

deprived of their initial attack, have their decay time adjusted, or continuous tones made to sound like bells being struck.

RING MODULATOR—A circuit for causing one sound source to be modulated
by another, causing deliberate intermodulation not possible by normal
mixing methods.

All of these items may be found in a single unit, such as the *Moog
Synthesizer*. This electronic music generator comprises several oscillators,
each tunable over 2 octaves; wave shaping circuits giving sine, saw-tooth,
triangular, or pulse signals; modulators; high pass and low pass filters;
white noise generator; reverberation; also a 4 way mixer. It is operated
by a 5 octave piano type keyboard controller, which in fact supplies a
control voltage to the oscillators, and a continuously variable ribbon
controller which permits gliding tones. Each module within the synthesizer has to be inter-connected with a number of patch-cords, and a work
sheet of this patching is made out for future reference. The output signal,
which is zero level in a 600 ohm line, is taken to a monitor amplifier and
also directly into a tape recorder, or a studio mixing console.

Any large-scale composition of electronic music involves a great deal of
time and labour, and it is virtually impossible to work to any form of
musical score. In fact the paper work (if any) for this style of music is
usually compiled after the composition has been recorded, and is used
merely for reference purposes. Electronic music provides a good avenue
for exploring the more unusual possibilities of magnetic recording.

Music Concrete

This type of music also relies on magnetic recording, although any kind
of sound source can be incorporated into the musical score including tones
from musical instruments. Once again the pitch, timbre, and decay time
of a musical note can be easily controlled, or its initial attack cut off the
front and the tape played backwards. Once a musical note has been
recorded, the relationship between its characteristics is fixed. But the pitch
may be altered by re-recording at a different speed, in which case the
timbre and decay time will also be altered. The entire quality of the note
will be changed so that its true origin will not always be recognized—
which is often desirable when creating music concrete.

CHAPTER X

Stereophonic Sound

STEREOPHONIC SOUND is only made feasible by the keen sense of direction in our hearing, as mentioned on page 19, and the logical development of stereo recording techniques is to simulate this directional effect. It may not seem obvious at first that stereo permits a far more life-like reproduction of sound, but a simple listening test will quickly prove that this is so.

It is probably easier to grasp a fuller understanding of stereo if one considers its effect with photography. Looking at an ordinary photographic print, both our eyes see identical images and we do not obtain any sense of depth or perspective. If we now look at a pair of stereo prints, photographed with a camera having two lenses spaced the same distance apart as the eyes, we gain another dimension. Provided that the left eye sees only the left picture, and the right eye the right picture, both images are merged by the brain and every object in the print assumes its original three dimensional shape. The picture, in fact, acquires an impression of depth. Closing one eye will cause this third dimension to disappear and the image returns to that of an ordinary flat photograph.

The Basic Principle

Exactly the same principle can be applied to our faculty of hearing, and the successful operation of stereophonic sound is based on the fact that we can hear with both ears. When a particular sound is heard, each ear hears basically the same sound wave but at a slightly different time. It is mainly this time difference which enables us to appreciate and sense the direction from which the sound came. Cover one ear, and our sense of direction is lost.

Our directional capabilities also vary according to the frequency of the sound, and the lower frequencies of the audible spectrum contribute nothing at all to stereophonic appreciation. This is because the human head itself determines the frequency at which the sense of direction diminishes, caused by the actual distance apart of one's ears. This distance averages from $6\frac{1}{2}$ to 7 inches (16·25 to 17·5 cm), which is exactly half the wavelength of frequencies in the region of 800 Hz to 1 kHz. Sounds reaching the ears will vary little in time difference at frequencies below 1 kHz since their wavelength will be greater than 7 inches (17·5 cm). It is therefore the difference in phasing of signals arriving at each ear which becomes progressively noticeable as the frequency is lowered.

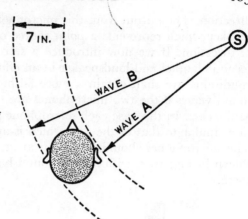

Fig. 10.1. Diagram explaining sense of direction.

At signal frequencies above 1 kHz the time and amplitude differences become predominant, causing our sense of direction to become alerted (Fig. 10.1). When sound waves from a particular source S reach our ears, wave A is heard at a fraction of a second before wave B, also slightly louder due to the shape of the head. This intensity difference is only about 3 db at 1 kHz, but at 10 kHz it is nearer 30 db if a sound of this frequency is directed at one ear. We can then immediately turn our head to the left or right and face the source of sound; the result being that each ear will then receive the same intensity and phasing of sound waves at all frequencies.

When an orchestra is playing, sound vibrations are radiated in all directions over a fairly wide area. In order to record a satisfactory pattern of these vibrations it would be necessary to have a large number of microphones, equally spaced both horizontally and vertically. Each microphone would have to be connected to a separate recording channel. Such a system is theoretically an ideal one, and would faithfully capture a complete wall of sound waves. If loudspeakers were placed in the positions occupied by these microphones, the same wall of sound could be reproduced with all the directional characteristics of the original. In practice it has been found that only two channels are really needed to create a good stereophonic effect in a practical manner, although more than two microphones are often employed.

Consider the case of a single microphone feeding into a single channel. The microphone will respond to all sounds occurring within its sensitive area, as shown by its polar distribution, without any discrimination as to direction. The output from this microphone is heard over a single loud-speaker which represents a point source of sound, again giving no sense of direction. If we now introduce a second microphone feeding into a second channel and loudspeaker in an effort to simulate normal listening conditions, we shall obtain a more faithful reproduction of the original sound waves if the two microphones are spaced the same distance apart as the ears. In this case each microphone should possess a polar distribution similar to that of the ear, which is approximately omni-directional. The microphones should be set up at an angle of 90° to each other as shown in Fig. 10.2, with a small sound baffle or acoustic screen between them.

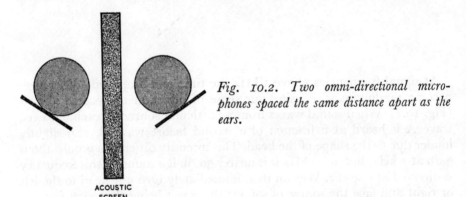

ACOUSTIC
SCREEN

Fig. 10.2. Two omni-directional microphones spaced the same distance apart as the ears.

The outputs from each microphone must be kept entirely separate, and the ideal listening condition for a true *binaural* effect is to wear head-phones. The general impression of stereo is at its maximum when the output from the left-hand microphone is heard only by the left ear, and the output from the right-hand microphone by the right ear. Although headphones give an excellent sense of direction they do not provide a satisfactory method of listening over long periods of time, even with light-weight moving coil headphones. It is also disconcerting to have the apparent sound source move as the head is turned. Therefore stereo sound is usually judged by listening to a pair of high fidelity loudspeakers, which means that the output from both channels will be heard by both ears without the complete separation that is possible with headphones.

So we arrive at the basic requirements for the recording and re-production of stereophonic sound, which consist mainly of two separate mono channels (Fig. 10.3). Each channel must be identical in amplification and frequency response, since any discrepancy between channels can

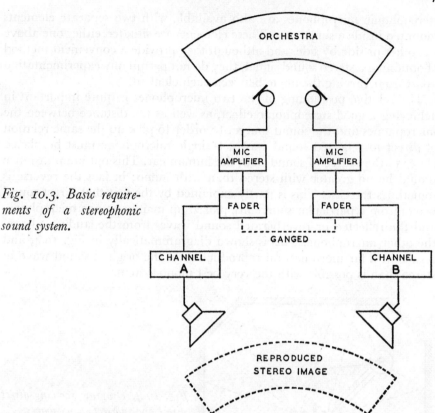

*Fig. 10.3. Basic require-
ments of a stereophonic
sound system.*

have a marked influence on the stereo effect. An important point is the use
of a ganged fader, which ensures that the signal amplitude passing through
each channel bears the same relationship to the signal amplitude reaching
each microphone. It is thought in some circles that a reduction in frequency range and signal-to-noise ratio can be tolerated in stereo without
any detrimental effect. This is only true in cases where expenditure is
limited, and to achieve the best possible realism the full frequency range
is required from every item of equipment, as well as the best signal-to-
noise ratio.

Stereophonic Microphone Techniques
Almost any type of microphone can be used for stereophonic recording,
although the polar distributions of the various types must be taken into
account before deciding on any particular arrangement. Numerous

stereophonic microphones are also available with two separate elements mounted inside a single case. These elements are situated either one above the other or side by side, and although they provide a convenient method of obtaining a stereo sound signal, they do not permit any experimentation apart from varying the angle between each element.

The relative positioning of the two microphones is quite important in achieving a good stereophonic effect, as well as the distance between the microphones and the sound source. In order to pick up the same relation of direct to reflected sound waves, a single microphone must be placed closer to the source of sound than the human ear. This optimum distance should be no greater with stereo than with mono; in fact the reverse is sometimes the case. This is partly explained by the fact that direct sound waves from a particular source are picked up mainly on one microphone, and the reflected or reverberated sound waves from the studio walls on the other microphone. This is shown diagrammatically in Fig. 10.4, and results in a far more natural reproduction of the original sound wave in stereo than is possible with the very best mono system.

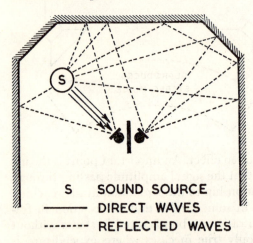

Fig. 10.4. Diagram showing direct direct and indirect sound waves.

S   SOUND SOURCE
——— DIRECT WAVES
------- REFLECTED WAVES

There are three basic techniques of microphone placement used for stereophonic recording. They are known as:

    1. The coincident microphone pair.
    2. The sum and difference method.
    3. The spaced microphone technique.

All of these arrangements will give a good stereophonic effect, although there is a considerable difference in the method of working with each one, as well as in the results obtained.

Coincident Microphone Pair

This is the method normally employed when a faithful recording of the original sound is required, as heard by an observer in the studio or at a concert. For music recording this means that the orchestra must be correctly balanced internally, so that the result from one pair of microphones will sound approximately the same as it does to the orchestra conductor. A *coincident microphone pair* implies that both microphones are placed as close together as possible, and directed to the left and right of a centre line between them and the orchestra. Under these conditions there is little difference in the time taken for a particular sound to reach both microphones, but there will be an intensity difference which results in two different amplitudes being passed on to the separate amplifier systems in the two recording channels.

It is therefore obvious that the outputs obtained from the left-hand and right-hand microphones used in a coincident system will depend on their directivity, as shown by their polar distribution. So to obtain the maximum amount of directivity, and channel separation, a pair of bi-directional ribbon microphones can be used close together at an angle of 90° to each other. This will still give a good frontal coverage across a fairly wide area with little overlapping, and the resulting polar diagram is shown in Fig. 10.5. The output from the microphone facing left is designated the A signal, and from the microphone facing right the B signal. This

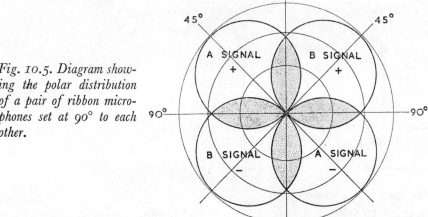

Fig. 10.5. Diagram showing the polar distribution of a pair of ribbon microphones set at 90° to each other.

terminology is used instead of L (left) and R (right) to avoid confusion due to language problems in other countries.

Referring to Fig. 10.5 it will be seen that all signals occurring in front of the two microphones will be in phase, and so will signals occurring at the rear of the microphones below the 90° axis. But care must be taken in a reverberant studio to avoid too many sound reflections reaching the rear of either microphone. Obviously any sound occurring to the left of the 0° axis will eventually be reproduced on the left-hand loudspeaker, and any sound occurring on the right of the axis on the right-hand loudspeaker. Therefore reverberation entering the rear of a microphone could be reproduced on the wrong channel. Furthermore neither direct or reverberated sound should be present near the 90° axis, since this represents an out of phase area between A and B channels. Sounds occurring in this area are apt to introduce phase distortion.

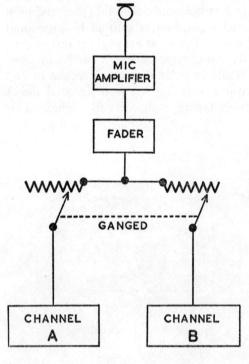

Fig. 10.6. Diagram illustrating the use of a panoramic potentiometer (pan-pot).

Panoramic Potentiometer

In order to achieve a satisfactory sound balance, it may be necessary to strengthen the volume obtained from a particular instrument, soloist, or section of an orchestra. This can be achieved by introducing a closer coincident microphone pair, placed on the same axis as the main pair to maintain correct positioning of instruments. When this is not practical, a single microphone can be used and its output fed into a network which divides the signal between A and B channels.

This network is called a *panoramic potentiometer*, normally referred to as a *pan-pot*, and it consists of a twin ganged fader (Fig. 10.6). One of the fader elements is wired in reverse, so that the signal fed into one channel is attenuated as the signal fed into the other channel is increased. By careful adjustment of the pan-pot the sound image from the single microphone can be superimposed over the main stereo image, the instrument or soloist being favoured retaining their correct position.

Sum and Difference Method

The *sum and difference* method is the result of a considerable amount of research into stereophony by the late A. D. Blumlein of the old Columbia Gramophone Company, and was the subject of a very important British Patent in 1930. This system is really a variant of the coincident method, and requires two microphones with different directional characteristics. For example an omni-directional dynamic microphone can be used together with a bi-directional ribbon, the ribbon facing sideways to the sound source and the dynamic straight ahead. Stereo signals are obtained by adding the outputs from each microphone for one channel, designated the M signal in international terminology, and subtracting the outputs from each microphone for the other channel, designated the S signal in international terminology. This arrangement has come to be known as the *M/S method*.

Condenser (capacitor) microphones are favoured for recording with the coincident system, for apart from their wide frequency range their directivity can be altered to suit the acoustics of the studio. This is achieved by altering the polarizing voltage, and is fully explained on page 96. Although two single condenser microphones can be placed side by side, it is sometimes more convenient to use a single stereo model with two condenser capsules contained in a common housing. The upper capsule is rotatable, and the polar response of each capsule can be varied through nine directional patterns. These include omni-directional, cardioid, bi-directional, and six other intermediate positions. The advantage of this flexibility becomes apparent when setting up for a recording session. Having adjusted the relative angle between the two capsules and approximately arranged the microphone distance, any further directivity adjustments can be made by remote switching on a directivity control box.

When recording sound sources covering a wide area, as in musical or choral works, the distance between the microphones and the performers has a marked effect on the apparent size of the sound source. If the microphone distance is too great, the *stereo image* of an orchestra will appear compressed and contain little stereo effect. On the other hand if the microphone distance is too small, the orchestra will appear to be spread out to the extent of being insufficiently covered. The correct position of a coincident microphone pair is found when the apparent width of the stereo image produces a satisfactory effect to the listener.

A refinement in stereophonic recording is a method of adjusting the width of the stereo image electrically by *cross-mixing*. This means feeding a portion of the A signal into the B channel, and vice versa, through a special width control circuit and attenuator. The result is an apparent reduction in the width scale, but by introducing a phase reversal the apparent width can be increased. Although such a control is useful, the effect is not as satisfactory as when the microphones are correctly positioned to obtain the desired width.

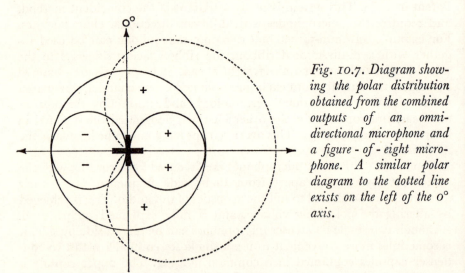

Fig. 10.7. Diagram showing the polar distribution obtained from the combined outputs of an omnidirectional microphone and a figure - of - eight microphone. A similar polar diagram to the dotted line exists on the left of the 0° axis.

The polar distribution obtained from these two microphones is shown by the diagram in Fig. 10.7, the dotted line representing the addition of the two polar curves. This indicates the sensitive area of sound being fed into one channel. A similar polar distribution is obtained on the left of the 0° axis by subtracting the two polar curves, and the result fed into the second channel. Professional practice is to use a pair of high grade condenser microphones with variable directional characteristics. One of the microphone capsules is adjusted to produce the familiar figure-of-eight pattern, and the other capsule is adjusted to give a cardioid characteristic. This combination reduces considerably the amount of reverberation from behind the microphones, as illustrated in Fig. 10.8, and enables a cleaner signal to be fed into both sum and difference channels.

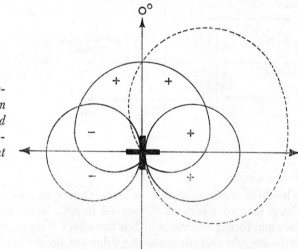

Fig. 10.8. Diagram showing the polar distribution obtained from the combined outputs of a cardioid microphone and a figure-of-eight microphone.

The actual sum and difference signals (which are out of phase with each other) must be produced electrically. In professional equipment they are usually obtained with two sum and difference transformers, which are *hybrid transformers*, each having one primary winding and two secondary windings. A primary winding is connected across each microphone line, and the four secondary windings are connected in pairs. One pair are wired in series to produce the sum signal, and the other pair are wired in series but out of phase to produce the difference signal. Another cheaper method is to use an amplifier with a valve or transistor stage to provide the necessary phase inversion between anode and cathode (collector and emitter) circuits. The addition of the in-phase (sum) and out-of-phase (difference) signals is then accomplished by a resistive network. The accuracy of this system depends on equal amplification of the two microphone signals. A simplified combining circuit which uses only a single transformer is shown in Fig. 10.9, with a phase reversal in the secondary windings producing the sum and difference signals.

Another point to be remembered is that if a single microphone is used with the M/S method, contributing an additional signal through a pan-pot, the output fed into each channel must be correctly phased with the main signal to avoid any unpleasant side effects.

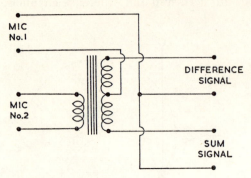

Fig. 10.9. *Circuit showing a single transformer used to obtain sum and difference signals.*

Width Control

The M/S method enables a large degree of control to be exercised over the apparent width of the stereo image. Reducing the output from the forward facing microphone has the effect of increasing the width scale, and reducing the output from the sideways facing microphone will make the sound appear across a narrower front. A certain amount of width control can also be introduced by varying the directional characteristic of the forward facing microphone.

Since the microphone with the figure-of-eight characteristic is facing sideways to the sound source, it is obvious that the signal picked up by this microphone will contain more than its share of the total amount of reverberation. Since the S channel obtains more of its signal from this microphone than the other, any attenuation in its output will therefore affect the amount of reverberation present in the overall stereophonic signal.

The sum and difference circuits previously mentioned form an admirable method of width control, with an attenuator in each circuit ganged in opposite sense. This arrangement gives a smooth control over the width scale from almost a point source to a wider than normal stereo image, and can be used in any stereo channel even when microphones are arranged as a coincident pair. Under these circumstances we are dealing with signals originating from A and B channels, not the M/S method, so another set of transformers is required after the width control to reconstitute the A and B channel information.

Spaced Microphone Technique

The third form of microphone placement is known as the *spaced microphone technique*, and employs a pair of omni-directional or cardioid microphones spaced several feet apart. This method is based on early experiments by the Bell Telephone Laboratories in America, and although it permits a good separation to be achieved between the two channels, the results are not always so clearly defined as those obtained from the previous two methods. The stereo effect with spaced microphones is obtained by a time difference between the two channels, and this difference is often sufficient to alter the phase by 180° on each channel of two sound waves from the same sound source. This can cause partial cancellation of sound to the listener, and total cancellation when attempting to combine the two stereo signals to obtain a compatible mono signal.

Another peculiarity of this technique is that sounds occurring near the centre between the two microphones appear to become suppressed or

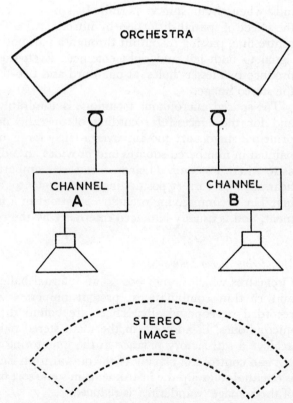

Fig. 10.10. Diagram showing the spaced microphone technique.

further away than sounds occurring at the sides, or directly in front of each microphone. Consequently if a moving sound is recorded, its distance from the microphones apparently increases about the centre line. This is technically called *spatial distortion*, although it is rather better known as the 'hole in the middle' effect. Spatial distortion can obviously be reduced by placing the microphones closer together, but this results in a reduction of the width of the stereo image and could amount to insufficient coverage at the extreme sides.

When using cardioid microphones an alternative position can be tried with both microphones facing inwards towards each other. The left-hand microphone is then connected to the right-hand channel, and the right-hand microphone to the left-hand channel. This results in a considerably improved sensitivity to sounds occurring within the central area. The main disadvantage is that sounds occurring too close to either microphone will be recorded on the wrong channel and appear misplaced on the stereo image. Therefore this crossed over arrangement can only be used successfully when circumstances permit. It is better recording practice to offset the effect of spatial distortion by introducing a third microphone on the centre line, passing its output through a pan-pot which delivers an equal signal to both left and right channels. Even this arrangement tends to produce two lesser 'holes' at one-third and two-thirds across the width of the stereo image.

The spaced microphone technique is admirably suited for large choirs, and for the successful recording of operatic performances where the principal singers are moving over a fairly large area. The floor is usually painted in numbered squares and provides an indication to the principals as to where to stand. Their own music is similarly numbered during rehearsals, and correct positioning is subsequently achieved during recording. The accompanying orchestra is set out in a normal concert arrangement, and is usually balanced internally by the conductor.

Wandering Stereo Image

Orchestras which do not possess an internal balance, such as pop groups and rhythm combinations, present numerous difficulties when being recorded stereophonically. There are bound to be a number of single microphones, in addition to the main stereo pair (if used), in order to achieve a satisfactory balance in the monitoring room. Although a pan-pot can control the placing of the output from each single microphone, it is essential to group the instruments in some sort of order so that the effect of their image 'wandering' is reduced.

This wandering is caused when the position of an instrument is placed by a pan-pot, and the same instrument is also heard over an adjacent microphone which is 'placed' somewhere else in the stereo image. Any alteration to the setting of the volume control faders on these microphones will cause the instrument to 'wander' in a disturbing and uncanny fashion. It is always better recording practice to place each instrument in the studio so that it is already situated in the position it will occupy in the final result.

Recording Equipment

The basic requirements for stereo recording are a matched pair of microphones, amplifiers, recorders, and monitoring loudspeakers, together with a mixing console for accurately balancing the signal to be recorded on each channel. Since the stereophonic effect relies on phase differences as well as amplitude differences between the two channels, particular attention must be given to prevent phase reversals when connecting all items of equipment. This is essential if the left-hand and right-hand channels are to record and reproduce the original sound waveforms in their correct phase relationship.

To indicate the polarity of microphones, cables, channel wiring, and loudspeakers, a system of colour coding is normally employed for all leads. However to ascertain that true polarity is always being maintained it is expedient to use a polarity tester such as the EMT type 160 unit. This battery operated device consists of a sender which injects an acoustical or an electrical pulse into any item of equipment, and a separate indicator with a phase sensitive circuit which shows polarity by means of a red or green light. Even microphones which have been rigged and are not very accessible can be reliably tested for polarity, which means that a final check can be made immediately before a recording session when all cable runs have been completed.

When testing the phase of loudspeakers a pre-amplifier is necessary to increase the sensitivity of the indicator by approximately 50 db. An accessory amplifier containing a built-in microphone is available for this purpose.

Another problem of equal importance to phase relationships is the need to ensure that *crosstalk* between channels is kept to a sufficiently low value. Crosstalk means the leakage of one channel into the other, and vice versa, causing a reduction of the stereophonic effect. Crosstalk which is independent of frequency, and is in phase with the main signal, causes a narrowing of the width of the stereo image. Crosstalk which increases with frequency tends to reduce definition and cause a blurr of the stereo image.

This blurring is due to the numerous frequency components of a particular sound not being recorded and reproduced in their true position, and can create a 'wandering' effect to a sound which is known to be fixed.

The usual causes of crosstalk can be traced to capacitive coupling between the leads or wiring of the two channels, so that care should be taken to ensure that long parallel cable runs are avoided. Other sources of trouble exist in disc and tape recorders due to coupling between the two channels of a stereo cutter head and a stereo record head. With disc recorders it is impossible to design a mechanical stylus suspension which is completely isolated, since the single stylus must respond to signals from both channels. Under these conditions a crosstalk figure of 30 db is considered a good separation. The stacked heads of a stereo tape recorder cause mutual induction due to the close proximity of the two coils, but by careful screening the channel separation can be kept as low as 50 db to 55 db.

All professional stereophonic recordings are originally made on magnetic tape, the transfer to disc and 'pre-recorded' tapes being carried out at a later date. Equipment used to record the 'master' tape must have superior electronic and mechanical specifications, since these tapes may have to be re-recorded several times before they finally appear as a stereo disc. The normal tape speed used is 15 i.p.s. (38 cms per second), and the timing accuracy between recorders is ± 2 seconds after 15 minutes running. The overall frequency response extends from 30 Hz to 18 kHz (± 2 db), with a signal-to-noise ratio of approximately 60 db.

Professional recorders always incorporate separate record and replay heads on each channel, permitting the choice of direct or tape monitoring on each track. The record and replay heads are vertically stacked in two mu-metal cases, their gaps accurately aligned to prevent phase displacement between channels, and the complete head assemblies potted in resin to eliminate any movement of the head components. To reduce crosstalk the individual heads are screened between each track, and additional screens fall into place across the front of the heads when a hinged section of the tape channel is closed.

A single oscillator supplies the record bias and erase current for all channels, and is generally tuned to a frequency well outside the audible range—normally 100 kHz. The master oscillator itself has a comparatively low output, and this is amplified by slave units in each channel. The idea behind using a single oscillator is to eliminate all possibility of beat frequencies or combination tones occurring between channels, as might happen if separate oscillators were employed which were only closely tuned.

Magnetic Reduction Transfers

Although stereophonic discs and tapes possess only two separate tracks for reproduction over two channels, it is quite possible that the original master tapes were recorded on several mono channels. Not all master recordings are made on $\frac{1}{4}$ inch tape, and both 1 inch and 2 inch (25 mm and 50 mm) tape recorders are commonly used. The current practice is to record either 8 or 16 tracks across 1 inch or 2 inch tape, with various sections of the orchestra (and vocalists) on separate tracks. Nearly all studios re-balance the orchestra *after* a session, and spend some considerable time making an 8 to 2 or 16 to 2 magnetic reduction by a transfer process. In this way reverberation and extra equalization can be added to the final master stereo tape, and the vocalists' track controlled separately to achieve the best results. The 'hole in the middle' effect can also be substantially eliminated by feeding all mono tracks into pan-pots during the reduction process.

There is limitless opportunity for experimenting, and if the first mixed master is not satisfactory it can be re-recorded again from the multi-channel master as many times as is necessary. The reduction process permits special effects such as the introduction of a tape echo, or a sound-on-sound technique called *Sel-Sync*. This feature permits any single record head or a combination of record heads to be converted into temporary replay heads whilst recording continues on the remaining tracks. Using this system a soloist may be recorded in sync with what has previously been recorded on other tracks, and even accompany himself. Magnetic reduction will then provide a composite stereo master, or even a mono master if required.

Magnetic reductions are usually carried out in a special transfer suite, with a mixing console containing reverberation facilities, filter units, and quadrant or linear faders. Each fader is fitted with a phase reversing switch, so that any material which will not combine without phase distortion can be quickly checked with the switch in either position. Only when the final mixed master tape has been prepared and checked is the material ready to be transferred on to an acetate lacquer disc or stereo copy tape.

Stereophonic Listening Conditions

The only accurate method of listening to stereophonic sound is to ensure that the sound being reproduced by the left or A channel is heard only by the left ear, and sound being reproduced by the right or B channel is heard only by the right ear. This means wearing headphones to obtain the necessary separation, which is not a very practical proposition over long periods of time. Furthermore headphones render the listener incapable of turning his head to localize the direction of any particular sound.

It is therefore usual to listen to stereophonic sound over a pair of carefully positioned loudspeakers. These should be a matched pair in every respect if the sound quality of the *stereo image* is to be maintained from one side to the other. We have already learnt that the location of sound is appreciated by means of time and amplitude differences between each ear, and these same differences must be reproduced from each loudspeaker if the stereo sound is to be clearly defined.

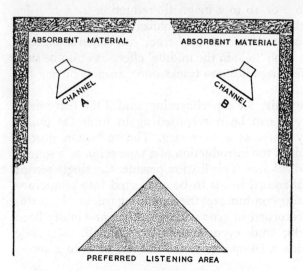

ABSORBENT MATERIAL   ABSORBENT MATERIAL

CHANNEL A   CHANNEL B

PREFERRED LISTENING AREA

Fig. 10.11. Diagram showing preferred stereophonic listening conditions.

In studio monitoring rooms a separate loudspeaker and monitor amplifier is used for each channel, although occasionally with 8-channel recording only 4 loudspeakers are used, 2 channels being fed into each. All monitors are accurately balanced for overall gain and frequency response, and the loudspeakers themselves correctly phased so that their cones move in the same direction for a particular sound. An EMT polarity tester is the quickest method of checking phase, although another method is to feed a signal of low frequency into all channels. An out-of-phase condition will immediately become audible due to a partial cancellation.

In order to appreciate fully the directional information being recorded by each channel, it is desirable for the direct sound waves reproduced by each loudspeaker to be directed at each ear. This is not always possible with a large installation, and the best position for each loudspeaker must be found by trial and error. If they are spaced too far apart there is the danger of creating a 'hole in the middle' effect; if they are spaced too close together the width of the *stereo image* will appear rather small. There is an optimum position for every room.

The same conditions apply to loudspeaker placing in the home. In the average sized room the two loudspeakers should be spaced 6 ft. or 8 ft. (2 m or $2\frac{1}{2}$ m) apart to achieve a satisfactory effect. The optimum listening distance will then be about 9 ft. (3 m) away, although it is essential to experiment before arriving at any conclusions. In a very small room the spacing between each loudspeaker may be only 3 ft. 6 in. (1 m), or up to 13 ft. (4 m) in a room 33 ft. (10 m) in length. The point here is that there is an optimum listening position which varies in distance with each loudspeaker spacing.

When listening to a mono channel with a single loudspeaker system, a little reverberation in the monitor room will pass un-noticed. However with stereophonic monitoring it is essential to cover any large areas of reflecting surfaces with curtaining or some other absorbent material, so that each loudspeaker can operate under rather 'dead' conditions. This will prevent reflected sound waves being generated near the loudspeakers and confusing the *stereo image* which is being created. It is not necessary to carry this damping to extremes, and Fig. 10.11 shows all that is required.

In order to generate a strong, direct sound wave at all frequencies, it is essential to use loudspeakers with forward facing cones, each loudspeaker angled in slightly to face the listener. Complete stereophonic coverage is seldom achieved over a large room, and a preferred listening area is formed which is roughly triangular in shape. The apex of this triangle is situated at a point between the two loudspeakers, at a distance corresponding to their distance apart. Listeners outside the preferred listening area will not be able to hear the same stereo image, due to the angle between them and each loudspeaker.

The stereo effect becomes more noticeable with sounds of middle and high frequencies, since it is a common feature of all moving coil type loudspeakers that high frequencies tend to be radiated along a narrow beam in line with the loudspeaker cone. This indicates that the listening position which gives the maximum fidelity and directional information is confined to the point of convergence of each loudspeaker axis: therefore it is at this point in the monitoring room that the recording engineer should sit whilst controlling the width and balance of the *stereo image*.

Another loudspeaker arrangement, found on domestic reproducers where space and cost are the deciding factors, relies on the fact that the ear finds it increasingly difficult to obtain stereo information at low frequencies. It is not unknown to use a single bass unit situated in the centre and fed from both channels, with two high frequency units placed one on either side and fed from each channel separately. The stereo effect is quite marked.

Stereophonic Broadcasts

Although English stereophonic broadcasts by the B.B.C. are limited in transmission time, they may nevertheless become a subject to be tackled by the recording engineer, so it is worth noting how stereophony is achieved. Briefly, transmissions of signals from both A and B channels are made with a single frequency modulated transmitter, using a frequency division multiplex system. The two sets of channel information are switched by a 19 kHz sub-carrier to modulate the main transmitter, and the stereo information is decoded at the receiving end by means of a multiplex circuit or multiplex adaptor. This ensures that the whole of the output from the tuner is passed to the loudspeaker for which it is intended.

Before attempting to record a stereophonic broadcast it is necessary to fit a low pass filter to remove the 19 kHz carrier frequency, and any higher harmonics, which might cause distortion and the generation of spurious combination tones. These can become audible as high pitched whistles due to interaction between the carrier frequency and the frequency of the h.f. bias on magnetic tape recorders. Low pass filters are already fitted to the better grade of f.m. tuner units, and also to certain magnetic recorders.

Any f.m. tuner without a decoding circuit will receive a stereo broadcast satisfactorily, but it will reproduce the signal in compatible mono. Similarly many f.m. tuner units can be fitted with an external decoder when it is desired to reproduce a stereophonic signal.

Quadrasonics

This is the term used to describe the newer four channel sound, which is an extension of the normal two channel stereo system. Quadrasonics require four sound sources which are fed through four amplifying systems into four loudspeakers. These four loudspeakers are normally placed in the four corners of the listening room, the usual stereo pair in front of the listener and an additional stereo pair behind. This provides a solid sound surrounding the listener, and in its purest form enables a more accurate simulation of concert hall conditions. At a live concert there is always some reflected sound waves coming back from the walls of the auditorium, which have phase and time delays in comparison to the direct signal and constitute reverberation. Quadrasonics enable this reverberation to be reproduced in its natural perspective, merely by placing an additional pair of microphones at the rear of the auditorium where the recording is to be made, and recording two extra tracks.

Existing studio equipment of 4 track, 8 track, 16 track, and 24 track recorders are admirably suited for quadrasonics, and the majority of tape masters today are recorded with this in mind. Naturally the presence of four channels enables numerous musical gimmicks to be performed, including the multiple 'panning' of static sounds. Mixing consoles designed for quadrasonics contain pan-pots with joy-stick controls, which permit mono sounds to be located at any point within the listening area, either between any two of the four loudspeakers or even where the listener himself is seated.

Quadrasonics are as great an advance over stereo as stereo was over mono, although pre-recorded material is currently available only on tape. The 8 tape track cartridge of the endless loop variety (see page 61) is the ideal method of packaging, since it will provide two four channel programmes with interleaved tracks. Quadrasonics will no doubt make their appearance on discs, and FM stereophonic broadcasts will be available on four channels.

CHAPTER XI

Motion Picture Sound

RECORDING SOUND for motion pictures is a specialized occupation, restricted to a small number of professional engineers normally associated with either the film or television industries. The production methods are slightly different for the two media, although the end product is virtually the same. Since this manual is not primarily concerned with television practices, the author intends to concentrate on sound recording for films, and on sound reproduction to large audiences.

Double Film System

The most important factor governing motion picture sound is the need for synchronization, since both sound and picture records must match each other exactly. Whenever possible sound is recorded on a separate piece of film from the picture as this permits the two to be independently edited. This is called the *double film system*, a technique which is practised by all professionals making 35-mm and 16-mm films. Separate recording of sound allows the editor to cut picture or sound wherever he wishes, making it possible to speed up the action by discarding footage or to slow it down by inserting extra material in either picture or sound track. It also makes it much easier to mix the sound recorded with picture with other sounds later, such as background music or effects. To indicate that the sound recording is separate from the picture the term *sep-mag* is used, an abbreviation of *separate magnetic*.

In order to maintain synchronism between picture and sound, motion picture recordings are made whenever possible on magnetic film as distinct from magnetic tape. Magnetic film consists of a normal film base of the same dimensions as camera film, perforated in the same way, but instead of being coated with photographic emulsion it is coated with iron oxide similar to that used on recording tape. Films shot on 35-mm film have sound recorded on 35-mm magnetic film, films shot on 16-mm have sound recorded on 16-mm magnetic film. Since picture and sound have the same physical characteristics and perforations it is possible to run the two in synchronism mechanically. In fact, there is one additional gauge of magnetic film, 17·5-mm, half the width of 35-mm and perforated to 35-mm standards down one edge only. It is normally run at the speed of 45 feet per minute and is used for recording with 35-mm picture film, its advantage being a considerable reduction in bulk. The picture camera and sound recorder are driven by separate motors from a three-phase mains supply, which gives the machines an electrical interlock and ensures that they run at exactly 24 frames per second.

Although the use of perforated magnetic film has many advantages for film work and is used for all stages of editing, mixing and the production of release prints, recorders using magnetic film tend to be large and bulky. With the development of small and extremely portable transistorized battery driven tape recorders, film producers have concentrated on quarter inch tape for making all original recordings. To solve the problem of synchronizing these recordings with picture a pulse, generated by the camera, is recorded on the same tape as the audio signal (see page 258). This pulse enables the selected sound takes to be subsequently transferred to 35-mm or 16-mm magnetic film, in synchronization with picture, for editing and mixing purposes.

Original magnetic recordings are treated as master rolls and kept in the recording department. The working copy used by the editor is usually a re-recording or *transfer* of the original, which is a safeguard against accidental damage to valuable recorded material. Further transfers can always be made as required, and the master rolls retained in good condition. They will eventually be bulk-erased and used over again. During the preparation of a final composite sound track, the first transfer may have to be re-recorded into a third, or even a fourth generation. Because of this continual re-recording, the transfer equipment must have a flat frequency response and a good signal-to-noise ratio.

Single Film System

An alternative method of synchronized recording is the *single film system*, where both sound and picture are photographed and recorded on a single roll of film in a special combined camera. This system is particularly suited for newsreel work and television interviews, where there is no requirement for complicated editing. At one time it was essential to use an optical sound track with single system cameras, which was known as a *com-opt* track, an abbreviation of *combined optical*, indicating that both the picture and optical track were on the same piece of film. Now that a magnetic band, or *stripe* as it is called, can be placed alongside the picture area on motion picture film it is possible to combine magnetic recordings on the same film as the visuals to which they relate. In this case the sound is known as a *com-mag* track, meaning *combined magnetic*. Cameras that record the sound on the same film as the picture are known as single system cameras, whether the result is an optical or a magnetic track. However, optical tracks for original recordings are very seldom used today.

Single system cameras have built-in magnetic record heads situated between the picture gate and the take-up sprocket. Sound is always recorded at a point ahead of the picture gate, meaning that the sound is not located alongside the picture frame to which is relates (see page 212). After development of the picture, an immediate synchronized playback is available for Telecine or other purposes.

Before the days of magnetic recording, all sound had to be recorded photographically using an *optical recording camera*, loaded with a special fine grain positive emulsion of high speed. This was developed to obtain a sound negative, and a print was delivered to the cutting rooms together with the corresponding picture print. Photographic or *optical sound tracks* are limited today to 35-mm release prints for exhibition in cinemas, for television, or prints on 16 mm for use in education, industry, television, clubs and the home. Prints for all these purposes have the sound printed on the same reel of film as the picture. Nowadays initial recording is carried out on magnetic tracks which are subsequently transferred, after all the stages of editing and mixing have been completed, on to an optical track by a studio or laboratory. The operation is described on page 213.

Compiling a Film Sound Track

Before detailing the recording equipment used in a film studio, it would seem preferable to describe the general requirements of a film sound track, and the part that the sound recording engineer has to play. The sound track commences with the actual material which is recorded at the time of shooting the picture, which will subsequently be referred to as the *sync track*. Each scene or take may last only a few seconds, and sequences are built up in the editing process as the film progresses. In a feature film the sync track will consist mainly of dialogue between the various artistes, although instructions from the director are occasionally heard and will have to be removed eventually.

It is imperative that the sync track is as good as possible, and scenes containing a lot of action and dialogue are often filmed several times to obtain a first class 'take'. Recording dialogue is not easy and straightforward, as consistently good results are expected and must be maintained. Conditions in a film studio do not favour the sound recordist, since it is not always possible to place the microphone in an ideal position because it must not be seen by the camera, nor must it throw shadows on to the picture area. The performance of some artistes can also be seriously affected if their attention is drawn to technical matters, apart from the fact that to repeat a certain scene might be an expensive proposition, or even impossible.

Film making is no longer confined to a studio, and it is common practice to transport artistes and film unit to the actual scene or locale demanded by the script. This involves travelling abroad with portable equipment, and recording out of doors where conditions for the sound engineer are far from ideal. There are often extraneous noises to contend with such as the sound of wind, traffic, onlookers, or even aeroplanes. The cameraman may be using a noisy generator for additional lighting, which cannot be sited far enough away from the microphone. Under such conditions the dialogue recording may not be of sufficient quality or intelligibility to warrant its inclusion in the final sync track. Such material is called a *guide track*, and is announced as such at the beginning of every take. This track is subsequently used as a guide for replacing the dialogue with a new recording, made under studio conditions.

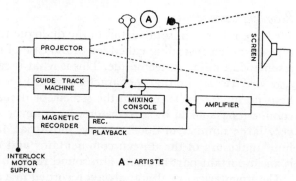

Fig. 11.1. Diagram showing the equipment necessary for the post-synchronization of dialogue.

Post-Synchronization

When the sync track has been edited it will contain dialogue which has been recorded in a variety of sets and locations. Material which is not acceptable will be replaced by a system known as *post-synchronization*. The scene containing the dialogue which is to be re-recorded is broken down into a number of sections which are then formed into loops, each loop of picture being exactly the same length as its corresponding loop of guide track, and containing not more than one or two sentences.

A simplified diagram showing the equipment necessary for post-synchronization is seen in Fig. 11.1. The picture is projected on to a screen in a small theatre, and the sound from the guide track is replayed over a loudspeaker. The artiste stands facing the screen and repeats the dialogue, at the same time copying his or her lip movements. The guide track is then switched from the loudspeaker to a pair of headphones worn by the artiste, or sometimes a single headphone, and the dialogue is recorded afresh via a correctly placed microphone. This new recording is made on a loop of 35 mm magnetic film, threaded on a recording machine with a special *loop bin*. As the loop goes round the previous recording is erased as each new one is made. When the recordist is satisfied that a good recording has been achieved, he operates a *check key* which switches off the erase head and allows the new recording to be replayed over the loudspeaker.

At the end of the session the freshly recorded magnetic loops are taken away for cutting into their correct positions in the sync track, replacing the original guide track which is then discarded. As a safety measure a magnetic transfer is made of all loops before editing commences, and this transfer is held as a master recording in case of accidents. Some studios prefer to run a quarter-inch tape recorder continuously during the post-sync session, in addition to the loop machine, so that the entire performance of each artiste is retained.

Recording Commentaries

We have referred in some detail to the dialogue track but there is another type of speech recording called for in the case of many films that requires a somewhat different technique. This is what is called *off screen narration* or *voice over*. It may be that a character is heard speaking his thoughts while he is no longer to be seen on the screen, or it may be a straightforward commentary spoken by a narrator who is never seen by the audience. A very large number of documentary, industrial, factual and instructional films make use of the unseen commentator and recording commentaries is an important part of many film sound recordists work.

Commentaries are almost always recorded in a studio, the commentator being placed in a commentator's booth or small recording room that has been treated acoustically. It is usual for the commentator to speak the narration while the picture is projected on to a small screen that is within his line of vision. However, it is preferable that he does not have to take his timing from the picture unaided. This would tend to distract him and make it difficult for him to concentrate on putting the most natural intonation into his voice. Very often he is cued by a producer who takes his cues from the screen or from a footage indicator just below the screen.

The placing of the microphone for commentary work is critical (see page 236) and it is important to rehearse the first paragraph or two, at the very least, to obtain the best setting of the controls both as regards input volume and compensation to produce the most natural reproduction of the commentator's voice. Script rustle can be very troublesome and scripts should be typed on one side of the paper only and each page either clipped to a board or placed inside a cellophane envelope.

Commentaries are normally recorded on magnetic film, or on quarter inch tape which is later transferred to film. Tape is more economical as a recording medium, and only selected takes need be transferred. Any errors in timing can often be corrected during editing, so that it is not always necessary to insist on timing accuracy at the recording session.

Sound effects

Both commentary tracks and sync tracks require building up with sounds from other sources—sounds which were not able to be recorded at the time of shooting. These consist mainly of sound effects and music, which will be added to the sync track during a final re-recording process. The sound effects will include all the backgrounds which are necessary to establish a location, and which will run continuously over a number of picture cuts. These background sounds can later be controlled in volume and perspective, leaving the dialogue on the sync track to be clearly audible. Dialogue which has been post-synchronized will be devoid of all background effects, and these may have to be specially recorded.

In addition there will be a number of synchronized or *spot effects* required, such as footsteps, doors opening and closing, car tyre squeals, pistol shots, telephone bells, etc. Footsteps are usually recorded by a post-sync process since synchronization and the type of floor surface will be critical. Otherwise recourse is made to a sound effects library containing material on magnetic film or quarter-inch tape. Effects not already on film are transferred to this medium as required. All sound effects must be synchronized and fitted into their respective places throughout the picture, and joined up into further rolls of film to await the previously mentioned re-recording process. The magnetic film used may be 35 mm or 16 mm. If the film was shot on 35 mm picture film it is usual to use 35 mm magnetic film at this stage, if the film was shot on 16-mm the music and effects tracks would normally be transferred to 16 mm magnetic.

During editing, the magnetic tracks on each roll are separated by film spacing, which usually has a photographic emulsion on one side. It is essential that this emulsion is kept away from the magnetic heads on the replay machines, to prevent a build-up of *emulsion corns*. The spacing is inserted so that its base is in contact with the replay heads, in line with the magnetic coating. Both straight and diagonal butt joins are used, held together with a special adhesive tape, so that alterations can be quickly made without losing any frames.

Music Recording

Film music is recorded in a specially constructed *scoring stage*, similar in plan to the music studio shown in Fig. 9.2 on page 170. Provision is made for projecting sections of the picture for which music is to be scored on to a full sized screen facing the conductor. Film music is always specially composed and recorded, since it must often vary in mood and tempo at precise moments, as demanded by the action.

During rehearsals and recording the conductor will have the sync track available to him on a pair of headphones, so that he can secure an accurate timing of his music with the dialogue. He will have allowed for this in his score, and arranged his dynamics so that the music will not cloud the dialogue but rather harmonize with it, assuming his conducting is accurate. He has various devices available to assist him, including a projected counter showing minutes and seconds, a film loop of 'clicks' to maintain tempo, and cue marks called *streamers* drawn diagonally across the picture film at strategic points.

To maintain synchronization at all times, the projector and magnetic recorder motors are electrically interlocked. After a satisfactory recording of a music section has been made, it is usually played back immediately together with the sync track. Both music and dialogue are heard over a high quality loudspeaker system, either in the monitoring room or directly on the scoring stage. When all music sections have been recorded and approved, the chosen takes on the master rolls of 35 mm magnetic film are transferred to provide a working copy. These transfers are then joined into music rolls, equal in length to the already edited picture, sync track, and sound effects, ready for re-recording.

In practice the films that have specially composed music are feature films, the higher budget documentaries and advertising commercials. There are a large number of documentaries, instructional and educational productions as well as advertising films made to budgets that do not permit special music to be composed and recorded for them. In such cases the producers draw upon the wide range of *mood music* available from a number of publishing houses on quarter inch tape or discs. If a skilful selection of appropriate passages from a number of recordings is made a very good music track can be built up although it may not, of course, follow the changes of mood in the picture quite as closely as a specially composed score. The selected passages are transferred to 35 mm or 16 mm magnetic film in the same manner as the specially recorded music. Royalties are paid to the publishing companies for the music used.

Re-recording

So far the ingredients for the film sound track are contained on separate rolls of 35-mm (or 16-mm) magnetic film, synchronized with the picture film, and consist of dialogue (sync track), sound effects, and music. There will be more than one roll of dialogue and one roll of music, so that sounds for one scene can be faded out and the following scene faded in— or sometimes overlapped in a sound dissolve. Sound effects may occupy any number of rolls from one to twenty or more, depending on the complexity of the situation.

Each roll of sound is threaded on a separate reproducing machine, with a *start mark* opposite the magnetic replay head. These machines are arranged to run with an interlocked motor system so that all reproducers remain synchronized to the picture projector. The audio output from each replay amplifier is taken to an individual fader on a *re-recording console* in a special theatre, where the combining process is carried out by two or more engineers under conditions which simulate the acoustic conditions of an average cinema. This includes a monitor equalizer circuit which slopes off the high frequencies as shown in Fig. 11.2, as occurs in larger auditoria.

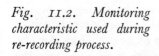
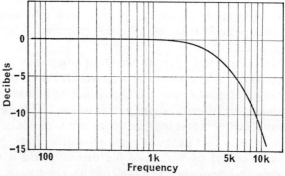

Fig. 11.2. Monitoring characteristic used during re-recording process.

To assist the engineers a special *cue sheet* is made out which indicates the nature and duration of all the sound tracks which have been laid for each roll of film, and also the exact footage within the roll at which each track occurs. Thus the progress of a reel can be followed in relating the footages on the cue sheet to those on an illuminated *footage counter* situated below the screen. Movement of the counter digits is controlled by a contact arrangement on the picture projector.

In addition to checking footages and watching the picture, frequency equalization will have to be made in order to match all the various sound tracks. Telephone simulators are frequently required for dialogue, and reverberation may have to be added in caves, churches, empty warehouses, etc. Background suppressors are also employed which automatically lower the level of the background between sections of dialogue, especially useful on exterior recordings. Band-stop filters may have to be switched in to remove narrow band interference from arc lamps, camera motor, or other high frequency sounds. It is also necessary to correct by ear for any frequency variations between the sync track and post-sync track.

Re-recording installations are now equipped with a reversible motor system, nicknamed *rock'n roll*, which enables the entire equipment to be run down in interlock and run backwards when required. This permits the repeated examination of a difficult section without having to unthread the projector and sound reproducers. When, after numerous rehearsals, the engineers have obtained a sound balance which is acceptable to the director, a take is made on a 35 mm or 16 mm magnetic recorder. If the take is not quite satisfactory, a new section can be inserted using the rock'n roll system and operating a record/replay switch at the appropriate times.

If the recording installation has been correctly aligned, it should be possible to record to playback sync, monitoring a signal from the replay head. This procedure requires the picture to be adjusted to coincide with the distance between the record head and the replay head, usually 2 frames retarded for 35 mm and 5 frames retarded for 16 mm on dual gauge recorders.

In the case of 35 mm films most companies retain the dialogue, music, and sound effects on three separate tracks recorded across a single roll of 35-mm magnetic film. This is done as a matter of convenience for the subsequent preparation of *foreign versions*. This operation only requires the music and effects tracks, to which is added a dialogue track in a language different to that of the original recording. Foreign version dialogue tracks are compiled by the post-sync method, and a new final sound track is made and despatched to the country concerned.

The 16-mm procedure is to mix the music and effects on to a separate magnetic track, known for short as an *M and E* track, the dialogue or commentary being retained on a separate track. Finally, these two tracks are mixed to produce what is known as the mixed master. Foreign versions can be produced at any time subsequently by mixing the M and E track with a new dialogue or commentary track recorded in the language required.

There now remains a transfer of the final three-track or single-track master from magnetic to optical, so that a sound negative is available for making *married prints* or *show copies*. There is a displacement of 20 frames on a 35 mm print, and 26 frames on a 16 mm print, between the frame of picture being projected and its corresponding frame of sound, the sound being ahead of picture. This is because the picture is projected with an intermittent motion, whilst the sound track must pass through the reproducer below the picture gate with an even and continuous motion. Therefore a loop of film exists between these two points.

Optical Sound Recording

To transfer magnetic sound into a photographic image, a special *optical recording camera* is necessary. Such a camera consists of a light-tight film magazine, a light-tight chamber containing the film transport mechanism, an exposure lamp, optical system, modulating device, and a synchronous driving motor. Two entirely different types of modulator are used, one producing a sound track of *variable area* and the other producing a sound track of *variable density*. Both types of track will reproduce equally well, although it has long been recognized that variable area is capable of giving greater sound volume.

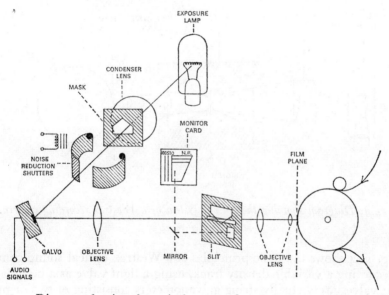

Fig. 11.3. Diagram showing the optical system of an R.C.A. recording camera.

Fig. 11.3 shows the general layout of an R.C.A. optical sound camera for recording a variable area track, using a mirror galvanometer as a modulator. Light from the exposure lamp is passed through a V-shaped mask and convex lens on to the mirror galvanometer. The shape of the mask is then reflected through a narrow horizontal slit, the image of which is focused on to the film through an objective lens system. Audio signals fed into the galvanometer windings cause the mask image to move vertically in front of the slit, and the result is a varying width of light falling on the film to produce a photographic trace of the audio signal waveform. To improve the signal-to-noise ratio of the system, a pair of mechanical shutters are fitted which close in outside the mask image when there is no audio signal. These shutters are biased from a special ground noise reduction amplifier, and lift out of the way at the commencement of an audio signal.

Instead of noise reduction shutters, some R.C.A. recorders employ a biased galvanometer. The bias voltage from the noise reduction amplifier is used to tilt the galvanometer so as to produce a very narrow bias line on the track. This line returns to its normal width when an audio signal appears and cancels the bias voltage.

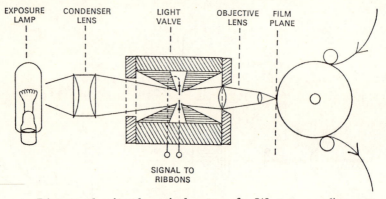

EXPOSURE LAMP   CONDENSER LENS   LIGHT VALVE   OBJECTIVE LENS   FILM PLANE

SIGNAL TO RIBBONS

Fig. 11.4. Diagram showing the optical system of a Westrex recording camera.

Fig. 11.4 shows the basic principles of a Westrex optical sound camera for recording a variable density track, using a light valve as a modulator. Light valves are virtually string galvanometers consisting of two or more metal ribbons, clamped under tension in a strong magnetic field. The passage of audio signals causes displacement of the ribbons, thus varying the intensity of the light falling on the film. The result is a varying exposure of constant width. If the ribbons are rotated through 90° so that they are vertical instead of horizontal, and a slit of fixed width is placed in front of them, movement of the ribbons will vary the width of the illumination on the fixed slit, which will produce a variable area track. Noise reduction is applied by biasing the ribbons so that they reduce the exposure on a density negative track and the width of an area negative track.

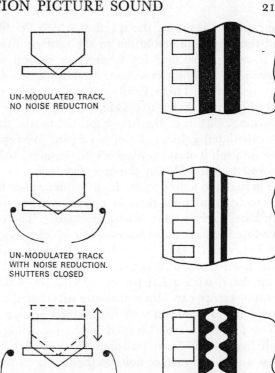

UN-MODULATED TRACK,
NO NOISE REDUCTION

Fig. 11.5. Diagram illustrating effect of noise reduction shutters on R.C.A. camera.

UN-MODULATED TRACK
WITH NOISE REDUCTION.
SHUTTERS CLOSED

MODULATED TRACK, SHUTTERS
SWUNG CLEAR.

Noise Reduction

The audio signal itself is used to control the noise reduction amplifier, the output of which is rectified and passed on to the modulator unit in the form of a d.c. bias. This bias is completely removed within 18 to 22 milliseconds after the commencement of an audio signal, and returns gradually after the cessation of any signal. Although this does not make any contribution to the overall signal-to-noise ratio of the system during modulation, it does offer a reduction of from 6 db to 10 db in background noise when there is no audio signal.

Frequency Response

Photographic sound tracks suffer from a restricted frequency response when compared with magnetic recording. The highest frequency which can be recorded on film is determined by the size of the slit through which the exposure is made, the speed at which the film is drawn past the slit, and the degree of resolution in the film emulsion. The speed is fixed at 24 frames per second (25 frames per second for British and European television), and film emulsions already possess fine grain properties with high resolution. Theoretically a slit of 0·002 in. (0·050 mm) is required to record frequencies up to 9 kHz, which is the upper limit with this type of recording. But since the image formed on the film is always greater than the calculated value, a slit of 0·0005 in. (0·0127 mm) is used in practice. The slit itself is of more generous dimensions, and the correct size of image is formed on the film by the objective lens.

There is also a progressive high frequency loss in photographic recording due to internal reflections in optical systems, internal reflections in the film base, and to some extent processing. The optical recording channel therefore includes a *film loss equalizer* which gives pre-emphasis to frequencies between 1 kHz and 7 kHz, and this equalizer is adjusted so that a print from the sound negative will be reproduced through a projector sound head with a flat frequency characteristic. Of course *azimuth* and focusing errors can also contribute substantial h.f. losses, but these errors should never occur in well maintained equipment.

Low pass filters are also used in the recording channel to prevent very high frequencies from reaching the modulator, since they would only cause additional surface noise as the film became worn. A filter of 7·5 kHz or 8 kHz is employed with 35 mm equipment, and approximately 6 kHz with 16 mm equipment. To produce a balanced sound the low frequencies must also be restricted, usually with a 60 Hz or 80 Hz high pass filter. Figs. 11.6 and 11.7 show typical recording characteristics necessary to obtain a satisfactory reproduction from a photographic print, on 16 mm and 35 mm respectively.

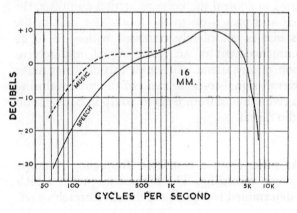

Fig. 11.6. Typical recording frequency characteristic for 16 mm photographic sound.

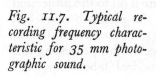

Fig. 11.7. Typical recording frequency characteristic for 35 mm photographic sound.

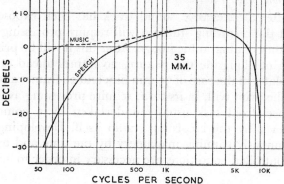

Signal-to-Noise Ratio

Under laboratory conditions a signal-to-noise ratio of at least 50 db to 55 db may be expected from an optical sound track, but a more practical figure is less than 40 db due mainly to auditorium conditions masking low level sounds. Modern reproducing equipment contributes very little background noise, due to transistor amplifiers and the use of *solar cells* instead of photo-electric cells. But audience noise and that due to other sources such as air conditioning have some effect, in addition to losses in cinema installations due to the fact that the sound has to pass through a perforated picture screen behind which the loudspeakers are usually installed.

Negative Exposure

The negative exposure in the sound camera is determined by an ordinary ammeter showing the current passing through the exposure lamp, which is a low voltage, thick filament type, passing a current of 6 or 7 amperes. Exposure will usually be adequate if the current variations are restricted to plus or minus one-eighth ampere of the optimum setting.

The film stock employed for variable area recording is a fine grain positive type emulsion, with a high contrast to maintain the dividing line between the recorded signal and the background. It also has a high resolution to give a well defined outline to the image, especially at high frequencies. The film stock employed for variable density recordings is also a fine grain positive emulsion, but it is of medium contrast since the range of frequencies and amplitude depend on variations in density. It is the exposure range which will control the dynamic range of variable density sound.

Sound Film Processing

After the negative sound track has been exposed in the sound camera at the recording studio it will require processing in the same way as any other photographic image. After this it will be printed on to the projection print alongside the picture, 20 frames ahead of the picture to which it relates in the case of 35 mm film and 26 frames ahead in the case of 16 mm. The print will, in its turn, require processing as well. Film processing is a specialized task usually undertaken by a commerical laboratory, and never by the recording studio itself. Developing is carried out on continuously running machinery by the time and temperature method, and controlled conditions are necessary in order to achieve acceptable results.

Sensitometry

Modern sensitized materials require precise handling in a laboratory, and the behaviour of film emulsions to exposure and processing is controlled by *sensitometry*, which means literally the measurement of sensitivity. In sound recording sensitometry is employed to determine the density and contrast of the developed image in relation to the illumination used to provide the exposure. This relation is a logarithmic one which is normally plotted on a graph, density being the vertical ordinate and log exposure along the horizontal plane. With film emulsion characteristics the slope or gradient of the plotted curve shows the change in density which corresponds to a change in exposure, which reveals the contrast of the emulsion. Contrast assumes more importance with variable density tracks than with variable area, the latter usually being developed to a density only.

Contrast is always measured in terms of *gamma*, gamma being the tangent of the angle formed by the straight portion of the exposure/density curve to the base. Fig. 11.8 shows two curves, one of high gamma (con-

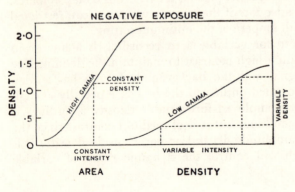

Fig. 11.8. Diagram showing the basic requirements for variable area and variable density sound negatives (not to scale).

trast) for use with an area track, and one of low gamma (contrast) for use with a density track. It will be noticed that both curves are only linear in their centre sections, which indicates the possible working range. The shoulder and toe of each characteristic is curved, and exposure in these regions would only result in distortion.

To determine negative exposure, a series of tests are made on the optical sound camera at different lamp currents. These are developed at the standard time for the particular developing bath, usually about 5 minutes, and the results plotted on an exposure graph. The correct exposure is the one which produces the required density in the middle of the working range. In addition a special test strip is exposed in a *sensitometer* which gives 21 steps of controlled exposure, and this strip is attached to each roll of sound negative as it is passed through the developer. The results are measured on a *densitometer* against a reference density, and from the resulting curve is determined the gamma.

A watch is kept on the gamma and developing time required to produce the specified density, since incorrect conditions can cause *chemical fog*. This is the term given to the colour of the unexposed but developed emulsion. Fog is always present to some extent, but it is only of any consequence with area recordings. It can be caused by light scatter within the sound camera itself, but with modern coated lens systems this effect has been substantially eliminated.

Cross Modulation

A variable area sound track is seen to be a copy of the original sound wave which has been traced out on film, the area on one side of the trace being opaque and on the other side transparent. Due to the nature of the photographic process it is not possible to achieve 100 per cent black and 100 per cent white, so a compromise must be made which will produce acceptable sound quality, low surface noise, and practical working conditions.

Photographic materials tend to diffuse all images slightly, and the working conditions must ensure that this *image spread* is kept under control. Ideally the image on a sound print should be of exactly the same dimensions as the optical image which exposed the sound negative. The effect of image spread is a distortion of sibilants, particularly the 'S' sound, which will appear exaggerated, split into two parts, or completely broken up due to the valleys and peaks of the recorded waveform being filled in (Fig. 11.9). To ascertain the precise processing conditions for both negative and positive which will minimize image spread, a series of *cross modulation* tests are carried out.

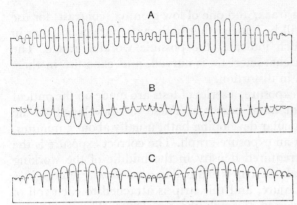

Fig. 11.9. Effect of exposure on photographic image. (A) Correctly exposed; (B) Under-exposed, distorted waveform; (C) Over-exposed, waveform filled in by halation.

The sound negative is exposed at various illumination levels whilst recording a combined audio signal of 400 Hz and 6 kHz at 80 per cent modulation. These tests are developed and a family of prints made at different densities from each negative density. All prints are then played on an optical reproducing machine, to which is connected a cross modulation analyser. This comprises a volume indicator and selective filters for eliminating either the high or low frequency content. The optimum print density is the one which produces the highest output from the high frequency, and the lowest output from the low frequency. Incorrect negative densities will be shown up as a 400 Hz modulation, due to changes in the average transmission of light through the film. If optimum conditions are only met at one end of the range of prints, then the negative density must be adjusted accordingly. This process should be repeated with every new batch of emulsion. Fortunately for variable area, slight errors in negative density can be off-set in printing. The usual negative density is between 2·8 and 3·2, with a gamma of 3 and a print density around 1·6. These figures will vary according to local conditions and the emulsions used.

Intermodulation
Variable density tracks suffer mainly from harmonic distortion due to incorrect processing, and a system of intermodulation is employed for processing control. A combined signal of 60 Hz and 4 kHz is recorded, the latter having 25 per cent of the modulation of the former, at a series of different lamp currents. A family of prints is made from each negative, all of different densities, and the results played through an intermodulation waveform analyser.

The analyser contains a band stop filter to suppress the low frequency, and the remaining high frequency is amplified, rectified, and filtered. The filter passes d.c. which is proportional to the amplitude of the high frequency signal, and this is fed to a meter which is calibrated in percentage intermodulation.

It is possible to achieve working conditions without elaborate signal generators and analysers by making test recordings of sibilant speech with several negative exposures. A listening test on the resulting family of prints will determine the most suitable processing. The usual figure for negative and print densities is between 0·04 and 0·05, and a low gamma of 0·40.

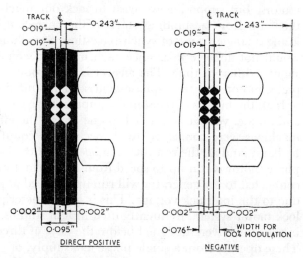

Fig. 11.10. A comparison between a direct positive and a negative recording.

Direct Positives

Improvements in sound quality can sometimes be obtained by eliminating the photographic negative entirely, adjusting the optical sound camera to produce what is called a *direct positive* recording. This is an original recording which has all the features of a photographic print, and requires a reversal of the noise reduction bias to the modulator in a density optical system, and changing the shape of the mask in an area optical system. Fig. 11.10 shows a direct comparison between a direct positive and a negative recording, the direct positive being wider to prevent the reproducing slit from scanning clear film.

Using an area track it is possible to compensate for any expected *image spread* during recording by altering the shape of the mask, which assists in cancelling out any photographic distortion. Direct positive recording has certain economical advantages, but mainly in the 16 mm gauge. Attempts are sometimes made to obtain a positive track with a reversal emulsion, but the distortion introduced by the reversal development process renders this system unacceptable for high quality recordings.

Interlock Motor Systems

Reference has been made to an *interlock motor system* for running several sound reproducing and/or recording machines in absolute synchronization. Normally a three-phase induction motor will only run at one speed when connected to a three-phase mains supply, and any number of machines will therefore run in synchronism when fitted with three-phase motors. But supposing we wish to lock our machines together, and run them up from a standing start to the correct operating speed without losing a single frame of synchronization. Switching on individual motors would not achieve this, since each machine would run up to speed at a slightly different time. The answer is to introduce an intermediate three-phase motor and three-phase generator mounted on a common shaft.

If all the motors of the sound equipment are connected to the generator, and an a.c. voltage is applied to one phase, the effect is the same as if all machines were connected by a mechanical coupling. Rotate one motor by hand, and all the rest rotate in *interlock*. If the large intermediate three-phase motor is run up to speed from the normal mains supply, all motors connected to the generator will run up to speed at precisely the same time, due to the interlock voltage. This is a brief description of the *selsyn* interlock motor system, frequently used in film studios. Older systems are still in use which were designed before the days of three-phase mains supplies. These operate from a single phase a.c. supply, or even d.c., and rely on a special generator to control the speed of the main motor through a tuned circuit incorporated in a valve amplifier.

Progress with motor and generator design has now eliminated the necessity of the continuously running selsyn system, and a number of interlock motors can be made to run up to synchronous speed by themselves. Another system is the Perfectone *synchro-start*, requiring a special generator which is used only whilst the motors are running up to speed. The motors then run synchronously on three-phase mains, and the generator shuts itself down.

Principle of Synchro-Start

When the interlock motors to be synchronized are switched on, the Perfectone motor-generator turns synchronously at 1,500 r.p.m. and feeds the interlock motors with 55 volts d.c. This voltage on each of the three phases keeps the motors locked in their starting position. Rotation of the motors is obtained by the gradual decrease of the generator speed to zero r.p.m., whilst the voltage applied to the motors rises from 55 to 240 volts. At the same time the frequency is raised from zero Hz (d.c.) to 50 Hz, and the entire operation requires 2 or 3 seconds. By reversing the process, all motors can be stopped in synchronism at any time.

In rock'n roll installations backwards running is obtained by reversing the connections to one of the three phases whilst all the machines are at rest, and for this reason the interlock voltage must be removed momentarily. Selsyn systems are also employed for this purpose.

Magnetic Film Recording

The principle of magnetic film recording is not very different from magnetic tape recording, and the same theories will apply as explained in Chapter 3. However, film base is considerably thicker than tape base, 0·005 in. (0·127 mm) against 0·002 in. (0·050 mm) for standard play tape, which makes film base less pliable. It requires a transport mechanism with a tight loop system so that the film is kept under tension and makes intimate contact with the record head. If contact is lost by only 0·001 in. (0·025 mm) there will be a reduction of 12 db at 1 kHz and 20 db at 7 kHz. Once a track has been recorded in this way there is no method of restoring such a loss.

It is also important that the magnetic head should be constructed with extremely hard-wearing laminations, since the film tension causes the oxide coating to have a very abrasive effect. Most magnetic film, and tape, has a polished coating to reduce the amount of head friction. Polishing is carried out during the drying operation by a process called *calendering*, and produces a completely flat surface which will make intimate contact with the magnetic head. Even so there are some coatings where the oxide particles clump together and do not respond to the normal process of recording, causing what are generally termed *dropouts*.

Magnetic Film Path

A magnetic film recorder has flanges or plates which accept 1000 ft. (300 m) rolls of magnetic film on standard cores. A single drive sprocket feeds the film into a tight loop system consisting of sprung filter rollers to maintain tension, and two sound drums which have a pair of dynamically balanced flywheels on their shafts. In addition the mechanical filter rollers have an oil-filled *dashpot* to absorb small speed fluctuations which would otherwise result in flutter. As with all film mechanisms there is a danger of introducing *sprocket hole modulation*, which is flutter caused by film perforations engaging or leaving the sprocket teeth, and this has a frequency of

96 Hz at a film speed of 24 frames per second—4 perforations per frame in the case of 35 mm film.

Separate record and monitor heads are located between the two sound drums, and their position is carefully adjusted to give a good tape/head contact with an adequate frequency response. Magnetic film recorders are not normally fitted with erase heads, since it is considered more convenient and less dangerous to bulk erase each roll of film before use. But film recorders used for post-sync channels are fitted with double-gap erase heads, also recorders in rock'n roll installations.

Frequency Response

The overall frequency response obtained with magnetic film recording is from 50 Hz to 12 kHz on 35 mm, and from 50 Hz to 10 kHz on 16 mm. The IEC recording characteristic for 35 mm film corresponds to a time constant of 35 microseconds with a signal of constant voltage applied to the input of the recording chain, and for 16 mm the time constant is 100 microseconds due to the slower linear film speed. In both cases the reproducing characteristic is that which gives a flat response when reproducing a sound track recorded with the above conditions. This standard is used mainly by the television industry.

Film industry equipment is usually aligned with a special calibrated test film type RCFM for 35 mm, and type M16MF for 16 mm (see appendix for details). The reproduce characteristic is adjusted first to give a flat response from the test film, and the record characteristic is then adjusted so that the same flat response is achieved. The permitted tolerances are very small (plus or minus ½ db) since original recordings are often transferred through several generations.

Magnetic Track Standards

Magnetic sound has an unlimited track width under sep-mag conditions, since the oxide coating extends across the full width of both 35 mm and 16 mm film. This permits multi-track recording on both gauges, and has resulted in international standards for track location and dimensions. For example all single track recordings on 35 mm film are 200 mil wide. 200 mil is in fact 200 thousandths of an inch (0·200 in. or 5·4 mm), but in the film industry the term *mil* is used instead of *thou* to express track dimensions.

Other 35 mm sep-mag standards are three tracks of 200 mil each, four tracks of 150 mil each, and six tracks of 100 mil each, centrally located between the perforations. There is also a 35 mm com-mag standard of a

35MM   35MM   35MM

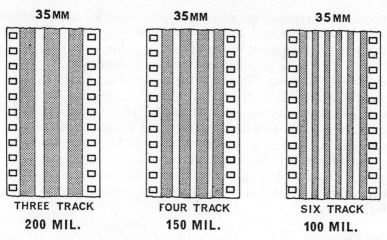

THREE TRACK   FOUR TRACK   SIX TRACK
200 MIL.   150 MIL.   100 MIL.

Fig. 11.11. Track positions used for 35 mm magnetic recordings.

single 100 mil track alongside the picture for television programme exchange, but this standard has not yet been adopted for cinema use due to the existing installations of optical reproducing equipment. The special com-mag standards for Cinemascope and 70-mm films are described on page 229.

16 mm sep-mag standards for single perforated film include a single 200 mil track located in the centre, a 200 mil track located at the edge, and a 100 mil track also located at the edge. 16 mm com-mag consists of a 93 mil track located at the edge, and a 26 mil track located outside the sprocket holes on double perforated film. Although some studios record three 100 mil tracks across 16 mm single perforated film, this is not strictly speaking an international standard (see appendix, page 259).

Magnetic Stripe

So far 35 mm magnetic film has only been referred to as fully coated, either completely across the film width or between the two sets of perforations. To facilitate sound editing and the writing of sync marks and numbers on the film, clear film base coated with a *magnetic stripe* 300 mil wide is used for the majority of single track transfers. There is also a small *balancing stripe* on the opposite side of the film so that spooling will remain even at all times.

Magnetic stripe is used extensively in all the narrow film gauges. A magnetic stripe 100 mil wide is available on clear 16 mm film base for ease in sound editing, and this also has a narrow balancing stripe.

Unexposed 16 mm picture negative is also pre-striped for magnetic recording in single system cameras. Sound recorded in this way is unaffected by the subsequent development of the picture, and the system enables good quality recordings to be obtained under newsreel conditions.

The method of striping film base is the same for any gauge, from 8 mm to 70 mm. The film is threaded over a roller on the striping machine, and comes into contact with an *applicator wheel*. This wheel feeds the oxide lacquer on to the film at a uniform rate and thickness. An alternative method uses an accurately positioned orifice which governs both the position and thickness of the stripe. The coated film is then passed over a drying rack which subjects the stripe to a considerable amount of heat, and it requires an interval of several hours to harden off before it can be used for recording.

Recording Equipment

The normal 35 mm or 16 mm magnetic recording channel consists of a mixing unit, amplifier rack, recorder, and power unit. All this equipment is either installed in a central recording room or a mobile truck, except the mixing unit which is mounted on a wheeled trolley and positioned inside the studio. The modern tendency is to use the much more portable battery driven quarter inch tape recorders now available, particularly when recording away from the studio. This enables the much more bulky magnetic film equipment to be dispensed with. Since there are no perforations on tape for synchronization to the picture film, a *pulse track* is recorded simultaneously with the audio signal to indicate the speed of the picture camera.

The most widely used tape recorder in the film industry is the Swiss made *Nagra*, which has a specification to equal that of any 35 mm recording channel. The Nagra's main feature is its long term speed stability and low wow and flutter content, made possible by a large diameter capstan mounted on the shaft of a moving coil motor. A *phonic wheel* is placed on the same shaft, and the frequency of the signal it induces into a magnetic head is compared against a standard reference. A servo mechanism maintains a constant speed by applying a correcting signal when necessary.

The Nagra model IV has electronic circuits of modular construction so that individual recorders can be equipped to meet specific requirements. It will record at 15 i.p.s. (38 cm/sec.), 7½ i.p.s. (19 cm/sec.), or 3¾ i.p.s. (9·5 cm/sec.), with European or American equalization. The overall frequency response is from 30 Hz to 20 kHz at 15 i.p.s., and from 30 Hz to 15 kHz at 7½ i.p.s., so that both these speeds are adequate for film use.

The signal-to-noise ratio at $7\frac{1}{2}$ i.p.s. is 70 db referred to maximum recording level.

Although the Nagra model IV is normally used with an external mixing unit, the outputs from two microphones can be mixed together within the recorder (only one microphone on Nagra model III). Pre-amplifier modules are available for dynamic microphones of 50 ohms or 200 ohms impedance, also for dynamic microphones whose impedance varies with frequency (see page 106). Other modules include a power supply for transistorized condenser microphones, a line pre-amplifier which converts a microphone input into a balanced line input, and a pre-amplifier which accepts the signal from a gramophone pick-up cartridge of the magnetic type and corrects it to RIAA standards. The signal from the two microphone inputs can be passed through a speech filter, which is in fact a low frequency attenuator with four positions. It is designed to compensate for room acoustics, but it can also be used to compensate for *bass tip-up* when speaking close to pressure gradient and cardioid microphones.

Other tape recorders with pulse track facilities include the British made Leevers-Rich, the Norwegian Tandberg, the Swiss Perfectone and Stellavox, also the German Uher. Only the Tandberg has a pulse system which is compatible with the Nagra without conversion.

Pulse Synchronization

Although quarter inch tape recorders are designed to run at a constant speed with electronically governed motors, there is still a need for some form of camera speed reference to obtain 100 per cent synchronization with the picture film. In the absence of perforations synchronization is achieved by recording a camera *pulse track* in addition to the audio signal. The pulse can be obtained from the normal a.c. supply to the camera motor, or in the case of battery driven motors from a special pulse generator attached to the camera itself. Cameras without a pulse generator can sometimes be fitted with a battery drive motor having crystal speed control, and a crystal controlled pulse circuit eliminates the need for a cable between camera and recorder.

The audio track is subsequently transferred to 16 mm or 35 mm magnetic film for editing purposes, and the pulse track is used to modify the speed of the tape replay machine so that it synchronizes with the magnetic film recorder and produces a sound recording that is exactly the same length as the picture to which it relates. This is achieved by connecting an external synchronizer (internal circuit board on Nagra model IV) which compares the amplified pulse track against a reference signal, usually derived from the mains supply feeding the film recorder motor. The phase difference between the pulse and the mains waveforms is translated into a simulated d.c. signal which controls the speed of the tape recorder motor.

An alternative system is to amplify the pulse track from tape head level (approximately 4 mV) to 230 volts with a power of 300 watts. The amplifier output is then used to drive the film recorder motor instead of the mains. This system has fallen from favour due to the heavy and expensive amplifier required. An older method sometimes employed is to display the waveform of the pulse track and the waveform of the mains supply on a double beam oscilloscope, and vary the speed of the tape recorder manually to keep the pulse waveform stationary, and therefore in sync.

The physical location of the pulse track on the tape is extremely important, since there are several different standards none of which are compatible. For example the DIN standard for pulse synchronization (No. 15·575) as employed in the Uher recorder is a single track 0·1 to 0·5 mm wide located in the centre of the tape, and horizontally polarized so that it is at right angles to the audio track. This type of pulse track is ignored by the audio head during replay, and the problem of *crosstalk* does not arise providing that the pulse frequency is around 50 Hz to 100 Hz. This is the frequency of the signal from the special pulse generator on professional cameras like the Arriflex and the Eclair.

The Nagra and Tandberg recorders superimpose a narrow push-pull pulse track in the centre of the tape, which also remains inaudible when the audio track is replayed with a *full width* head. A *half-track* head would only scan one half of the push-pull track, which would then cause audible *crosstalk*. The Perfectone and Leevers-Rich recorders use one half of the tape width for audio and the other half for the pulse track, so that there is no possibility of *crosstalk* between the two (see appendix, page 258).

The external synchronizer used for automatic speed control during transferring can also be employed with an alternative reference signal, such as a camera pulse. This permits *post-sync* shooting against a pre-recorded tape, giving synchronous playback of musical material with extremely portable equipment.

Another type of sync pulse is employed with multi-track tape recorders when all tracks are required to carry audio information. A 14 kHz tone is modulated with 50 Hz or 60 Hz, using a ring modulator, and superimposed on one track with the audio signal. During replay the 14 kHz tone is isolated from the audio signal with suitable filters, and de-modulated to obtain a 50 Hz or 60 Hz pulse. This pulse is amplified and used as a control voltage to synchronize the recorder capstan motor during transfer to magnetic film.

Wide Screen Film Processes

There are two types of wide screen film processes which employ multi-track magnetic sound, Cinemascope and 70 mm productions. The Cinemascope com-mag standard contains four tracks as shown in Fig.

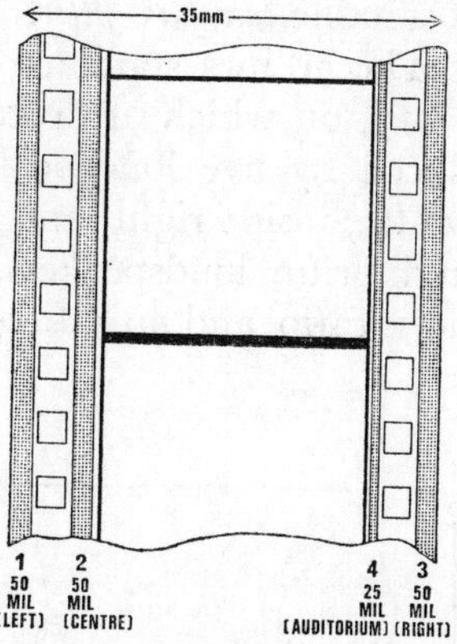

Fig. 11.12. Track positions used for 35 mm Cinemascope films with stereophonic sound.

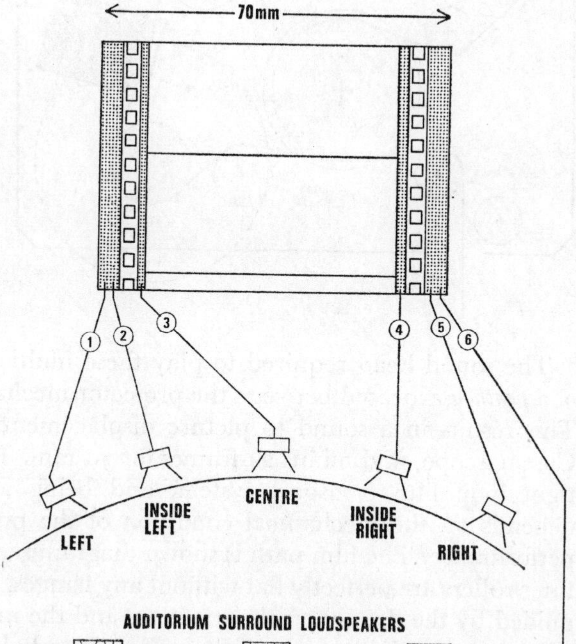

Fig. 11.13. Track positions used for 70 mm Todd-A.O. films with stereophonic sound.

11.12, three 50-mil tracks which are reproduced by three loudspeaker systems behind the screen—left, centre, and right, and one 30-mil track reproduced by loudspeakers surrounding the auditorium. Since the signal-to-noise ratio of the fourth track is rather poor, a *gating amplifier* is used in the reproducer to reduce the gain when there is no audio signal. The gating circuit is controlled by a 12 kHz tone recorded on the fourth track a little ahead of the audio signal, and this tone is isolated from the loudspeakers by a suitable *low pass filter*.

The 70 mm standard contains four magnetic stripes as shown in Fig. 11.13, on which are recorded six 50-mil tracks. Five of these are reproduced by five loudspeaker systems behind the screen—left, inside left, centre, inside right, and right, and the sixth track is reproduced over the auditorium loudspeakers. The auditorium track has an adequate signal-to-noise ratio, and no gating amplifier is normally required in the reproducer.

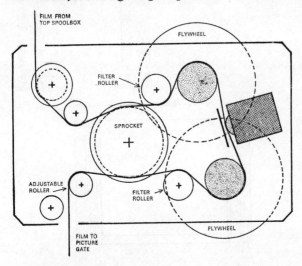

Fig. 11.14. Film path of pent-house magnetic sound head for 35 mm and 70 mm films.

The sound head required to play these multi-track recordings consists of a *penthouse* located between the projector mechanism and top spool box. This results in a sound to picture displacement of minus 28 frames for Cinemascope, and minus 24 frames for 70 mm. The penthouse contains a tight loop film transport system, and being a pull-through device it depends on the mechanical condition of the projector for a flutter free performance. The film path is shown diagrammatically in Fig. 11.14. The filter rollers are perfectly flat without any flanges, the film being accurately guided by the flanges on the sprocket, and the magnetic head is mounted on an adjustable base plate between the two balanced sound drums.

Frequency Response

The overall frequency response of these multi-track magnetic recordings is from 50 Hz to 12 kHz, plus or minus 2 db. The recording and reproducing curves are shown in Figs. 11.15 and 11.16, which shows the amount of high frequency equalization necessary in recording to produce a flat playback characteristic. The slight amount of bass pre-emphasis below 200 Hz in the recording curve corresponds with a shelf in the reproducing curve, and also produces a flat overall characteristic. The reason for this is to limit the amount of bass correction necessary on the projection equipment, and assist in maintaining a low motor hum and interference level around 50 Hz and 100 Hz. Fortunately the position of the penthouse is well away from the projector motor, minimizing the possibility of hum being induced into the magnetic head.

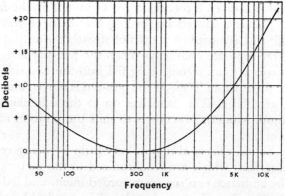

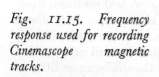

Fig. 11.15. Frequency response used for recording Cinemascope magnetic tracks.

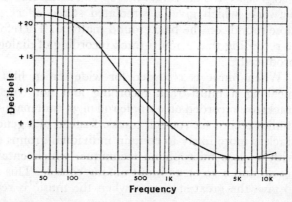

Fig. 11.16. Frequency response used for replaying Cinemascope magnetic tracks.

Multi-Track Recordings

Although both Cinemascope and 70 mm motion pictures are exhibited with multi-track recordings, not all of the original recordings which make up the finished product are themselves stereophonic. Only the music is recorded multi-track, the dialogue and sound effects being recorded on a mono channel. The main reason for this is convenience of operation during filming, apart from the obvious economy of equipment.

Originally all the dialogue for Cinemascope pictures was recorded stereophonically, and the artistes voices followed them across the screen in a natural manner. But when two scenes filmed from different angles were cut together, the voice of the artiste who was speaking at the time would jump from one side of the screen to the other. This made the dialogue recording appear to lack continuity of direction, although such movement may have been technically correct. So the stereophonic recording of dialogue was abandoned in favour of a single mono recording, which is given a pseudo-stereo treatment in the final re-recording process.

This is achieved by feeding the dialogue through a *pan-pot*, which in this case is a triple fader which divides the output from a mono source over three separate channels. When the pan-pot is in a central position, there is still a small signal being fed into the two side channels, usually about 12 db down in level. As the pan-pot is moved one way or the other, there is a gradual shift in emphasis on to the side channels instead of a sudden jump. Modern practice is to shift the position of the dialogue as little as possible.

Sound effects also gain very little by being recorded stereophonically. *Spot effects* which are synchronized to the picture and relate to something the audience can see are recorded mono and fed through a *pan-pot*, which enables the effects to be placed in a suitable position across the screen. *Background effects* are sometimes spread across all tracks by a special resistive network, which gives a simulated stereo effect providing there are no close sounds on the background material. Therefore it is only in the final re-recording that a multi-track recording of dialogue and sound effects is produced.

When music is recorded for wide screen film processes, it is strictly speaking a multi-track recording and not true stereo. Three 200-mil tracks are recorded on a single roll of 35 mm magnetic film, although some studios record six 100-mil tracks. Instead of a general area of sound, each track is more likely to contain individual groups of instruments recorded with a close microphone technique, which entails a multi-microphone set-up and a 20 or 25 input mixing console. This method has been found to give the greatest clarity when the music is reproduced in very large auditoria. It also permits the overall balance of the orchestra to be adjusted during the final re-recording.

Electronic Printing

When a final master magnetic recording has been made for a Cinemascope or 70 mm picture, it is treated as a sound negative and re-recorded to provide what is termed a *printing master*. This may contain three, four, or even six tracks in the case of a 70 mm production, and is used for re-recording the sound on to each picture print to produce a *show copy*. The studio which recorded the printing master supplies a frequency film recorded on the same equipment, which enables the operator of the printing machine to line up his equipment with that of the studio, both for frequency response and the level on each track.

The *electronic printing* installation consists of a master replay machine, amplifiers, frequency compensators, attenuators for track balancing, and a magnetic printer. To avoid the generation of *combination tones* between several bias oscillators, a single crystal controlled 60 kHz oscillator is used with separate slave amplifiers for each track. The audio input of the printer is at high impedance so that more than one printer can be fed from a single master replay machine. Printing is carried out at 24 frames per second, since this is the only speed at which sound quality can be accurately checked. Each track is sampled by the operator who wears headphones, and sync is checked simultaneously on a picture viewer with a rotating prism to 'arrest' the image.

The printing of 70 mm show copies can be carried out from either a four or six track printing master. In the case of a four track master the signal on the centre and outer tracks is split 50/50 to provide a new signal source for the inside left and inside right tracks. The result is often indistinguishable from that obtained from a six track master, and enables a studio with only four channel equipment to successfully produce a printing master for a 70 mm picture. It is not unknown for a single mono recording to be spread over the five main tracks, the inner side tracks receiving a signal 6 db down, and the outer side tracks 12 db down.

Reels are joined into 2000 ft. (600 m) lengths for printing, and are subsequently delivered in this length. The picture is already printed on each show copy before it receives its magnetic stripe and sound transfer, and must be protected from the possibility of scratching in the film path of the printer. This is the final stage in the production of Cinemascope and 70 mm productions, and the completed copies are despatched to the client.

CHAPTER XII

Microphone Techniques

THIS CHAPTER is intended as a guide to microphone selection as well as operating technique, and the ideas expressed are the result of practical experiences by many sound engineers. Although the numerous examples given do not constitute the only solutions to the problems raised, they did prove to be successful at the time. The final choice of microphone and of microphone placement will depend on whether the recording is to be out-of-doors or in a studio, the studio acoustics, the artistes, and where music is concerned the instruments. There are no hard and fast rules to microphone placement; therefore the best way to learn is by practical experience under a wide variety of conditions, and by not being afraid to experiment.

Microphone Connectors

The two most frequently used connectors are the Tuchel and the Cannon type XLR, both containing three pins and an interlocking feature between male and female types. Many microphones, including the Beyer and Sennheiser Ranges, use a Tuchel or Cannon plug as an integral part of the microphone body; whilst other microphones designed for boom mounting, such as the A.K.G. D25 and the R.C.A. 10,001, have a short pig-tail from their body with a connector on the end. The standard wiring for Tuchel plugs is pin 1—audio, pin 2—cable screen, pin 3—audio. The standard wiring for Cannon plugs is pin 1—cable screen, pin 2—audio, pin 3—audio. Most professional equipment is designed to operate with balanced microphone lines, and the microphone cable usually terminates in a male plug with a female socket on the tape recorder, mixing unit, or amplifier.

Microphones are rather delicate and very susceptible to damage, so for inspection or changing connectors never place a microphone down on a workshop bench without first making sure that the bench is clean, and preferably covered with a sheet of clean paper. Dynamic and Ribbon microphones both employ large magnets which attract metal filings and metal dust, and these can ruin a microphone's performance or even cause a short circuit between the diaphragm and case. It is wise to keep a microphone in a protective bag or case when not in use, and foam filled cases with snap or zip fasteners are provided by some manufacturers.

Condenser microphones do not possess magnets and are not so prone to damage from metal filings, but the diaphragm construction is equally delicate and care should be exercised in handling them. In fact care should be exercised when handling all microphones, so that damage from mis-use does not occur at some inopportune moment. Should a microphone become suspect, it should be tested against a similar microphone of known quality and the outputs compared. If the performances of the two microphones do not match fairly closely, the faulty one should be returned to the manufacturer or agent at the first opportunity. It is not wise to completely dismantle a microphone oneself, since special tools are often needed and further damage could ensue.

Some of the condenser microphones available today have an output level which is too high for the average mixing unit or microphone input on a tape recorder. Therefore some form of attenuation must be inserted in the microphone line, and to maintain impedance relationships an H type pad is to be preferred—made up from five small resistors which may be hidden inside a Cannon connector. Fig. 12.1 gives the values for a 10 db pad and a 20 db pad, suitable for a circuit impedance of 200 ohms.

Fig. 12.1. Circuits for attenuator pads at 200 ohms impedance.

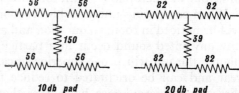

10 db pad   20 db pad

Microphone Directivity

No single microphone can ever be suitable for all recording applications in a studio, which partly accounts for the large variety of microphone types available. Of course frequency response is of prime importance, and this should be as wide and as smooth as possible to obtain realistic results. We saw in Chapter 5 that different microphones have different directional characteristics, and the significance of this is not always fully understood.

For example, when using an omni-directional microphone fairly close, room reverberation and random sound pick-up will seldom present any problems due to the relative strength of the direct speech wave. As the sound source-to-microphone distance increases, the indirect sound due to reverberation begins to cause a 'colouration' of the signal. This colouration becomes audible at a microphone distance of about 12 in. (30 cm), and assumes serious proportions at 24 in. (60 cm) and over. This is the distance at which it is wise to discontinue the use of a non-directional microphone, unless the colouration is required or a wide-angle pick-up is essential. Out of doors these colouration problems can still exist, and an omni-directional microphone should only be used for close-up work.

Therefore to obtain a greater working distance, a microphone with directional characteristics is essential.

Bi-directional microphones of the ribbon type enable the working distance to be increased from 2 to 3 times as compared with an omni-directional type for the same quality sound; always assuming that the axial frequency response of both microphones is the same. This ability of being able to pick-up or *reach* from a greater distance is due purely to the directional effect, and does not necessarily infer greater sensitivity. The directivity assists in ignoring reverberation and background noise, thus allowing the volume control to be advanced to compensate for the increased microphone working distance. Bi-directional microphones are most suitable for voice and music recordings under studio conditions, where they can be set up and left in a fixed position. For all recordings where the microphone is continually on the move, such as in film and television studios, the trend is away from bi-directional microphones and in favour of microphones with uni-directional or cardioid characteristics.

When comparing uni- and bi-directional microphones, little difference will be noticed in room colouration and ambient noise pick-up. But should any unwanted sound occur in a particular direction behind the microphone, the uni will prove superior since it is relatively insensitive at the rear and can be orientated to reduce the troublesome sound. All uni-directional microphones have a cardioid polar distribution, and both terms are used to describe the same type of microphone. Any type of microphone element can be designed as a cardioid, providing that the sound path to the rear of the diaphragm is 180° out of phase with sound arriving at the front. By varying the rear aperture the degree of directivity can be controlled. No cardioid is completely dead at the rear, the front-to-back ratio being around 15 to 20 db for a well designed unit.

Cardioid microphones can be used for dialogue recording up to distances of 6 ft. (2 m) or 8 ft. (2·6 m) quite satisfactorily before sound colouration becomes objectionable. Beyond this distance it is advisable to employ one of the highly directional types as described on page 99, bearing in mind that accurate placing of such microphones is essential.

Announcements and Commentaries

For recording announcements in public places where there is a high level of background noise, a uni-directional or cardioid microphone will give the best separation between wanted and unwanted sound. Satisfactory results can be achieved with an omni-directional microphone, providing it is used at a working distance of about 6 inches (15 cm), or if the background noise is low. Announcing studios, and commentators booths, are usually confined spaces where acoustic treatment alone will not give sufficient correction to eliminate sound colouration. Here again a uni-directional or bi-directional microphone is to be preferred, and an omni-directional microphone should not be considered unless working very close.

If sound reflections due to acoustics or items of equipment still cause colouration, they can be prevented from reaching the front of the micro-phone by placing a screen behind the announcer. A suitable screen would be a frame covered with acoustic tiles, sheets of Celotex, or some other absorbing material. Under highly reverberant conditions it may also be necessary to use a folding screen with two or three sections, and to cover the top over as well. If proper screens are not available, blankets will help in an emergency; but be careful not to hang them too close to the micro-phone or they will absorb too much h.f. and cause the speaker's voice to sound dull.

The correct working distance for the microphone can be found by trial and error, since different speakers will require different working distances. The microphone should be positioned about 12 to 18 inches (30 to 90 cms) away, and directly in line with the speaker's mouth or slightly above it. Excessive sibilance can be controlled by turning the microphone slightly sideways. A point to bear in mind is the rustle of paper scripts, which can reach alarming proportions if not kept under control. Commentaries should be typed out on single sheets of paper, each one numbered and clipped to a piece of card to minimize handling noises or slipped inside a cellophane envelope.

Lectures and Speeches

When recording lectures or speeches delivered from a fixed position such as a dais or rostrum, there is often no time or opportunity for any rehearsal to obtain voice level and quality checks. A simple solution is to use a lavalier type microphone which will maintain a fixed relationship with the speaker, but this will sacrifice sound quality, apart from the fact that it may be impossible to attach a lavalier microphone. A single high grade omni-directional microphone with a smooth, wide frequency response can be fixed to the rostrum, and this will produce better sound even with an itinerant speaker who fails to appreciate the importance of speaking to-wards the microphone and at the same distance from it throughout his performance—or being at all times *on-mike* as the saying is.

If the speech is being made in noisy surroundings out-of-doors, or indoors under conditions of poor acoustics, a cardioid microphone will give a better voice pick-up due to the suppression of unwanted sounds occurring from behind the microphone. But due to the increased directivity there will be a significant drop in voice level should the speaker turn his head to one side or the other, and it may become necessary to use two cardioid microphones. The best solution is to position the microphones close together and pointing outwards at an angle of 15° to 25°. The greater the angle the greater the freedom of movement offered to the speaker before he is *off-mike*. Should any sound reinforcement system be employed from the same microphones, there may be problems of feedback into the loudspeakers. This can sometimes be solved by spacing the two microphones apart and facing inwards, so that they still combine to give a uniform output. In all cases it is essential to use two matched microphones, and to ensure that their outputs are connected in phase electrically.

Plays and Drama

When recording a play it is obviously possible to tape a live stage performance, placing two or more directional microphones amongst the footlights. But due to the working distance being rather great, and some of the actors movements being decidedly off-mike, there will be too much reverberant sound for the recording to be a success. It is therefore better recording practice to arrange a special performance on the stage with the house curtains drawn together to isolate the empty auditorium. By using a pressure gradient microphone of the ribbon type, its unique directional characteristics can be employed for simulating both near and distant speech with acceptable quality.

The normal speaking distance between an artiste and the microphone should be about 2 ft. (0·6 m), often described as a 'script and a half'. Merely standing to one side of the ribbon will increase the perspective quite considerably, so that the artiste will not have to move his or her position very much. The professional will often employ more than one microphone, so that a number of artistes can be recorded with a near perspective without getting in each others way.

Drama presentations contain more problems than a play, and the variable acoustics of a drama studio, together with reverberation facilities, are usually essential. In addition there may be sound effects and music to be fed into the recording from tape or disc sources. Microphones must be carefully positioned so that they only pick up the artiste they are intended for, all other artistes being in the dead area of the microphone. This is fairly easily accomplished with bi-directional ribbon microphones, but would be impossible with omni-directional types. As in all recording situations it is experience which helps far more than reading textbooks.

Dialogue Recording

Conditions in a film or television studio do not favour the sound recordist when attempting to record dialogue, since it is not always possible to place the microphone in an ideal position because it must not be visible from the camera viewpoint. Even when it is out of picture it may cause shadows from lamps. Occasionally it is possible to hide the microphone behind an article on the set and by this means achieve a position close to the artiste. In general, however, the fact that the microphone must be kept out of picture means that except in close-ups the recording engineer can rarely bring his microphone as close to the actor as he would like. The microphone itself is mounted on a *microphone boom* which enables it to be easily and silently moved. A tubular arm can be racked in or out to follow the movements of artistes, and a turret mounting enables the microphone to be rotated through almost 360° by means of a separate control. A tilt control is sometimes included. The operator stands on a platform which can be raised with the tubular arm to a suitable height. The entire boom can be contracted sufficiently to pass through a normal doorway should the occasion arise.

A microphone suspended from a boom should not be moved too quickly, as noise can be generated from the boom mechanism and by the swishing of air over the microphone case. A directional microphone is always used, positioned above the artistes and directly in front of them. It should point directly at the speaker's mouth at an angle of approximately 45°, but may be tilted down to cover more than one artiste when no other course is possible. Once the artiste is allowed to get too far away from the microphone, intelligibility is reduced due to colouration. If the artiste gets too close there will again be a loss of intelligibility due to excessive *bass tip-up*. The correct distance is about 2 ft. to 3 ft. (0·6 m to 0·9 m) with a dynamic microphone, and from 3 ft. to 4 ft. (0·9 m to 1·2 m) with a ribbon microphone. At greater distances than these sound colouration due to reverberation will become noticeable.

Should the artiste turn his or her head without the microphone being moved accordingly, the sound pick-up will be of poor quality and the artiste is said to be *off-mike*. The operator should always try to anticipate artistes' movements, and so achieve the best position and balance between the direct sound and reflected sound from the walls of the 'set'. It is the job of the *sound mixer* to listen to the dialogue on high quality moving coil headphones, and so determine the working distance between microphone and artiste, listen for intelligibility and 'fluffs' in delivery, and also for overlaps. Overlaps occur when one artiste speaks before another artiste finishes, which makes track editing sometimes impossible.

Dialogue Quality

The sound quality of dialogue recorded in the manner just described will depend on the type of microphone in use, the microphone position, and the constructional details of the set. A small, boxy set with bare furnishings will produce more colouration than an open set containing a carpeted floor area and soft furnishings. Another factor which affects sound quality is the use of two microphones in close proximity. Distortion can be introduced due to a time and phase difference between signals arriving at each microphone from the same source, and this constitutes bad recording practice. The correct procedure when it becomes essential to use two microphones is to make a quick cross-fade from one to the other, or better still key one in and the other out simultaneously so that the outputs from both microphones cannot be heard at the same time.

Microphones used for dialogue recording should have frequent checks for sensitivity, frequency response, and overall quality to ensure the absence of internal noise—especially with condenser microphones. Ribbon microphones can lose some of their sensitivity if the ribbon sags due to sudden air blasts, and dynamic microphones can lose their bass response if accidentally dropped or otherwise damaged by shock.

Dialogue should never be recorded on a channel with a flat frequency response, due to the increase in bass response under set conditions. Low frequencies are also accentuated when the recording is reproduced at a higher level than the recording level, and when the voice is lowered during recording and has to be further amplified during reproduction. These effects can be minimized by using a *dialogue equalizer*, which is always left in circuit to correct any over-emphasis of frequencies below 200 Hz. In fact low frequency attenuation is introduced starting at 800 Hz, and slowly tapering off until at 100 Hz the response is 10 db to 12 db down in level with respect to 1 kHz. The reason for this will be appreciated by referring to Fletcher's curves for the human ear on page 18, which illustrates how the ear's frequency response alters with volume. Shouted dialogue on the other hand will have a very low bass content, and the dialogue equalizer may have to be removed altogether to achieve a good result.

In addition to bass attenuation, a certain amount of lift is given to the middle frequencies between 2 kHz and 5 kHz, usually with a peak of from 3 db to 6 db at around 4 kHz. This lift is designed to increase intelligibility, especially as these frequencies are rolled off in the cinema reproducing equipment, and further attenuated in the actual cinema auditorium itself. Film sound tracks of the photographic or optical type will not contain any frequencies above 7·5 kHz, although magnetic tracks extend up to 12 kHz. One trouble which occurs as a direct result of lifting the middle frequencies is *sibilance,* which occurs mainly with the letter S. This sibilance is most pronounced with persons wearing dentures, and can be minimized by turning the microphone slightly to one side—or edge on—during the initial recording.

Volume Level

The sound mixer must contain all volume levels within the dynamic range of the recording system, although this may mean no more than raising a whisper or lowering a shout. In addition to the headphone (or loud-speaker) monitor, the mixer has a volume meter to assist in gauging volume level fairly accurately. The average dialogue level should be 10 db or 12 db below 100 per cent modulation, which allows an adequate margin for signal peaks such as shouts. D.B. meters and V.U. meters which only indicate the r.m.s. value of a signal are increased in sensitivity by 6 db so that better use can be made of the scale. This means that average dialogue will be reaching to −6 db on the meter. Recorders using peak programme meters, or a modulometer like the Nagra, should show dialogue peaking to around 80 per cent to 100 per cent, depending on the *ballistics* of the meter and the amount of *overswing*. The monitor volume must be adjusted in relation to the meter, so that a comfortable listening level is obtained at normal recording levels.

Whispered speech can cause concern, since it can be heard quite clearly on headphones and yet hardly move the needle on the volume meter. This is quite normal, and to raise the volume until the needle showed the usual level would be quite wrong. In addition a whisper increases the high frequency content of the voice, which could also increase *sibilance.* Record-ing a generally quiet voice can prove difficult, however, and a request for the artiste to speak up will result in a far better recording than merely increasing the setting of the volume control. This is due to the increase in bass with quiet voices, which disappears when the same voice is slightly projected.

Shouts are best dealt with by raising the position of the microphone above the artiste, or taking the microphone further away so that more indirect sound will combine with the direct sound to produce a less peaky waveform. At the same time the volume control may have to be reduced to prevent excessive overload. Slight overload is unavoidable, and is perfectly acceptable since shouted voices are rough sounding aurally. Loud sounds, such as gunshots, doors closing, telephone bells, can occur during a quiet dialogue scene. If the volume control is well advanced these intrusions will be magnified larger than life. Even though blank cartridges are used with gunfire, the steep wavefront of each shot must be kept within reasonable limits. A reduction of from 10 db to 20 db below the volume setting for dialogue may be necessary, so it is wise to take steps to see that such noises do not occur over dialogue, but in between lines.

Dialogue Perspective

We are all accustomed to binaural hearing which gives us a sense of direction and perspective. Experience tells us how far away is the sound source, due to the ratio of direct to indirect sound waves. Out of doors there is very little indirect sound, and one has to judge distance by volume and quality. When viewing a close-up on the screen, one expects to hear close-up sound, and when viewing a long-shot, one expects to hear long-shot sound. Since the microphone is a monaural device, the microphone working distance is varied to obtain *dialogue perspective* and thus maintain realism. But the microphone position should always be closer to the artiste than the camera position to obtain the correct perspective, and about one half of the camera to artiste distance is a good compromise.

A further complication is the acceptance angle of the lens used on a film or television camera. With long focus lenses the microphone will have to be positioned much closer than with a lens of normal focal length. With some of the wide angle lenses in use today it is sometimes difficult to get a microphone in position at all without it being seen or casting shadows due to lighting. Sound volume also plays an important part in obtaining dialogue perspective, lowering the volume for sound occurring further away. But in general it will be the microphone position rather than volume which determines dialogue perspective, and an experienced sound mixer will record all his dialogue at a more or less constant volume, varying only the microphone position as he thinks fit.

Artistes can also require a certain amount of balancing on the volume control, so that one artiste will not appear weak when playing against another with a strong voice. Professionals with trained voices are usually alive to this situation, and will endeavour to modulate their voices accordingly. But in practice some assistance by the sound mixer is required to achieve a satisfactory balance.

Recording Out of Doors

The quiet recording conditions enjoyed in a studio are abandoned when using a microphone out of doors, and it is essential to take precautions against wind noise if successful recordings are to be guaranteed. Microphone diaphragms can be blasted by very small currents of air, and these are nearly always present outside. Even the slightest wind can cause a rumbling noise which is frequently as loud as the sound you are trying to record.

Ribbon microphones are out, since they are far too sensitive and likely to sustain permanent damage. Dynamic microphones are to be preferred, either omni-directional or cardioid, since they are robust and stand up extremely well to rough handling. Condenser microphones are seldom used out of doors because of the power supply problems and their more complicated circuitry, and there is an infrequent need for high fidelity. However, transistor condenser microphones can be employed, such as the Sennheiser directional type 805 described on page 101. Generally speaking cardioid microphones are not always satisfactory out of doors due to the special port openings which make them susceptible to wind noise, and omni-directional microphones are to be preferred for close work.

The first requirement is a satisfactory *wind shield*, and this item is made available by the manufacturers of high grade microphones. It may consist of a plastic or metal frame covered with silk, or a specially moulded foam plastic covering. Neither of these shields affect the high frequency response of the microphone, but they must be a very tight fit to eliminate all wind problems. Some condenser microphones require two shields, a small spherical shield covering the diaphragm and a large overall shield covering the entire microphone. This idea of two separate shields is technically superior, since it includes a volume of air trapped between the two shields, and air itself is the best insulator.

Recording in the rain is another occupational hazard, and this requires the further precaution of a specially made *rain shield*. Rain drops on the microphone or wind shield will record as low frequency plops. Holding an umbrella over the microphone is no solution as the rain striking the nylon or silk covering can be heard. The best solution is to obtain a dome shaped mould, such as a plastic kitchen colander, and cover it on the outside with plastic sheeting. This in turn is covered with thick felt glued into position, and the colander turned upside down to protect the microphone.

In general all dialogue will appear weaker out of doors due to the absence of any reflective surfaces, and the microphone working distance must be kept fairly close. The sound mixer may have to abandon his overhead position in sunny weather, since the angle of the sun may cause microphone shadows on the artistes. The only alternative is to position the microphone underneath the camera's field of view, directed upwards. This will give a satisfactory dialogue recording although footsteps may predominate, especially on gravel.

When it is impossible to position a microphone anywhere near the artistes, the use of a *radio link* and *lavalier microphones* can often produce satisfactory recordings. The dialogue perspective may not be quite correct for the scene, but there are occasions when some kind of recording is far better than none at all. When using a v.h.f. radio link the receiver aerial should be kept in line of sight with the artistes, and preferably as close to the scene of action as possible. This will ensure maximum signal being picked up and the best signal-to-noise ratio. Naturally each artiste will have a separate transmitter which will require a separate receiver, and it is essential to have a good supply of *fresh* batteries.

Explosions and Gunfire

Sounds of high intensity such as explosions and gunfire must be carefully recorded if they are to retain a natural sound. Do not use your best condenser microphone for this type of work, but choose a good omni-directional dynamic mounted on a substantial stand. The microphone should be angled away from the explosion if the direction of the sound source is accurately known. This will allow the shock wave to pass by the microphone diaphragm without doing any damage. The full bass response must be left in the microphone and the recording channel, otherwise the recording will sound restricted and false. Obviously the fader setting will have to be reduced to contain the initial impact, but it should be quickly restored to normal to obtain all the aftermath and reverberation of the explosion.

Gunfire can also prove disappointing if the recording channel does not have a good bass response, or if the microphone is incorrectly positioned. The preferred position is in line with, or slightly in front of, the gun muzzle, and never immediately behind. The working distance should be at least 18 ft. (6 m) out of doors, although this will depend on the size of the gun. Small arms fire may require a closer position to prevent the recording from sounding like a small firework. Once again the fader can be brought up again after the initial impact. With all explosive sounds a certain amount of overload is inevitable and perfectably acceptable, although care should be taken with volume indicator meters which should be made insensitive or switched off altogether.

Quiet Sounds

There are occasions when you may wish to record particularly quiet sounds, so quiet that you can only just hear them aurally by careful listening. For example the ticking of a wrist-watch may be no louder than the ambient noise in the studio, room, or recording booth, so that even with a microphone held fairly close the sound of the watch is not particularly clear. The answer lies in surrounding both the watch and the microphone with some sound absorbing material such as a coat or a blanket, which will isolate the ambient noise and show a remarkable improvement.

The same principle applies in larger studios which contain excessive reverberation for the job in hand. *Acoustic screens* are used to reduce the working area, shutting off part of the studio to reduce the unwanted reverberation.

The Piano

This is the most difficult instrument to record with any realism because there is no single point source of sound. The bass and treble notes are at least 5 ft. (1·5 m) apart on a full scale concert grand, and the problem is where to position a microphone so as to obtain a satisfactory balance over 7 or 8 octaves. A single ribbon or condenser microphone suspended about 8 ft. (2·6 m) away with the piano lid fully raised is ideal for concerto type performances, but for jazz playing and for film and television where the microphone must be concealed, an omni-directional microphone is the only answer—mounted inside the piano on a base with a sponge rubber mat underneath.

The microphone should be positioned near the top strings and behind the strut holding the lid. An improved balance can sometimes be obtained by introducing a second omni-directional microphone about halfway along the lower bass strings, especially if the piano is to be used without its lid which normally acts as a bass reflector. In any case a stereo recording of a piano will demand two microphones, and some experimentation will be required to determine the best position to secure a good effect.

It is a mistake to attempt to record a piano in too small a room, since a standing wave pattern will be set in motion which will give the piano a wavering tone, similar to mechanical flutter. Attempts to reduce standing waves by hanging curtains on the walls are only a partial answer, since curtains are notorious for absorbing high frequencies and this will reduce the brilliance of the recording. Naturally the room acoustics will have less effect when using a close microphone position than when using a more distant pick-up.

A singer accompanying himself (or herself) at the piano requires a slightly different microphone position, and a single ribbon can be used for voice and piano. It should be positioned about 1 ft. (0·3 m) in front of the performer, and tilted downwards so as to pick up some of the piano. Of course a separate microphone for the singer is the better procedure, and the use of a two microphone technique to balance the bass and treble sounds from the piano.

Copyright

Unless permission has been obtained from the copyright owners before recording takes place, it is an offence to record any copyright dramatic or musical performance whether live, recorded, or broadcast, and to use such a recording for personal gain. The English Copyright Act of 1956 clearly states what does and what does not constitute an infringement of copyright, and defines a recording as the aggregate of sounds embodied in a record of any description, and capable of being reproduced.

Several different coyrights are usually involved. First there is the author's copyright in any dramatic, musical, or similar work. This lasts all through the author's lifetime and for 50 years thereafter. Even then a second author, or musical arranger, can alter the original work or present it in a different way and so create a new copyright. Once again this will last until 50 years after death.

A second copyright exists in the actual recording of any copyright material, and this is owned by the company or individual who made the recording. In the case of commercial gramophone records and library mood music, both these copyrights must be cleared and the necessary royalties paid before use is made of these records.

There is a third copyright in the actual broadcasting of any copyright material, either live or recorded. The official view of the B.B.C. is that prior permission must be obtained from the copyright holders before taping a programme, and such tapes must only be used privately.

A fourth copyright exists in the performing right of a work, which means that having legally made a recording of copyright material, permission must be sought and a licence obtained before such a recording can be replayed or broadcast in public. Fortunately one does not have to search out authors, composers, or recording companies in order to legally use their material. The Mechanical Copyright Protection Society and the Performing Rights Society deal with all business on their behalf. There is also the Sound Film Music Bureau which is a central clearing house for all the copyrights which exist in music for film and television, and music cue sheets must be submitted to them for assessment of royalty payments.

Appendix

REFERENCE BOOKS

A TEXTBOOK OF SOUND by A. B. Wood. Publisher—Neill and Co. Ltd. (1949).

ACOUSTICS by G. W. Mackenzie A.M.Brit.I.R.E. Publisher—Focal Press Ltd. (1965).

AUDIO CYCLOPEDIA by H. M. Tremaine. Publisher—Howard W. Sams of New York. (1959, reprinted 1969).

ELECTRICITY AND MAGNETISM by R. C. Brown BSc. Publisher—Longmans (1964).

ELECTRONIC AND RADIO ENGINEERING by Terman. Publisher—McGraw Hill (1955).

ELECTRONICS by A. Van Der Ziel. Publisher—Allyn and Bacon Inc. (1966).

ELEMENTS OF SOUND RECORDING by J. G. Frayne PhD. and H. Wolfe PhD. Publisher—John Wiley and Sons Inc. (1949, reprinted 1959).

PRINCIPLES OF ELECTRICAL ENGINEERING by Timble and Bush. Publisher—John Wiley and Sons Inc. (1951).

TRANSISTORS—THEORY AND CIRCUITRY by K. J. Dean. Publisher—McGraw Hill (1964).

TRANSISTOR MANUAL by General Electric Corporation of America (1964).

MICROPHONES by A. E. Robertson B.Sc. AMIEE. Publisher—Iliffe and Sons. (1963).

FROM MICROPHONE TO EAR by G. Slot. Publisher—Cleaver Hume Press (1960).

RADIO DESIGNERS HANDBOOK by F. Langford-Smith. Publisher—Iliffe and Sons (1967).

MAGNETIC RECORDING TECHNIQUES by W. Earl Stewart. Publisher—McGraw Hill (1958).

MUSICAL ENGINEERING by H. F. Olsen PhD. E.E. Publisher—McGraw Hill (1952).

APPENDIX 249

TEST DISCS

DECCA	71123	50 Hz to 10 kHz in bands	Mono 7 in. 45 r.p.m.
DECCA	LXT5346	30 Hz to 18 kHz in bands	Mono 12 in.
DECCA	SKL2057	40 Hz to 12 kHz in bands	Stereo 12 in.
DECCA	SKL4861	Balance, phase, tone, wow and flutter, crosstalk, music bands.	Stereo 12 in.
DEUTSCHE GRAMMOPHON	101497	Balance, phase, music, voice, and effects bands.	Stereo 7 in. 45 r.p.m.
EMI	TCS101	30 Hz to 20 kHz in bands	Stereo 12 in.
EMI	TCS102	30 Hz to 20 kHz gliding tone	Stereo 12 in.
EMI	TCS104	30 Hz to 20 kHz in bands, with gliding tone on side 2.	Mono 12 in. (lateral)
EMI	TCS105	30 Hz to 20 kHz in bands, with gliding tone on side 2.	Mono 12 in. (vertical)
POLYDOR	220497	Balance, tone, phase tests, music and effects bands.	Stereo 7 in. 45 r.p.m.
SHURE	TTR-101	"An audio obstacle course" Phase and trackability tests. (for high grade pick-up arms)	Stereo 12 in.

MAGNETIC TEST TAPES (¼ INCH)

AMPEX GREAT BRITAIN LTD., Acre Road, Reading, Berkshire. Tel. 0734 84411.

31334–01 3¾ i.p.s. (9 cms per second) 200 μSec characteristic. 40 Hz to 8 kHz in bands.

31331–01 3¾ i.p.s. (9 cms per second) 120 μSec characteristic. 40 Hz to 8 kHz in bands.

31321–01 7½ i.p.s. (19 cms per second) NAB characteristic. 40 Hz to 10 kHz in bands. (Full-width track).

31321–04 7½ i.p.s. (19 cms per second) NAB characteristic.
40 Hz to 10 kHz in bands. (Four-track).

31323–01 7½ i.p.s. (19 cms per second) 70 μSec characteristic.
40 Hz to 10 kHz in bands.

31336–01 3¾ i.p.s. (9 cms per second) flutter test.

31326–01 7½ i.p.s. (19 cms per second) flutter test.

(Note: 15 i.p.s., ½ inch and 1 inch test tapes also available.)

BASF (U.K.) LTD., 5a Gillespie Road, London, N.5.
Tel. 01–226–2011.

Calibration Tape 9	3¾ i.p.s. (9 cms per second) full track tape recorded to 90 μSec characteristic. Range 30 Hz to 16 kHz in bands, also section for azimuth alignment.
Calibration Tape 19H	7½ i.p.s. (19 cms per second) full track tape recorded to 50 μSec characteristic. Range 30 Hz to 18 kHz in bands, also section for azimuth alignment.
Calibration Tape 19S	7½ i.p.s. (19 cms per second) full track tape recorded to 70 μSec characteristic. Range 30 Hz to 18 kHz in bands, also section for azimuth alignment.
Calibration Tape 38	15 i.p.s. (38 cms per second) full track tape recorded to 35 μSec characteristic. Range 30 Hz to 18 kHz in bands, also gliding tone from 30 Hz to 16 kHz and section for azimuth alignment.
Short Calibration Tape 38	15 i.p.s. (38 cms per second) full track tape recorded to 35 μSec characteristic. Bands of 63 Hz, 1 kHz, 6·3 kHz, 8 kHz, and 14 kHz, each of 5 seconds duration. Used for routine alignment checks.
Calibration Tape 4·75	1⅞ i.p.s. (4·75 cms per second) full track tape recorded to 120 μSec characteristic. Range 30 Hz to 10 kHz in bands, also section for azimuth alignment.

Stereo Test Tape 38 — 15 i.p.s. (38 cms per second) test tape used in conjunction with Calibration tape 38 for aligning stereo recorders. Contains (1) Tone level section of 1 kHz for 15 seconds on each channel, (2) Track position section of 1 kHz, (3) Azimuth alignment section of noise containing frequencies from 5·6 kHz to 16 kHz across the full tape width, (4) Cross-talk section of 63 Hz for 8 seconds on each channel, 1 kHz for 8 seconds on each channel, and 10 kHz for 8 seconds on each channel.

Alignment Tape — $3\frac{3}{4}$ i.p.s. (9 cms per second) tape used for adjusting replay heads. Noise is recorded to four-track standard, with track 3 erased. Frequencies 5·6 kHz to 16 kHz. When replayed at $7\frac{1}{2}$ i.p.s., frequencies become 11·2 kHz to upper limit of recorder, and at $1\frac{7}{8}$ i.p.s. frequencies become 2·8 kHz to 8 kHz.

Azimuth Test Tape — Used for aligning replay heads at tape speeds of $7\frac{1}{2}$ i.p.s., 15 i.p.s., and 30 i.p.s. A high frequency is recorded on two 2·75 mm edge tracks, and their phase relationship is switched alternatively from $+ 45°$ to $- 45°$ every second at 15 i.p.s. The replay head is correctly adjusted when there is maximum output without level variations. In stereo recorders both replay channels must be phase-correct.

(Note: Calibration tapes for $\frac{1}{2}$ in. (12·5 mm) and 1 in. (25 mm) tape widths are also available, recorded to the standard 35 μSec characteristic.)

EMI ELECTRONICS LTD., Installation and Maintenance Division, Blythe Road, Hayes, Middlesex. Tel. 01–573 3888.

SRT 14A — $3\frac{3}{4}$ i.p.s. (9 cms per second) full track tape recorded to 120 μSec characteristic. Range 40 Hz to 10 kHz in bands, preceded by spoken announcement.

SRT 15A — $3\frac{3}{4}$ i.p.s. (9 cms per second) full track tape recorded to 200 μSec characteristic. Range 40 Hz to 8 kHz in bands, preceded by spoken announcement.

SRT 18   7½ i.p.s. (19 cms per second) full track tape recorded to 70 μSec characteristic. Range 30 Hz to 16 kHz in bands, preceded by spoken announcement.

SRT 17   15 i.p.s. (38 cms per second) full track tape recorded to 35 μSec characteristic. Range 30 Hz to 20 kHz in bands, preceded by spoken announcement.

(All above tapes contain a section of 3 kHz tone for checking wow and flutter, also a section of stroboscopic markings as a speed check.)

TBT.1A   7½ i.p.s. (19 cms per second) full track tape recorded to 100 μSec characteristic for domestic machines. Range 40 Hz to 12 kHz, preceded by 8 kHz section for azimuth alignment.

TBT.2A   3¾ i.p.s. (9 cms per second) full track tape recorded to 120 μSec characteristic for domestic machines. Range 40 Hz to 8 kHz, preceded by 6 kHz section for azimuth alignment.

TUCHINGS ELECTRONICS LTD., 14 Rook Hill Road, Friars Cliff, Christchurch, Hants. Tel. 0425–2 2019.

Test Tape No. 1   7½ i.p.s. (19 cms per second) half-track tape recorded to 70 μSec characteristic. Range 40 Hz to 10 kHz in bands, preceded by spoken announcement. Track 2 carries 7·5 kHz tone for azimuth alignment.

Test Tape No. 2   3¾ i.p.s. (9 cms per second) half-track tape recorded to 140 μSec characteristic. Range 40 Hz to 7·5 kHz in bands, preceded by spoken announcement. Track 2 carries 5 kHz tone for azimuth alignment.

Test Tape No. 3   7½ i.p.s. (19 cms per second) full-width tape recorded to 70 μSec characteristic. Contains white noise in one-third octave bands from 40 Hz to 10 kHz, preceded by spoken announcement.

Test Tape No. 4   7½ i.p.s. (19 cms per second) half-track tape recorded to 70 μSec characteristic. Contains white noise in one octave bands from 100 Hz to 6·4 kHz, preceded by spoken announcement. Track 2 carries full range unfiltered white noise.

Test Tape No. 5   Full-width tape of unfiltered white noise (track 3 blank) for azimuth and vertical head alignment. Can be used without test equipment at all tape speeds on half-track and four-track recorders.

TEST FILMS AVAILABLE FROM THE SOCIETY OF MOTION
PICTURE AND TELEVISION ENGINEERS, 9 EAST 41st STREET,
NEW YORK.

35-mm MULTI-FREQUENCY TEST FILM (Code Number APFA)
A variable area photographic sound print used to obtain the
electrical frequency response at the output of the power amplifier.
Each print is individually calibrated and correction factors are
provided. This is a laboratory type film normally used by manufacturers and in equipment installation. Each frequency is
preceded by a spoken announcement.

Hz	Hz	Hz	Hz
1000	200	1500	5000
40	300	2000	6000
55	400	2500	7000
70	500	3000	8000
100	700	3500	9000
150	1000	4000	10,000

35-mm MULTI-FREQUENCY TEST FILM (Code Number ASFA)
A variable area photographic sound print normally used in
routine theatre servicing. Each frequency is preceded by a spoken
announcement.

Hz	Hz	Hz	Hz
1000	300	2500	5000
40	500	3000	6000
70	1000	3500	7000
100	2000	4000	8000

35-mm OPTICAL SOUND FOCUSING TEST FILM (Code Number
A9KC).
A 9000 Hz tone used to check focus and azimuth settings of
optical sound-heads. Tone recorded at 1 db below 100 per cent
modulation. Normally used by manufacturers and laboratories.

35-mm OPTICAL SOUND FOCUSING TEST FILM (Code Number
A7KC).
A 7000 Hz tone used to check focus and azimuth settings of
optical sound-heads. Tone recorded at 1 db below 100 per cent
modulation. Normally used for servicing theatre equipment.

35-mm BUZZ-TRACK TEST FILM (Code Number ABZT).

A photographic sound print used to determine the correct placement of the scanning beam slit, containing edge tracks of 300 Hz and 1000 Hz with opaque centre. When beam is correctly adjusted both frequencies are heard in equal balance, or no sound is heard at all.

35-mm 1000 Hz BALANCING TEST FILM (Code Number ABLN)

A photographic print designed to adjust the output level from two or more projectors.

35-mm 3000 Hz FLUTTER TEST FILM (Code Number A3KC).

An original photographic recording used to measure wow and flutter content in sound reproducers. A flutter bridge is required to make this measurement. Total film flutter is less than 0·08 per cent.

35-mm MAGNETIC 3-TRACK MULTI-FREQUENCY TEST FILM (Code Number RCFM).

An original recording of three 200-mil tracks, recorded at a level of 10 db below 3 per cent distortion. This film is intended as a reference standard in adjusting recording and reproducing systems. Each film is individually calibrated and correction factors are provided.

Hz	Length	Hz	Length
1000	30 ft. (10 m)	1000	17 ft. (5·5 m)
50	17 ft. (5·5 m)	3000	17 ft. (5·5 m)
65	17 ft. (5·5 m)	5000	17 ft. (5·5 m)
80	17 ft. (5·5 m)	7000	17 ft. (5·5 m)
100	17 ft. (5·5 m)	8000	17 ft. (5·5 m)
200	17 ft. (5·5 m)	10,000	17 ft. (5·5 m)
400	17 ft. (5·5 m)	12,000	17 ft. (5·5 m)

35-mm MAGNETIC 3-TRACK AZIMUTH ALIGNMENT FILM (Code Number 3TM-8).

An 8000 Hz tone recorded on three 200-mil tracks for adjusting the azimuth of heads on magnetic reproducers. (Not for use in theatre projectors.)

35-mm MAGNETIC 3-TRACK FLUTTER TEST FILM (Code
Number 3TM-3).

A 3000 Hz tone recorded on three 200-mil tracks for measuring
flutter on magnetic reproducers. A flutter bridge is required to
make this measurement. (Not for use with theatre projectors.)

35-mm MAGNETIC 3-TRACK BALANCING TEST FILM (Code
Number 3TM-1).

A 1000 Hz tone recorded on three 200-mil tracks for measuring
the output from magnetic reproducers. (Not for use with theatre
projectors).

35-mm MAGNETIC FOUR-TRACK CINEMASCOPE TEST FILMS
FOR PROJECTORS

(1) 1000 Hz level balance film   (Code Number SL-1)
(2) Multi-frequency test film   (Code Number MF-1)
(3) Loudspeaker balance film   (Code Number LB-1)
(4) Stereophonic test film (picture & sound) (Code Number ST-1)
(5) Flutter test film (3000 Hz)   (Code Number FL-1)
(6) Loudspeaker phasing film   (Code Number LP-1)
(7) Constant level test film (8000 Hz)   (Code Number AZ-1)
(8) Channel four test film (with 12 kHz/1 kHz)
                                           (Code Number CH-4)

16-mm MAGNETIC MULTI-FREQUENCY TEST FILM (Code
Number M16MF).

A single track recording, 200-mil wide, the edge of which is not
more than 5-mil from the non-perforated side of the film. Each
frequency is preceded by a spoken announcement.

Hz	Hz	Hz	Hz
400	300	3000	7000
50	500	4000	8000
100	1000	5000	9000
200	2000	6000	10,000
			400

16-mm MAGNETIC SIGNAL LEVEL TEST FILM (Code Number
M16SL).

A single track recording, 200-mil wide, of a 400 Hz tone. Recorded
at 5 db below coating saturation to provide an absolute reference
level.

16-mm MAGNETIC FLUTTER TEST FILM (Code Number M16FL).
A single track recording, 200-mil wide, of a 3000 Hz tone. An external flutter bridge is required to make the measurement, and the total flutter recorded does not exceed 0·1 per cent.

16-mm PROJECTOR TEST FILM (Code Number SPTF).
A photographic print used for demonstration purposes, containing music, dialogue, and piano recordings.

16-mm MULTI-FREQUENCY TEST FILM (Code Number PH.22).
A direct-positive photographic recording for checking the output of a sound-head and power amplifier. Each film is individually calibrated and correction figures are given. Each frequency is preceded by a spoken announcement.

Hz	Hz	Hz	Hz
400	300	3000	7000
50	500	4000	400
100	1000	5000	4000
200	2000	6000	—

16-mm SIGNAL LEVEL TEST FILM (Code Number PH22.45).
A direct-positive recording of a 400 Hz tone, designed to provide an absolute standard of recorded signal level. The specified level is approximately 2 db below 100 per cent modulation, and is about equal to the highest level that is possible in commercial practice.

16-mm SOUND FOCUSING TEST FILM (Code Number PH22.42).
An original negative recording of either a 5000 Hz or a 7000 Hz tone with a square-wave track. The square-wave track provides a more sensitive indication of azimuth errors than a sine-wave track.

16-mm BUZZ-TRACK TEST FILM (Code Number PH22.57).
An original negative recording of 300 Hz and 1000 Hz at each edge of the normal track position, with an opaque centre. When scanning beam is correctly adjusted, both frequencies will be heard with equal loudness, or no frequencies at all.

(NOTE: Six-Track 35-mm and 70-mm Multi-Frequency Test Films can be obtained from the TODD A–O Organization, Hollywood, U.S.A.)

DIN TEST FILMS AVAILABLE FROM BASF (UK) LTD.,
5a Gillespie Road, London, N.5.

Calibration Film 16   Used for the alignment of 16 mm magnetic recorders
                      and reproducers at a transport speed of 25 frames
                      per second. Recorded to 100 μSec characteristic
                      across full film width. Range 30 Hz to 14 kHz in
                      bands, also section for azimuth alignment.

Calibration Film 35   Used for the alignment of 35 mm magnetic recorders
                      and reproducers at a transport speed of 25 frames
                      per second. Recorded to 35 μSec characteristic
                      across full film width. Range 30 Hz to 16 kHz in
                      bands, also section for azimuth alignment. (Avail-
                      able in 17·5 mm film width.)

(NOTE: When these films are replayed at a transport speed of 24 frames
       per second, the frequencies will be 4 per cent lower whereas the
       level tolerances will be the same.)

CARE OF TEST TAPES AND FILMS

All test tapes and films must be carefully handled and stored if they are
to retain their accuracy over extended periods of time. In particular
magnetic heads and other components in the threading path should be
cleaned and demagnetized before threading a test tape or film, thus
preventing the possibility of dirt pick up or partial erasure.

Tapes should always be kept in their boxes, preferably on spools with
large diameter hubs, and isolated from extremes of humidity and temperature. They should also be stored under the tensions which exist after a
normal playing run, and not after a high speed wind or rewind. After
extensive use, high frequencies will tend to be down in level by as much
as 2 db, and flutter figures may appear to rise. This is caused by demagnetization, deformation of the tape due to stretch, and an increase in
drop out frequency as a result of tape wear. Both tapes and films will
benefit from being periodically cleaned by passing them through a felt
strip of velvet cloth during a normal run.

STANDARD TRACK DIMENSIONS FOR
TAPE SYNCHRONISING SYSTEMS

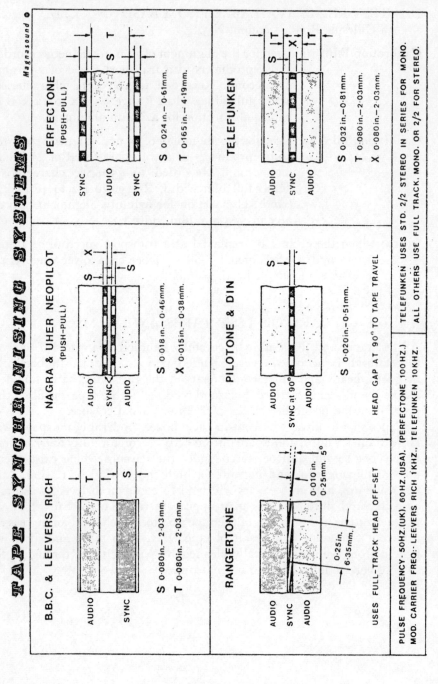

Magnasound

B.B.C. & LEEVERS RICH

AUDIO

SYNC

S 0·080 in.— 2·03 mm.

T 0·080 in.— 2·03 mm.

RANGERTONE

AUDIO

SYNC

AUDIO

0·010 in.
0·25 mm.   5°

0·25 in.
6·35 mm.

USES FULL-TRACK HEAD OFF-SET

NAGRA & UHER NEOPILOT
(PUSH-PULL)

AUDIO

SYNC

AUDIO

S 0·018 in.— 0·46 mm.

X 0·015 in.— 0·38 mm.

PILOTONE & DIN

AUDIO

SYNC at 90°

AUDIO

S 0·020 in.— 0·51 mm.

HEAD GAP AT 90° TO TAPE TRAVEL

PERFECTONE
(PUSH-PULL)

SYNC

AUDIO

SYNC

S 0·024 in.— 0·61 mm.

T 0·165 in.— 4·19 mm.

TELEFUNKEN

AUDIO

SYNC

AUDIO

S 0·032 in.— 0·81 mm.

T 0·080 in.— 2·03 mm.

X 0·080 in.— 2·03 mm.

TELEFUNKEN USES STD. 2/2 STEREO IN SERIES FOR MONO.
ALL OTHERS USE FULL TRACK. MONO. OR 2/2 FOR STEREO.

PULSE FREQUENCY - 50 HZ. (UK) 60 HZ. (USA).   (PERFECTONE 100 HZ.)
MOD. CARRIER FREQ:- LEEVERS RICH 1 KHZ., TELEFUNKEN 10 KHZ.

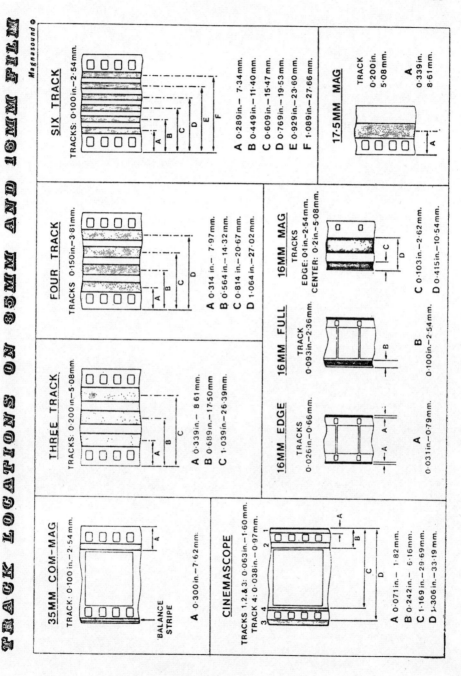

Index

Absorber
  membrane, 152, 171
  panel, 152
Absorption
  coefficients, 150
  factor, 146
  units, 149
A.C., 33
A.C. Voltmeter, 37
Acetate lacquer disc, 66, 74
Acoustic
  baffle, 93
  gain, 99
  lens, 145
  screens, 169, 175, 177, 245
  tiles, 146
  treatment, 169
Acoustical resistance unit, 144
Acoustics, studio, 147
Active networks, 125
Advance ball, 68
Air-borne sound, 148
Alignment
  azimuth, 58
  of magnetic heads, 58
  tapes, 58
Alternating current, 33
Alternative reverb, units, 154
Amperes, 30
Amplifier
  audio, 112
  bridging, 114
  compressor, 121
  gating, 182
  limiting, 121, 178
  line, 114
  microphone, 114
  operational, 125
  power, 114
  push-pull, 115, 118
  transistor, 116
  ultra linear, 116
  voltage, 112
Amplitude, 14
Anechoic chamber, 88
Announcements, 236
Anti-pop shield, 180
Anti-static fluid, 85
Applicator wheel, 226
Asbestos wool, 146
Attenuators, 235
Attenuation distortion, 164
Audio
  amplifiers, 112
  frequencies, 17
  oscillator, 36, 37, 182

Auditory
  canal, 17
  perspective, 171
Azimuth, 58, 216

Background effects, 232
Baffle, loudspeaker, 140
Balance stripe, 225
Balanced line, 110
Ballistics, 241
Band stop filter, 127, 211
Banjo, 166
Base, 116
Basic
  sound principles, 12
  stereo principles, 184
  transistor configurations, 117
Bass
  clarinet, 166
  double, 166
  drums, 168
Bass reflex cabinet, 140
Bass tip-up, 88, 94, 227, 239
Bassoon, 166
  contra, 167
Beat frequency, 14, 41
Bel, 17, 35
Berliner, 9
Bias
  compensator, 77
  d.c., 42
  high frequency a.c., 41
  oscillator, 42
  quiescent, 119
  rejection filter, 43
  the need for, 40
  voltage, 113
Bi-morph element, 80, 92
Binaural, 186, 242
Blake, professor, 10
Blattner, 10
Blattnerphone, 10
Boom, microphone, 239
Brass instruments, 167
Breakaway point, 121
Breath shield, 180
Bridging amplifier, 114
Broadcasting
  stereo, 202
  studios, 156
Bulk eraser, 63

Cables, microphone, 109
Calendering, 223

Calibration
    discs, 249
    films, 253 to 257
    tapes, 47, 249 to 252
Capacitance, 28, 32
Capacitor, 32
Capstan, 55
Capsule, 95, 120
Carbon microphone, 91
Cardoid microphones, 90, 236
Cartridges, 59
    ceramic, 80
    compatible mono, 82
    crystal, 80
    magnetic, 80
    miniconic, 81
    photo-cell, 81
    tape, 59, 61
Cassettes, 59, 60
    D.C. International, 61
Celeste, 168
Cell, photo-electric, 10
Cello, 166
Ceramic
    cartridge, 80
    microphone, 91, 109
Chamber
    anechoic, 88
    reverberation, 152
Check key, 208
Chemical fog, 219
Chimes, 168
Choirs, 179
Cinema loudspeaker, 144
Clarinet, 166
    bass, 166
Coercivity, 40, 48
Coil
    hum bucking, 54
    speech 93, 131
    voice, 131
Coincident microphone pair, 189
Collector, 116
Column loudspeakers, 144
Combination tones, 15, 41, 233
Combined
    magnetic, 205, 225, 229
    optical, 205
Commentaries, 208, 236
Copyright, 246
Com-opt, 205
Com-mag, 205, 225, 229
Compatible mono, 82
Compiling a film sound track, 206
Compression, 24, 121
Condenser microphone, 95, 109
Conditions for recording, 147
Connectors, microphone, 234
Consoles
    mixing, 159
    re-recording, 211

Contact microphone, 102
Cor Anglais, 166
Cornet, 167
Contra-bassoon, 167
Cross
    mixing, 192
    modulation, 219
Crossfield head, 53
Crossover distortion, 118
Crosstalk, 53, 123, 197, 228
Crystal
    cartridge, 80
    microphone, 91, 109
Cue sheet, 211
Cutter head, 68
    moving coil, 68
    moving iron, 68
Cutting a stereo disc, 73
Cutting stylus, 66, 68
Cycle, 13
Cymbals, 13
Cymbalum, 168

Dashpot, 223
DB., 17, 35
DB. meter, 162, 241
D.C., 33
D.C. International cassettes, 61
Decibel, 17, 35
De-esser, 122
De-fluxer, 63
Definite pitch, 168
Demagnetisation, 62
Demagnetizer, 63
Densitometer, 219
Density of track, 220
Dialogue
    equalizer, 128, 160, 240
    perspective, 242
    quality, 240
    recording, 239
Difference tones, 15
D.I.N. (Deutscher Industrie Normen), 44
Direct
    current, 33
    positive, 221
Direction, sense of, 19, 184
Directional microphones, 98, 243
Directivity, 99, 235
Disc
    acetate lacquer, 66, 74
    frequency test, 249
    preener, 85
    recording head, 68
    recording machine, 67
    pressings, 75
    stroboscope, 76
    wear, 84
Distort box, 128

Distortion, 26
  attenuation, 164
  crossover, 118
  frequency, 26
  harmonic, 26, 39, 112, 220
  intermodulation, 27
  phase, 15
  spatial, 27, 196
  tracing, 79
  transient, 27
  volume, 27
Division of units, 31
Dolby system, 123
Domestic loudspeaker, 143
Doppler effect, 22
Double bass, 166
Double film system, 204
Double play tape, 49
Drain, 119
Drama studio, 158
Drop-out, 48, 223
Dual concentric loudspeaker, 136
Dust bug, 85
Dynamic
  microphone, 86, 93, 108
  range, 26
Dynalizer, 128
Dynes per cm², 107

Ear, the human, 17
Early loudspeakers, 130
Echo, 16, 146
Edge tones, 166
Edison
  Thomas, 9
  phonograph, 9
Eddy current brake, 76
Effects
  background, 209
  spot, 209
Eigentones, 151
Electrical power, 31
Electronic
  music, 181
  printing, 233
  organs, 181
Electromagnetic
  cutter heads, 68
  loudspeakers, 131
  pick-up cartridges, 80
Electrostatic loudspeaker, 137
Elliptical stylus, 79
Emitter, 116
Emulsion corns, 209
English horn, 166
Equalizer, 125
  dialogue, 128
  film loss, 129, 216
  hi-lo, 126
  mid-range, 129

Equalizer—continued
  presence, 129
  telephone, 128
Erase head, 52
Explosions, 244

Faders
  linear, 160
  quadrant, 160
  rotary, 160
Farad, 32
Feedback, 157
  negative, 116
Ferrite, 52
Fidelipac cartridge, 61
Field effect transistors, 119
Film
  loss equalizer, 129, 216
  path, 223
  processing, 218
  recording, 213, 223
  reproduction, 216
  wide screen processes, 229
Filters, 125
  band stop, 127, 211
  high pass, 84, 126, 216
  low pass, 83, 126, 216, 230
  radio frequency, 43
  rumble, 84, 129
Finishing groove, 71
Fletcher's curves, 17, 18
Fluid
  anti-static, 85
  tape jointing, 65
Flute, 166
Flutter, 54
  echoes, 151
Foldback, 161
Folded horn, 140, 142
Footage counter, 211
Foreign versions, 212
Four track, 56
French horn, 167
Frequency
  correction, 83
  correction standards, 45
  distortion, 26
  dividing network, 133, 138
  fundamental, 20
  range, 17, 19
  response, 20, 71, 215, 224, 231
  test discs, 84, 249
  test tape, 249 to 252
  test films, 253 to 257
Fringe effect, 59
Full width head, 228
Fundamental frequency, 20

Galvanometer, 213
Gamma, 218
Gate, 119
Gating amplifier, 182, 230

Generator
 audio, 36
 pulse, 227
 white noise, 182
Germanium, 116
Glissando, 167
Gongs, 168
Glockenspiel, 168
Gramophone, 9
 turntables, 75
 pick-up arms, 77
 pick-up cartridges, 80
Grid swing, 113
Groove dimensions, 69
Guide track, 207
Guitar
 acoustic, 166
 electric, 102
Gun-fire recording, 244

Half nut, 67
Half track, 228
Hand capacity, 110
Hangover, 131
Harmonic distortion, 26
Harmonics, 20
Harp, 166
Head block, 54
Headphones, 186, 199, 241
Helmholtz resonator, 151
Hertz, Heinrich, 13
Hi-Fi, 28
High frequency bias, 41
High pass filter, 84, 126, 216
Hill and dale, 9, 66
Hi-lo equalizer, 126
Horn, 134
 English, 166
 French, 167
 loudspeaker, 134
 re-entrant, 135
Hum bucking coil, 54
Hybrid transformer, 33, 193

I.E.C. (International Electrotechnical
 Commission), 44
Image spread, 219, 221
Impedance, 34
 matching, 137
In phase, 14, 134
Indefinite pitch, 168
Inductance, 28, 32
Inductor, 32
Infinite baffle, 140, 142
Insertion loss, 125
Instruments
 brass, 167
 percussion, 168
 string, 165
 wind, 167
 woodwind, 166

Intensity scale, 17
Integrated circuits, 124
Interlock motor systems, 211, 222
Intermodulation, 133, 220
Internal balance, 173

Jointing
 fluid, 65
 tape, 65
Jolson, Al., 11
Junction transistor, 117

Lacquer disc, 66, 74
Lateral cut disc, 9, 66
Lauste, Eugene, 10
Lay-out of
 dance orchestra, 177
 jazz group, 178
 symphony orchestra, 173
Lavalier microphone, 103, 243
Lead-screw, 67
Lead-in groove, 71
Lead-out groove, 71
Lectures, 237
Lens, acoustic, 145
Lee de Forest, 10
Light valve, 10, 214
Limiter, 121
Limiting, 121
 amplifier, 121, 178
Line
 amplifier, 114
 balanced, 110
 microphone, 99
 unbalanced, 110
Linear fader, 160
Lip microphone, 102
Listening conditions, stereo, 199
Location recording, 207
Long play tape, 49
Loop bin, 208
Loudness, 24
 control, 25, 129
Loudspeaker
 baffle, 140
 cinema, 144
 column, 144
 domestic, 143
 dual concentric, 136
 early types, 130
 electrostatic, 137
 enclosures, 140
 horn, 134
 line course, 144
 moving coil, 131
 placing, 171, 200, 230
 re-entrant horn, 135
 volume, 163
Low pass filter, 83, 126, 216, 230

Magnetic
  film path, 223
  frequency response, 43
  heads, 51
  recording (film), 223
  recording (tape), 39
  recording (theory), 39
  reduction transfers, 176, 199
  reverberation unit, 63
  stripe, 205, 225, 230
  tape, 47
  tape splicer, 65
  track locations (film), 259
  track standards, 224
  transfer characteristic, 40
Magnetophon, 11
Mandolin, 166
Marimba, 168
Marker space, 71
Married print, 212
Masking, 16
Master disc, 75
Mechanical organs, 181
Membrane absorbers, 152, 171
Microbar, 107
Microfarad, 32
Microphone
  boom, 239
  cables, 109
  capsule, 95
  carbon, 91
  cardioid, 90, 99
  ceramic, 91
  condenser, 95, 109
  connectors, 234
  contact, 102
  crystal, 91, 109
  directional, 98
  directivity, 99, 235
  dynamic, 86, 93, 108
  lavalier, 103
  line, 99
  lip, 102
  loading, 105
  moving coil, 86, 93
  parabolic, 99
  polar diagrams, 88, 89, 90, 100, 101
  pressure gradient operated, 87
  pressure operated, 86
  radio, 104
  ribbon, 87, 94, 109
  sensitivity, 106
  techniques, 234
Mid-range equalizer, 129
Mil., 224
Millihenry, 32
Miniconic cartridge, 81
Mixing consoles, 159, 211
Mobius loop, 59
Modulation lead powering, 98
Modulation noise, 50, 123

Monitor
  loudspeaker, 163
  room, 147, 159, 171
  volume, 163
Monophonic, 29, 66
Mood music, 210
Moog synthesizer, 183
Mother disc, 75
Moving coil
  cutter head, 68
  loudspeaker, 131
  microphone, 86, 93
  pick-up, 80
Moving iron
  cutter head, 68
  pick-up, 81
M/S method, stereo, 191
Multiplex, 202
Multi-track
  heads, 53
  recording, 232
Multi-microphone technique, 174
Multivibrator, 182
Mu-metal, 51
Music
  concrete, 183
  electronic, 181
  orchestral scale, 21
  organ, 180
  recording, 165, 209
  studio, 168
Musical instruments, 165 to 168
Mute, 165, 167

Nagra Recorder, 226
N.A.B. (National Association o
  Broadcasters), 44
N.P.N. transistors, 117
Need for bias, 40
Negative
  exposure, 217
  feedback, 116
Networks
  active, 125
  frequency dividing, 138
  passive, 125
Noise
  air-borne, 148
  levels, 23
  reduction, 215
  reduction system, 123
  structure borne, 147

Oboe, 166
Obstacle effect, 15
Octaves, 22
Oersteds, 40
Off-mic, 238, 239
Off screen narration, 208

Ohms Law, 30
On-mike, 237
Operational amplifiers, 125
Optical
  recording camera, 206, 213
  sound processing, 218
  sound recording, 213
  sound tracks, 206
Orchestral
  combination, 172
  internal balance, 173
  lay-out, 172, 176
Organ
  electronic, 181
  mechanical, 181
  music, 180
Oscillator
  audio, 37
  bias, 42
Out of doors recording, 242
Out of phase, 14, 19
Overswing, 241
Overtones, 20, 21

Panel absorbers, 152
Panoramic potentiometer, 190, 232
Pan pot, 191, 232
Parabolic microphone, 99
Parastat, 85
Passive network, 125
Peak programme meter, 163
Penthouse, 230
Percussion instruments, 168
Permeability, 40, 51
Phantom powering, 98
Phase, 14
  distortion, 15
Phase-splitter, 115
Phon, 17
Phonic wheel, 226
Phonograph, 9
Photo-cell cartridge, 81
Photo-electric cell, 10
Photo diode, 120
Photo transistor, 120
Photographic sound recording, 213
Piano, 168, 245
  keyboard, 221
Piccolo, 166
Pick-up
  arms, 77
  cartridges, 80
  ceramic, 80
  crystal, 80
  moving coil, 80
  moving iron, 81
  variable reluctance, 80
Picofarad, 32
Piezo-electric effect, 80

Pinch
  effect, 71
  roller, 55
Pitch
  definite, 168
  indefinite, 168
Pizzicato, 165
Plate reverberation, 154
Plays and drama, 238
P.N.P. Transistors, 117
Podium, 174
Polar
  diagrams, 88, 89, 90, 100, 101
  distribution, 88
Polarizing voltage, 95, 96, 137
Pole faces, 132
Pole pieces, 51
Port, cabinet, 141
Post synch, 207, 228
Potential divider, 30
Poulsen, Valdemar, 9
Power amplifier, 144
Preener, 85
Presence equalizer, 129
Pressure
  gradient operation, 87
  operation, 86
  roller, 55
Print through, 50, 123
  factor, 50
Printed circuit, 124
Printing master, 233
Processing
  disc, 74
  sound film, 218
Proximity effect, 88, 94
Pulse
  generator, 227
  synchronisation, 227
  track, 226, 227
  track dimensions, 258
Push-pull amplifier, 115, 118

Quadrant faders, 160
Quadrasonics, 29, 202
Quadruple play tape, 49
Quick loading systems, 59
Quiescent bias, 119
Quiet sounds, 244

Radio link, 104, 243
Radius compensation, 71
Rain shield, 243
Reactance, 34
Record head, 51
Record wear, 84
Recorded surface, 71
Recorder, 166

Recording characteristic,
   disc, 72, 73
   film, 216, 217, 231
   tape, 45
Recording
   choirs, 179
   commentaries, 208, 236
   conditions, 147
   console, 159, 211
   dialogue, 239
   effects, 209
   equipment, 197, 226
   frequency response, 71
   head, 51
   machine, 67
   multi-track, 174, 229
   music, 165
   out of doors, 242
   speeds, 56
   studio, 146
   tape, 47
R.I.A.A. (Recording Industry Association
   of America), 72
Reduction transfers, 176, 199
Reed, 166
Re-entrant horn, 135
Reflected sound, 146, 188
Remanence, 48, 52
   curve, 41
Replay head, 52
Re-recording, 210
   console, 211
Reproducing stylus, 78
Resistance, 28, 30
Resonance, 17, 27
Resonant frequency, 34, 35
Resonator, Helmholtz, 151
Reverberation, 16, 146
   chamber, 152
   plate unit, 155
   spring unit, 154
   time, 146
Ring modulator, 182
Ringing, 131
Room
   monitoring, 171
   resonances, 28
   vocal, 170
Rock 'n Roll system, 212
Rotary fader, 160
Rumble filter, 84, 129

Sabine, professor, 149
   formula, 149
Saxophone, 167
Scoring stage, 209
Sel-sync, 199
Selsyn, 222
Semiconductor, 81, 116
Sense of direction, 19, 184

Sensitometer, 219
Sensitometry, 218
Sep-mag, 204, 225
Shield
   anti-pop, 180
   breath, 180
   mu-metal, 51
   rain, 243
   wind, 243
Show copies, 212, 233
Sibilance, 241
Signal-to-noise ratio, 25, 217
Silicon, 116
Sine wave, 37
Single film system, 205
Skating, 77
Small domestic loudspeaker, 143
Solar cells, 217
Sound
   absorbtion coefficients, 150
   absorbtion factor, 146
   absorbtion units, 149
   air-borne, 148
   effects, 209
   film processing, 217
   isolation, 147
   mixer, 239
   traps, 148
   waves in air, 13
   velocity, 12
Source, 119
Sousaphone, 167
Spaced microphone techniques, 195
Spatial distortion, 27, 196
Speech
   coil, 93, 131
   waves, 22
Speeches, 237
Splicer, tape, 65
Spool sizes, 49
Spot effects, 209, 232
Sprocket hole modulation, 223
Stacked heads, 53
Stampers, disc, 75
Standard play tape, 48
Standard recording characteristic
   disc, 72
   film, 216, 217, 231
   tape, 45
Standard track dimensions,
   film, 221, 225, 259
   pulse, 258
   tape, 56, 60, 62
Standing waves, 28, 151, 180
Start mark, 211
Stereophonic
   broadcasts, 202
   discs, 66
   disc cutting, 73
   film sound, 232
   image, 192, 200, 201

Stereophonic—*continued*
  listening conditions, 199
  microphone techniques, 187
  pick-up, 82
  principle, 184
  wandering image, 196
  width control, 192
Streamers, 210
String instruments, 165
Stripe, 205, 225, 230
Stroboscope disc, 76
Structure borne sound, 147
Studio
  acoustics, 149
  drama, 158
  lay-out, 156
  music, 168
  talks, 157
Stylus
  pressure, 79
  pressure gauge, 80
  recording, 69, 70
  reproducing, 79
Sum and difference method, 191
Swarf, 69
Sync track, 206, 210
Synchro-start principle, 222
Synthesizer, 183

Talk back, 157
Tape
  base, 47
  coatings, 47
  deck, 54
  double play, 49
  hiss, 123
  joining, 64
  long play, 49
  playing times, 49
  quadruple play, 49
  recording, **39**
  selection, 48
  splicer, 65
  standard play, 48
  transport mechanisms, 54
  triple play, 49
Telegraphone, 9
Telephone simulator, 128
Theory of magnetic sound, 39
Thou., 224
Threshold of
  feeling, 18
  hearing, 18
  pain, 18
Timbre, 21, 23, 25
Tone controls, 83
Tracing distortion, 79
Track dimensions
  film, 221, 225, 259
  pulse, 258
  tape, 56, 60, 62

Track location
  cartridge, 62
  cassette, 60
  film, 221, 225, 229, 259
  pulse, 258
  tape, 75
Trackability, 77
Tracking force, 79
Transcription unit, 75
Transfers, reduction, 176, 199
Transient distortion, 27
Transistor, 116
  amplifier, 116
  cartridge, 81
  condenser microphone, 97
  configurations, 117
  field effect, 119
  integrated circuits, 124
  junction, 117
  N.P.N., 117
  P.N.P., 117
  photo, 120
  voltmeter, 37
Triangle, 168
Triple play tape, 49
Trombone, 167
Trumpet, 167
Turntables, 75
Tuba, 167
Tweeters, 134, 139
Twin track, 56
Tympani, 168

Ultra linear, 116
Unbalanced line, 110
Uni-directional microphone, 90, 95, 98, 236

Valve
  amplifiers, 112
  voltmeter, 37
Variable
  area recording, 213
  density recording, 213
  reluctance cartridge, 80
Velocity, 12
  microphone, 94
Vibraphone, 168
Videotape, 64
Viola, 165
Violin, 165
Vocal
  chords, 23
  room, 170
Voice
  coil, 131
  effort, 24
Voltage amplifier, 112
Voltmeter, 37
Volts, 30

Volume
  distortion, 27
  indicators, 161
  level, 241
  units, 161
V.U.'s., 161
V.U. meter, 162, 241

Wandering stereo image, 196
Wavelength, 13
Watt, 31
Wax platter, 66
White noise generator, 182

Wide screen films, 229
Width control, 194
Wind shield, 243
Wind instruments, 167
Woodwind instruments, 166
Wow, 54

Xylophone, 168

Zero level, 17, 36
  dbm, 36
  dbv, 36